MW01518912

INGER!

INGER!

A Modern-Day Viking Discovers America

by James N. Sites

ScanAm Communications
Ashland, Kentucky
2006

Dedication

This book is dedicated to my private, personal, perpetually perplexing Norwegian Viking, with a 4-D *skaal*! for helping me re-discover my own country during the six amazing decades recounted on these pages. *Tusen takk, Inger!*

ISBN: 1-931672-38-5

Cover & Book Design by Brett Nance

Published By:
ScanAm Communications
P.O. Box 669 • Ashland, KY 41105
606-326-1667 • JSFBOOKS.com

Foreword

Inger! is a true, modern saga of discovery—a distant echo of the amazing feat of Viking seafarers who, 500 years before Columbus' voyage, sailed "beyond the sunset and the baths of all the western stars"[1] and discovered America. This saga, however, deals with the most remarkable person I've ever met: **Inger**. From Norway. AND with America and our times—yours, too—and the tumultuous recent happenings in this crazy, mixed-up, unpredictable world of ours.

Before getting too far along, however, it might be helpful to recall how some people feel about foreigners coming into the USA. While I was born in Pittsburgh at a time when it was truly The Big Smokey, my mother came from Kentucky—from a remote "holler" near the small town of Olive Hill. Strangers, as you may have heard, were hardly welcome in those parts. Not to mention "revenooers." In fact, all such were lumped together as "G-D furriners" and given one hot reception if and whenever they dared put in an appearance.

So it was that shortly after World War II ended, I came to visit Mom with a very special new friend I had met on my last ship, outbound from Scotland to the USA. Yet here in tow was the absolutely unthinkable—a bonafide, 100% dyed-in-the-wool, through-and-through foreigner. I came with no little fear and foreboding. And what happened? Well, the two fell into each other's arms! Mom, in fact, came to contend that in this very special case, the G-D didn't mean what you might think at all: It meant *Grande Dame.*

Well, I aready knew the real meaning. That's why I wanted to introduce Inger to Mom in the first place. And now I'd like to introduce her to you, too. <u>You</u> decide which is right....

Good reading! *Jim Sites*

---

[1] *The quote's source? See book's last lines.*

Chapter I

High-pitched laughter cut though the cold gray mist swirling across the River Clyde and hit the two young officers striding across the Liberty ship's slippery boatdeck with the impact of a close-up siren. Both skidded to a stop, traced the jarring sound to an approaching Scottish motorlaunch, then looked at each other with a mixture of amazement and alarm.

"What in holy creation is THAT?" bellowed the Third Mate, wiping his eyes to see better. He pulled his rainslick tighter around his neck. I did, too. It wasn't raining; it was just raw and wet, all over. Mid-March in this windswept Greenock anchorage downriver from Glasgow was no joke. Even the gyrating seagulls were complaining, forecasting still worse weather to come.

"Women!" I answered, letting out a low whistle. I wasn't sure whether to express my feelings with a "wow!" or "oh my gawd!"

The launch cut its motor, drifted in toward the looming ship and tied up at the gangway. And there before us, laughing and chattering in a lilting foreign language, stood the source of our wonder—seven of the fairest young women I had ever seen. Mostly tall and blond, they bounced out of the launch and up the gangway with striking ease and carefreeness, despite their strangely ill-fitting, bulky clothing. And how excited their faces! They beamed like the sun breaking out. One raised her head, her bright eyes moving up to us on the boatdeck, and smiled. White teeth sparkled—and, oh, how her eyes danced! I was so entranced I just gawked.

"Scandinavians," the mate announced with a touch of awe.

Boston Irish, Bernie Doyle didn't often show awe, even to friends like me—the ship's Third Assistant Engineer. He and I were the same age—24, and he was equally thin and tall—almost six feet, with a similar mop of brown hair and blue eyes. However, his ever-agitated angular face showed he was suffering from a much worse case of war damage. One of his ships had been torpedoed the year before, and went down in a holocaust of exploding ammo and fire. He survived, but his nerves didn't. So his eyes wandered around incessantly whenever he spoke. Like now. I could see them searching for something—for inner peace? I wondered—up around the mist-shrouded mast-tops.

Okay, so they're Scandinavians, I thought, but what else were they? And why were *they* coming aboard our ship instead of the Army officers we thought we would be taking home? And where were they going?

The ship's busy-bee purser, Bill Lamar, seized with unaccustomed flutter, met the new passengers at the top of the gangway and led them right past Bernie and me on the way toward their rooms. And here again came the one with the big smile. Only this time the smile was bigger...and more radiant. I opened my mouth to say *welcome aboard!* but no words came. I croaked, grimaced when I meant to grin, and finally managed to nod my head—all the while feeling my stomach turning funny flipflops.

Lamar continued to fawn over his charges like a mother hen clucking over her chicks. Other crew members scrambled alongside the ship's railing and bid the newcomers a much noisier, raucous welcome.

"Hey, Bill, bring dem dolls aft!" one called. "We got plenty room aft."

"The ship's stern!" another shouted. "Come see our stern."

Doyle spun his eyes, shook his head and moaned, "Oh, oh, here comes trouble."

I knew what he meant. Five months had now passed since the *SS William B. Travis* loaded 10,000 tons of grain in Philadelphia for what we supposed would be a short trip to Genoa. Short, indeed! Instead of going home, we were then ordered to Casablanca to pick up phosphate fertilizer for Gdynia, Poland. Next came Copenhagen, where we loaded ballast. And, now, here we lay in Scotland taking on fuel for the long voyage home, back to the USA.

True, we had hit some interesting ports—and, in one case, a dangerous one. Yet, everyone aboard was getting restless. During the war the American merchant marine had multiplied ten-fold from 50,000 men to 500,000—one of whom was me. Yet, the war had ended 10 months before in Europe, and 7 months before in the Pacific. Leaving us dead-tired of it all. It was high time we wartime seamen, who had carried fightingmen and the stuff of victory into every battle zone, quit the briny deep and became landlubbers again.

As for me, I found I had long since contracted an acute form of seasickness—meaning I was simply sick of the sea. I was sick of nearly four years of rolling, rattling, careening ships (I had served on seven such tubs). I was sick of narrow bunks and close quarters, of wretched food and dubious water, of longing for the transforming touch of a woman, of battling to stay afloat in raging seas...or, sometimes even worse, of staring endlessly at long lines of gray ships plodding gray seas under gray skies. Not to mention dodging enemy submarines in the North Atlantic and dive bombers in the Mediterranean. I was aching to get away from conflict and back into the real world—though after witnessing firsthand the reign of terror imposed by the Red Army "liberators" of Poland, I was no longer sure which was real.

More immediately troublesome, though, was the fact that a half-dozen crew members had gotten into trouble wherever we went. Nor did it help ease shipboard strains that the 30 men in the deck force, the Black Gang and the steward department were almost all black, while the 13 officers were white. And how did our ancient Captain Sandy McPherson respond when we went to him with reports of unruly crew conduct?

"Get their names!" he would shout: "They'll be duly reported when we get to port."

He would then retreat into his room and lock the door.

So the shipboard circus went on and on. And would now pick up pace, I feared.

Finally persuaded of the imminent problem of having attractive young women aboard, however, the captain decided to lay down some laws. He banned the girls from the main deck, where the crew had its quarters, and sealed off the two ladders leading up to the boatdeck. Here the newcomers would be staying in rooms built earlier for Army brass when the *Travis* had served as a troop transport. Armed guards would then be posted outside their quarters.

To which Third Mate Doyle cracked, "Sure hope I get guard duty!"

Bernie and I happened to be on deck when our passengers arrived because we both had just come off the 8-12 morning watch—he on the bridge and I down below. There, the fireman and oiler and I had teamed up to bring the No. 2 boiler back on line and warm up the Liberty's big triple-expansion reciprocating engine. Wifts of burning Bunker C oil now drifted downwind from the stack, mingling with vague fish odors from the Clyde and that rarest of cargo-ship rarities—the lingering fragrance of women's perfume. The ship was ready for departure. This was now heralded by a deafening blast of her steamwhistle, which set off a crescendo of receding echoes among the barren surrounding hills. The anchor winch whirred up forward and the screw began to thrash the water aft. Throbbing with new life, the *Travis* slid slowly downstream. Next stop after two more weeks of ocean: Baltimore.

We were going home!

The buzz of departure brought the passengers scurrying out of their rooms and back onto deck. They ran excitedly from rail to rail to catch a last glimpse of Scotland through the mists. Wind from the ship's forward motion drove the chill drizzle into their faces, wiped away the big smiles and made them burrow deeper into their coats, which struck me again as not only ill-fitting but completely out of style for such pretty young women. Were they all that poor? I wondered. Or since the war's devastation had uprooted millions from their homes in Europe, could these be DPs—displaced persons?

The mystery was solved by Purser Lamar, who joined me in the lee of the ship's housing and related that the seven were Norwegians, on their way to various US universities under the first postwar exchange scholarships. They were in their early 20s, and their names sounded like a cast from a Norse saga—Sigrid, Kari, Ragnhild, Ingebjorg, Hilde, Lillimor and Inger. They had boarded another Liberty in Copenhagen a week before we docked there...but, to everyone's horror, that ship (the *SS Byron Darnton*) had piled up on a reef in a violent storm just outside the mouth of the Clyde and broke in two. The Scottish coast guard had managed to save everyone aboard. But in abandoning ship in heavy seas, the girls were forced to leave behind almost all their private possessions. Present apparel was courtesy of the Red Cross.

Advance weather reports, like the seagulls' warnings, were bad, and the *Travis* began to heave in rising sea swells even before we got out of sight of land. Our initial course, as announced by the captain, was set for due south. We planned to run south past the Azores, then turn due west and follow the 37th parallel all the way to Hampton Roads and Chesapeake Bay. The aim was to get clear of the raw weather we had experienced in Poland and elsewhere here in the north and find spring, sun and smooth seas for the voyage home. No objections there!

At dinner that evening in the officers mess, I got my first close look at the by-now-famous seven. And, oh, what a grand look it was! Slender, energetic and strikingly good looking, they radiated strength and good health. And where was the make-up? There was none! How would American girls stack up against these northerners? I asked myself. The answer: They would have one tough time of it. Clad in colorful knitted sweaters and slacks, they swept into the room behind Lamar, and were seated by the ship's unusually solicitous steward at the room's far end. The off-duty officers at the other tables abruptly stopped talking and stared, their food forgotten. "Squareheads," the Second Mate had termed them in a loose moment—but that they weren't. In fact, there didn't appear to be a single square shape anywhere in sight. And in terms of brightness, I decided that even the dumbest could beat the Second Mate hands-down.

Two of the group had taken on a dull gray-green pallor—seasick, I guessed. Four others were talking and laughing as though they hadn't a care in the world. And then there was the final one—the only one who could fit Lamar's description of a "knockout." Nor was that meant only in terms of beauty, for two others were no less pretty. But this one was different. She stood out. She had poise. She had *presence*—though I wasn't sure what that meant either. Calm yet alert, she sat as straight as an SP on shore patrol and surveyed the room with wide-set blue eyes, the corners of her full mouth turned up in a tiny smile. She finally focused on me. Suddenly, a gleam of recognition must have hit, for there and then the tiny smile exploded into a dazzling display of pure art. And with it that special sparkle I remembered from the boatdeck. It set the whole room a-glow.

It also set my shipmates a-glow. A score of eyeballs followed her smile and found its target. And than the razzing began:

"Hey, Jim, what's your secret?"

"Oh, Third, may I have this dance?"

The final straw was piled on when Lamar sailed by, bent over and croaked out a whisper that could be heard around the whole room: "Her name's INGER!"

By then my face must have looked as though it was swabbed with red-lead paint. I stole a peek at Inger, who took in the whole incident with a tinkling laugh. She tossed her head, deep blond hair tumbling over her shoulders, and turned back to her companions.

Whew! I breathed, hacking at the food on my plate. Feeling increasingly warm under the collar, I stumbled to my feet and, without glancing at the girls again, bolted from the room. I was glad for the chance to return to the engineroom for the 8-12 evening watch—for the chance to get absorbed in work again. And while I went, I heard a small inner voice needling: "Don't forget you're a ship's officer. You canNOT get involved with passengers."

Easier said than done....

The very next evening three of them invaded my last sanctuary. Led by Purser Lamar [the traitor!], they came hobbling down the engineroom's three steep ladders into the very bowels of the ship. From afar I could see that one was Inger. I closed my eyes...hard. *This can't be happening,* I muttered. When I dared look again, they had reached the floorplates. And there I stood, surrounded by three stunning blondes—all smiling, expectant, waiting. I backed up against the operating desk, feeling like some cornered beast. *The fates have lined up against me,* I thought, *there's no way out but surrender....*

Lamar, the very soul of joviality, said: "Third, these lovely young ladies wanted to see the engineroom. And here they are! Meet Inger, Kari and er...ah...Ragnhild." My, how he butchered the pronunciation! He then slithered over and, in an aside for my ears only, continued: "Actually, what they really wanted to do was meet that lean engineer with the wavy hair and the friendly grin."

"Ah, so now you've also become a mindreader!" I retorted. "Thanks, you rat..."

Bill turned and left...and left me wondering what to do or say. For here, at last, was Inger herself—her expressive eyes following my every move. And what did I say? Nothing! My tongue again got tied in knots. Inger, however, saved the day. What are all these gauges for, she wanted to know. And how do you use this "funny thing" with the handle that says FULL, SLOW, STOP etc? [She was referring to the telegraph to the bridge, where Officer Doyle was then running the deck show.] And see how the flames roar in the boiler fireboxes! And how that monstrous engine thunders and hisses! (As it turned the big steel shaft leading aft under the 4th and 5th cargo holds all the way to the prop and the churning sea.)

In order to hear anything in this bedlam of noise, one had to get very close or shout. By mutual consent, I suppose, we chose the former. What a solution! Now I saw close up a woman with solid cheek bones and a small nose, arched eyebrows over big blue eyes, with marked concentration lines between them, and laughter crow's feet at the corners—plus, of all things, dimples that danced in and out of the cheeks as she smiled and talked. It was a face that showed a wondrous mix of intelligence, good humor, strength and sensitivity. But the main feature was her eyes: They looked at you—and into you—with a startling openness and honesty. I concluded that Diogenes might just as well hang up his lantern and look no further.

Pulling myself away with great effort, I put a new pot of coffee on the hotplate behind my stand-up desk. On deck, it was biting cold, with rising wind and waves battering the ship. Yet, here below in this wonderworld of engines, boilers, dynamos, pumps and condensers, it was warm and pleasant—despite the ship's lurching and the racket. Which embodied a strange phenonomen: If the slightest noise were out of cadence in the over-all cacophony, the trained ear could detect it immediately...and react. Like now. The strange noise was people laughing....

"The engineroom is really the heart of the ship," I told the visitors, adding in a lame effort to sound cute: "In fact, down here we run our own racket."

The reaction? Polite smiles. They just didn't get the double entendre. So no more joking around! I decided. Especially since Inger, who knew a few things about language, assured me that it's hard to grasp double meanings unless you're a near-native in a language.

Continuing more seriously, I said that here is created the power not only to make the ship go but also to provide the electricity, water and heat and repair services for all aboard. And, as the Third Engineer, I was in charge of the ship's electric system. (Which was sometimes a downright shocking job, I was tempted to tell them—but held my tongue.)

What about the bridge? one asked.

Yes ma'm, that's the brain of the ship—though that doesn't necessarily mean it's *peopled* by brains, I quickly added, thinking of our captain.

I also warned that we were all now considerably under the ocean, whose surface was some 14 feet up around the top of the boilers. Well, that didn't phase them at all. For here were people whose ancestors had lived by and on the sea for untold centuries. But it had once disturbed me plenty; during submarine attacks, with depth-charge explosions repeatedly slamming against the hull like satanic sledgehammers, I had horror-visions of the whole side of our torpedoed ship caving in right on top of me and my buddies here below...and sending us straight to Davy Jones' locker.

As the engineroom warmed up my visitors, they decided to shed their unneeded sweaters—with my help, of course. They shouldn't have. For, oh, how Inger filled out her blouse! Showing them around the engineroom, I also noted that no woman I ever knew wore slacks with such grace. Long legs combined with narrow hips and an even narrower waist and those bulging blouseworks to create a fabulous figure. I found it increasingly difficult to take my eyes off her.

My fireman and oiler were also impressed. In fact, they reacted to the visitors with goggle-eyed delight when I introduced them, their teeth gleaming like white pearls in their dark faces. No trouble-makers, these, I assured the girls, who looked apprehensive. One was from Alabama and the other from New York's Harlem, and both were studying my well-worn engineering books with me during the idle periods on watch. It was my hope that this would help prepare them for later Coast Guard exams and a better position in the Black Gang.

During our talk over coffee Inger proved herself amazingly open, direct and totally devoid of affectation. In fact, all three girls seemed as natural and refreshing as a Nordic breeze—Kari the tallest, Ragnhild the heaviest, and Inger the…well…just right! She spoke English with that lilting accent I had noticed when she first came aboard, and continued to ask enough questions to fill a quiz show. Like, in the first place, how on earth had I ever gotten here?

Well, I thought that was putting the prop in front of the ship. The big question was how *they* had gotten here.

"The shipwreck? Oh…*det var en mareritt!*" exclaimed Ragnhild in Norwegian.

"It really *was* a nightmare—the whole night!" Inger added in response to my puzzled look. And this is the story she told, emotions running the full gamut over her face, while the other two chimed in occasionally for extra emphasis:

Sailing westward, their previous ship had rounded the northernmost tip of Scotland and headed south toward the Clyde in a violent night-time storm. It never arrived…but smashed into a reef just outside the river's mouth. Right under a lighthouse! All that night, waves pounded the ship onto the rocks, with each shock rending the passengers' nerves with visions of ultimate disaster. Meanwhile, distress flares shot into the rainy sky, crisscrossing the glaring beams of the lighthouse, while the radio cracked out SOS signals. Daybreak showed cracks widening in the ship's hull; it was beginning to break up. Then came rescue! A Scottish coast guard launch finally swept through the waves, and everyone got into the lifeboats and off the doomed ship just before it broke in two with a thunderous roar.

"You're heroes," I said. "Er…a…heroines!"

"No, no, we were just scared…and lucky," Inger replied. "The real heroes were the seamen who somehow…I really don't know how…managed to lower the lifeboats into the sea without the waves smashing the boats against the ship and…and drowning us all."

Even so, I *was* impressed. It seemed to me that the girls' harrowing experience on this one trip beat anything I had gone through in all my 13 crossings of the sub-infested Atlantic.

Inger wasn't so easily put off concerning her first question, though. For some reason she persisted in wanting to know more about me. How had I gotten here? Well, I wasn't so sure myself. Who was during those war years? But I tried to hit the high points—avoiding anything personal—as her startlingly honest eyes continued to probe mine:

Actually, my present role in the *Travis* engineroom was somewhat unique, even though, originally, I hardly knew the difference between a pump and a generator. It all began when I joined the US Merchant Marine during the first year of America's involvement in World War II—a wild time when undefended oil tankers were being knocked down daily by Nazi U-boats along our East Coast like sitting ducks in a shooting arcade. My enlistment launched five months of basic seamanship training at Sheepshead Bay in Brooklyn, followed by a couple grueling years of sea duty as a fireman and oiler, mainly in the North Atlantic and the Med, but once out to the Persian Gulf. I then spent four glorious months "away from it all" at the USMS Officers School at New London, Connecticut, where I graduated at the top of my engineers class. (*That* got Inger's attention!)

My next move—last Summer—was to the Nordberg Diesel school in Milwaukee, Wisconsin…after which, in its boundless wisdom, the government routed me to a diesel-powered tanker tied up at a pier in Norfolk, Virginia. I took one look at the ship's ancient Burmeister and Wain diesel engine and concluded that I for one would never, ever be able to get that monster running again. Fortunately, I didn't have to. After six weeks, tugboats came alongside and towed us up the James River, where the ship was tied up in the US reserve fleet. And what a forlorn sight that presented! Here sat scores of once-proud veterans of the seven seas that had helped win the war, abandoned and rusting away. They obviously weren't going anywhere now. (Or ever more?)

I continued to relate that this past September, I signed on the *Travis* as Third Engineer for what I assumed would be my last trip to sea. We sailed to Cherbourg with a load of canned foods for a desperately hungry Europe (and as a bonus got three days off to travel by train to see an overjoyed, free-at-last! Paris). Once we returned home, though, I got what looked like bad news from the Chief Engineer. The First Engineer and the Second were leaving, he said. "And say, Jim, couldn't you stay on for one more trip? You'll be the one guy who knows what's going on down below."

Was that an order? Or an offer? Whatever, I told Inger, that's how

I came to be here on this last voyage. Reluctantly. But not right now!

The new First—Williamson Smith, inevitably called Smitty—turned out to be a friendly, fatherly, rotund graduate engineer who was more than double my age...and had ten times the technical knowledge. Trouble was, he had been crippled when his ship was hit by Nazi off-shore shelling during the Allies end-run disaster at Anzio, Italy, and could barely get down the ladders for the 4-8 watch. The new Second, in turn, turned out to like alcohol...a lot! He had put away vast quantities of wine in Italy, unmentionables in Casablanca, vodka in Poland, aquavit in Copenhagen and scotch in Glasgow. Under these various influences, he would then drone out a long-winded song with a Latin beat that soared repeatedly into this refrain:

You're the girl that I adore.
And when our money is all spent, I will go to sea for more.
Fine girl you are!

Meanwhile, one hardly ever saw the Chief; he and the Captain spent all their time in each other's quarters playing an endless card game. Thus, running the engineroom fell much on one very green green-horn named Jim. It was a miracle the ship moved at all!

But the most miraculous of all miracles, I was beginning to sense, must surely lay in the chain of events that kept me aboard the *Travis* for this final trip to sea. For how else could I ever have met Inger?

Inger! I abruptly woke up to the fact that it was almost midnight—time for eight bells to sound and the new watch to begin—and here we stood still talking! So the girls left...fast, promising to come back the next night. And that they did—all seven! Word had gone around that the best coffee on the ship was brewed down below on the 8-12 watch. And who loves coffee more than Scandinavians? So down the ladders they came, leaving little room for the crew to work. While I found the company absolutely grand, the First did not. Hereafter, he ruled, no more than two visitors could be below at any one time, for the rest of the trip. This meant, in essence, Inger and one other. And sometimes just Inger. I didn't protest at all!

The next day dawned with sobering weather portents. The wind was picking up along with the waves; the barometer had fallen below 29; and the sun, blinking through dark, racing clouds storming across the horizon, appeared as dull as a 25-watt light bulb. It reminded me of a favorite saying my grandfather used to recite: "Red sun in the morning, to a sailor it is warning...."

"'Fraid we're in for it," Third Mate Doyle said when I stopped by the bridge on the way to the engineroom. He was fuming over the 700 measly tons of ballast the port authorities had allowed us to take on in Copenhagen. The captain had asked for twice that amount, to no avail. And now the ship was being hit by a full-scale gale and riding high and light as a cork on mountain rapids.

"And what about our passengers?" I ventured.

"You couldn't possibly mean Inger? No, that couldn't be! Well, don't worry. Those Vikings'll do okay. They got salt water in their veins."

That was hardly reassuring. On my first trip to sea our ship ran directly into the tail-end of a hurricane near Nantucket. The bulk sulfur loaded in New Orleans kept shifting in the holds each time the ship rolled, almost capsizing her. We battled for a long, harrowing night to stay afloat, finally returning to New York to reload the cargo. No more complacency about the sea after that! I now stood in awe before a raging sea, when man and his creations seem pitifully small and helpless and utterly dependent on fate. Yes, the sea *is* a glorious thing. It's endless, timeless, restless, uncompromising, untamable—perhaps the last pure thing on earth. A vast reservoir of food and minerals. The aboriginal nursemaid of us all. Carrier of trade and travel routes to the four corners of earth. Yet, oh how dangerous at times! Like right now....

Worse, this infernally tublike, wallowing Liberty was nothing to inspire confidence. Libertys with their all-welded construction had compiled a notorious record of breaking up in storms and simply disappearing...with all hands. And now the *Travis* was pitching and rolling uncontrollably, with the screw coming out of the water on wave-crests and its normal thump-a-bump song of power giving 'way to a frightening race-away series of sharp cracks.

"Just hope we don't throw the screw," I muttered to the oiler on my watch.

Doyle must have shared my concern, for just then he phoned from the bridge and called for lower engine speed to reduce vibration.

Visiting the bridge at the end of my watch, I saw firsthand the frenzy I had felt below. Immense black-gray clouds hurtled overhead above the mast-tops, trailing ragged, spinning streamers. In flashing gaps blinked a faint-blue lifeless sky. And even as I watched, the clouds thickened and the sky vanished. Enraged winds shrieked through the cables, slid along the deck and slammed into the deckhouse. They whipped the sea into mountains of foam, filled the air with piercing spray and hurled roaring waves against the bow, lifting and tossing the ship like a drunken giant.

"Gusting up to 60 knots," the mate yelled over the din.

The short, wiry helmsman, feet spread wide and knuckles white against the wheel spokes, struggled to meet the mounting waves at just the right oblique angle. At this moment, he had become the most important person aboard. For all were all now relying on him alone to keep the ship from being broadsided by the five-story-high waves...and sent straight to the bottom.

But where had the passengers gone? Looking game but scared, they were holed up in the officers salon, I was told. All but one, that is. For there, peeking around the boatdeck housing at the wild sea, was a familiar face. Scrambling down from the bridgewing, I lurched along the tilting deck and almost collided with Inger as I turned the corner. She looked shaken. I laughed, waved my arm outboard and shouted over the uproar:

"Wow, isn't this some show!"

Inger swayed backward and tightened her grip on the doorway stanchion. "It's *fantastisk!*" she cried out. "I never dreamed the sea could be so vill...wild."

The shifting, slanting, staggering deck drove us closer, and I gripped Inger's arm to keep her from falling. She stared as though hypnotized as the leaping waves crashed over the deck, lifted the hull and sped on beneath, leaving the ship hanging breathlessly in midair, then plunging it shuddering into the next trough. My stomach plummeting apace, I asked shakily:

"Say, aren't you seasick?"

"Yes, a little. But mostly dizzy."

Brushing back her wind-tossed hair, she turned to go inside. But just then a giant wave caught the ship heeled far over, deluged the starboard lifeboats and poured across our feet. The deck caromed like a crazed elevator. Our knees buckled and Inger fell heavily, spinning in the receding stream of foaming water and sliding directly toward the lifeboat opening and the yawning hell beyond.

I dove for Inger and caught her arm with one hand, clawing at the steel deck with the other in a desperate attempt to stop our deadly slide. We banged up against the boat davit. Reacting instinctively, I threw out my leg...and it held. And there we hung for a small eternity, suspended between life and death, my slippery grip loosening steadily. Then, as abruptly as it had rolled to the right, the shuddering ship rose on the next wave and rolled steeply to the left. We slid away! Scrambling to my feet, I half-dragged, half-carried the distraught Inger along the careening deck and into the passageway.

Stunned, disheveled, soaked with seawater, Inger broke into wrenching sobs. I wrapped my arms around her and leaned against the bulkhead for support, holding her tight. Slowly, finally, she stopped. Then, still trembling, she raised her head and flung her arms around my neck...and kissed me. I was stunned! It was a quick yet wonderfully soft kiss, strangely warm through the icy seawater streaming down over our faces.

"Oh, thank you...thank you, Yim...Jim...Jimmy." she breathed. "You saved my life!"

And with that she broke away, leaving me shocked, speechless, staring into nowhere.

Shaking myself hard, I squished my way down to the galley and asked the gaping steward to send a tureen of hot soup up to Inger. Had she ever earned it! I then took a hot shower, put on dry clothes and got set to go down below into the dissonance-filled engineroom.

Was the ship going to make it? An even chance was the best we could hope for, Doyle said. And tonight would tell the story....

Toward midnight and the end of our watch, I began to detect the slightest change in the sea's pounding. Or was I just being misled by hope? No, there it was...in the engine's beat! Despite the creaking from every seam, the off-beat hammering was beginning to moderate. I put in a call to the bridge, and Bernie confirmed it: The wind *was* slackening! And better weather was on the way…tomorrow. But forget about sleep, he said. This meant another bad night of tossing and turning in your bunk and bracing yourself against every next shock.

Daybreak brought sighs of relief from everyone. The wind was abating…and even though mountainous waves still marched endlessly across the angry seascape, their violent cresting was subsiding. By mid-afternoon we all began to relax as the ship's crazed roller-coasting gave 'way to normal pitching and rolling.

And the passengers? I got only brief glimpses of them that day and next. Evidently, our nerve-wracking battle with the sea, coming on top of their shipwreck, had proven too much. It was almost as bad as the torture and killing and deprivation of the five-year-long Nazi occupation of Norway, they told the purser. And, mister, you can't get worse than that! For his part, Lamar found himself doubling…willingly…as both nursemaid and room-service waiter. With no lack of galley volunteers lending a hand. I sent words of encouragement with him to Inger and fretted over how she would act next time we met.

I needn't have worried. Thanks to the purser's blandishments and their built-in resilience, the girls showed their old exuberance when they finally appeared on deck again. The ship was back on course and fairly racing along at our normal running speed of 11 knots, rising and falling gently on long, even sea swells. The sun broke through the scattered clouds occasionally and, best of all, the air was getting noticeably warmer. An after-crisis, good-to-be-alive mood pervaded the ship.

When I saw Inger again in the officers mess, I went straight over to her, took her hand and asked as off-handedly as I could how it was going. She smiled…off-handedly, too…and quipped for the benefit of her pals:

"*Utmerket!* It was really *ingenting*…nothing."

But she pressed my hand…hard…and held it for one extra second. Yes, she did remember! I felt a surge of joy and announced grandly that all—meaning Inger—should visit the engineroom again soon. First Engineer Smitty just shook his head.

Inger and Ragnhild paid a visit that very evening. I stopped by the refrigerator room on the way down below and purloined some chicken drumsticks. I then proceeded to fry these on our hotplate while the guests watched with no little wonder. Such delicacies in Nazi-occupied Norway? Forget it!

A regular party atmosphere developed. The girls had been collecting "Americanisms" and were trying to fathom their mysteries. With the fireman and oiler joining in the hilarity when they could get away from their duties, Inger asked:

"What means 'to pull your leg'?"

Then Ragnhild: "Or 'to paint the town red'? Or 'be a wet blanket'?"

I choked out answers of sorts in between chuckles. And was further hit with:

"How 'bout being 'a dark horse'? Or 'a white elephant'? Or 'a bull in a china shop'?"

Then came more animals: "What do I get when I 'buy a pig in a poke'? Or 'go on a wild goose chase'? Or 'let the cat out of the bag'? And speaking of bags, what happens when I'm 'left holding the bag'?"

Inger found it all plenty bewildering, even though she said her major field of study in America was going to be English/American literature. "Don't Americans ever speak plain ol' straight English?" she pleaded.

"No," I replied, smirking ever so little, "in fact, the Brits say we don't speak English at all. That means you're going to have to learn a whole new lingo."

I found my favorite Norwegian a lot of fun. In repose, Inger was much like the others. But once involved in discussion, an amazing change took place. She became excited, animated—showing that keen interest and rare warmth toward others I had noticed before. And when she laughed, she threw back her head in unrestrained exuberance, baring a mouthful of magnificent, evenly set, gleaming teeth...and the whole place danced! I got the feeling that if a woman's quality were ever to be judged by her teeth, like a horse, Inger would win the Kentucky Derby.

I was dying to be alone with her, but wasn't at all sure I should be. Once in a while, our eyes would meet for a longer-then-normal moment, and I would feel my heart skip a beat. Things *were* different between us now. Yet I kicked myself for even thinking there might be anything more. Remember the fairytale, dare a cat look at a queen?

How could an ordinary seaman—one with no money, no connections, no particular plans or promise for the future—imagine someone like Inger being interested in *him*? I vowed to withdraw and avoid her as much as possible.

As the *Travis* steamed past the Azores and turned west, it ran into blissful days of balmy weather And the Norwegians turned out en masse, like sun-starved heliotropes, to blot up every ray of sunshine. In scanty garb. In fact, as scanty as possible. This was upsetting the crew, some killjoy told the captain.

"Them clothes got to go!" he exploded. "Er...I mean, it has to stop!"

Catching me coming up from watch that day, Inger took my reluctant hand and said excitedly: "Come, see what I've found!" She then led the way to the very top of the ship, to one of the former anti-aircraft gun turrets—now stripped of its weapons—and urged me to climb over and sit down. That was plenty inviting, for she had arranged lifejackets as cushions inside the three-foot-high barrier.

"You've been avoiding me," she said with a mock frown. "And I thought for sure we were friends...."

We were out of the wind, and the sun fell full and warm where we sat on the north side of the turret. Inger was dressed in a pair of worn slacks, which she had scissored off to reveal those long, lovely legs. Seeing that was tough enough. Still worse, she wore a man's shirt with the shirttails tied under her chest to reveal the maximum of midriff, and which now strained precariously against a single button. *What the devil!* I sighed, abandoning my last resolve, *surviving the war was easy compared with this....*

There was truly magic in the air. The *Travis* drifted along on gentle sea swells like a painted ship on a painted sea. But unlike Coleridge's ancient mariner, we gladly embraced the bloody sun at noon, which, high above the mast did stand, no bigger than the moon. After the punishing storm and many sleepless nights, it was balm for jangled nerves and rent spirits.

Then and in the days that followed, Inger asked repeatedly about "that wondrous land" beyond the setting sun. And about me. She had always dreamed of going to America one day...and now her dream was coming true! But she was worried over leaving her family and friends back in Oslo and whether she would really like America. Even worse, she worried over whether Americans would like her...and accept her. Would they?

Well, I considered that the most unnecessary question I ever heard! As far as I was concerned, there had to be something wrong with anyone who didn't like Inger.

"As for America, I hardly know where to start," I said, wondering ever so tentatively if Inger and I might somehow explore it together. I went on to say that our country is big and nothing if not varied. It's seashore and mountains and prairies and desert and swampland, the cold north and the hot south, huge cities and small towns, farms and vast forests. And the people are just as varied. They come from everywhere. That's why our national motto is so fitting: *E pluribus unum.* Somehow, against all odds, we've managed to pull a huge mess of diverse peoples and states and ways of life into one big, sprawling, amazingly well-working unit.

"So, Inger," I concluded, "your image of America really depends on where you grab it—where you land on it. In fact, where *will* you land? I mean, where will you be studying?"

"Kalamazoo College, in Michigan!" Inger said that with considerable bravado, even though all she knew of that far-off place was that Glenn Miller's band had recorded a lively song about it. "Think I can learn about America there?"

"Yep, they play baseball there, too."

"Oh? Oh-h-h-h...."

I saw she was completely puzzled, so hastened to add:

"Well, you should know that my brother Ernie—he's three years older—is a professional ballplayer. Rose all the way up to Spring training with the Pittsburgh Pirates in '43. Roomed then with one of the game's greats—Honus Wagner. But then Uncle Sam grabbed him. So while I was dodging torpedoes in the Atlantic, Ernie was playing baseball...imagine that!...for the US Navy at Bainbridge, Maryland. But the point he makes is this: You can never really know our national character unless you know our national sport. For here you'll see every player trying his best to stand out as an individual star...but knowing that the real key to winning is teamwork. So, Inger, go see all the baseball games you can sandwich in between your studies—both the formal ones in town and the pickups on sandlots. It'll be confusing at first. But, by golly, I think you'll learn to love it...AND America!"

Almost out of breath from my soliloquy, I switched back and asked: "But how on earth did you decide to go to Kalamazoo?"

"I didn't. They offered me a scholarship...and I took it!"

Inger then related that during the raw years of Nazi occupation of Norway, she had gotten a job in a leather-goods store to help support the family. Then, during evenings she turned with intense concentration to studies, which she had always before shrugged off as some peculiar joke. She had cleared "gymnasium," passed her "artium" exams (boy, was I ever confused by those words!) and then enrolled in a tough study schedule at the University of Oslo. So she already had the equivalent of a US Bachelor of Arts degree. (This made me feel pretty small, since all I could show was one tiny year of prewar college.)

When US and British forces arrived in the heady days of liberation, Inger scored a touchdown (though she didn't exactly use that US-ism). She got a job as a three-way English-German-Norwegian interpreter for the Americans, helping our troops inventory and dispose of Nazi war materiel in Norway. As proof, she proudly displayed a letter from the commander of the USA's Task Force A. This cited her "high degree of intelligence and sound judgment" on the job, plus her "loyalty, dependability and efficiency" and unusual "cheerfulness, character and appearance."

"Hell, even a blind man could see you got that!" I broke in.

Such sterling service had been rewarded by what Inger felt was a thoroughly American gesture of generosity: She was awarded that scholarship for a year of study toward her Master's Degree...at Kalamazoo.

"You know the place?" she asked anxiously. "It sounds so exotic. Like Indians...and pioneers...and the frontier...and...."

"Not really, dear Inger," I replied, inadvertently slipping in that "dear." Actually, I didn't want to throw cold water on her vision. "But I do believe that's all a thing of the past—say, over a hundred years past—back when that area was settled as part of our Northwest Territory."

"But dear Inger," I continued (since I had gotten away with that once, I boldly tried it again), "don't you have a last name? Or is Inger sort of like a stage name—requiring nothing more? Who *is* Inger?"

A big laugh came with the answer: "Ah, you've never heard of Erling Krogh?"

"No...." I shook my head slowly, trying to make a connection.

"Well, that's my father. He's one of Norway's greatest operasingers. And its most beloved folksinger, too. If you were from the upper Midwest, where so many Scandinavians settled, you would know all that. There, they call him 'Norway's Caruso.' And my mother's from Denmark. She's a pianist...and often serves as Pappa's accompanist. So my older sister Grete and my younger brother Erling and I grew up in a home filled with music. And my full name? It's Inger Marie Krogh. But please, don't change—just call me Inger."

Ah, there's the secret! NOW I knew why Inger was different. Who else did I know that had graduated beyond church hymns and hillbilly and cowboy songs and jazz? No one! Including me. And Inger wasn't talking about the modern stuff that's designed to excite and inflame...but about music that enriches and inspires. While opera to me was as remote and exotic as New York's Met or Milan's La Scala, it was Inger's first love.

Inger went on to tell me that she had grown up as a fun-filled rascal of sorts in the Majorstua area on the west side of Oslo. She had proved herself a "romp" in the sandbox and a tough competitor on the playground—the first out on cross-country skis in Winter in Nordmarka's forests on the north side of Oslo and the first to dive into the icy fjord waters in Summer. She didn't just play at being a Viking; she *lived* the role. And forward boys had discovered early on that she could hold her own in a snowball fight or hand-to-hand combat.

At home, Inger's Pappa had provided inspiration while Mamma directed a tough, no-nonsense Danish upbringing...in both behavior and spending. This showed up in her favorite commands: *Ikke skab deg!* [Don't show off!]; *Si ikke noe vrovel!* [Don't talk nonsense!] and *Ta deg sammen!* [Pull yourself together!]. With Mamma, you didn't sit around at home listening to the radio or playing games or snacking on the sofa with your friends; you either studied or worked or got out. And when you came in, you took off your shoes and parked them by the door and changed to slippers. At mealtime, you sat straight at the table and ate plain, wholesome foods. [And no complaints, please, for, as Mamma said, *hunger is the best cook!*] What's more, you didn't get money to ride around Oslo on *trykken*; you walked.

The upshot of this "tough love" raisin'? It gave Inger what I suspected from the beginning—an enviable inner solidity and personal security. And that fantastic body I was seeing was no gift from the gods—even though they may have handed down the potentials through Inger's parents. It was developed through a strenuous life of hiking, biking, skiing, swimming, etc, etc.

"No free love?" I ventured.

"Du, da!" she retorted. "You Americans watch too many movies. Sure, Scandinavians have long engagements. Some might even live together for a while. But it's all meant to lead to a permanent relationship. Even marriage. No pro...mis...cu...ity!"

She bungled the word, then said it again, emphatically.

"And what about your present status, Inger?" It was my turn to be apprehensive.

"Status?"

"Yeh, you know, boys, boy-friends. Are you engaged? Or somethin'?"

"Ja, once," she replied slowly, a distant look clouding her eyes. "But that's all past now."

She turned and faced me directly: "You rascal, you've got me talking my head off...about me. Now it's your turn. What about you?"

That's easy, I replied...and gave her the mercifully short version—that I was born in a true mixing-bowl neighborhood in Pittsburgh—almost on top of the J&L steel mill in Glenwood. But when the city virtually shut down during the Depression and the family income dried up, my sister and brother and I were shipped off to my grandfather's small farm along the Ohio River...in southern Ohio. There, I grew up in a world much like Tom Sawyer's—with riverboats and occasional raging floods, a one-room schoolhouse with pot-bellied stove and McGuffey's Readers, revival meetings and the *Holy Bible*, 4th of July picnics and American Legion parades and the Boy Scout *Handbook*. Plus dawn-to-dusk work hoeing corn and pitching hay, chopping wood and cutting the grass, feeding the chickens and slopping the hogs, firing up castiron kettles for the weekly wash and helping with baking and canning. *Whew!* I felt worn out just thinking about it.

"Yet, so help me, Inger, I loved it! And you won't believe this, but I also loved school and my studies—something I guess I got from my schoolteacher mother."

"So, how do you do...? I mean how *did* you do in school?" asked Inger. (Now, why would she be so all-fired interested in *that,* I wondered.)

"Well, highschool went like a breeze. Even became class valedictorian." (Inger nodded vigorously.) "But it wasn't like I was that good—just that the competition wasn't much."

I added that, like her, this had led to a scholarship of sorts—for a year's tuition at Marshall College across the river in Huntington, W. Va. There I had taken pre-med studies while working at the library in order to eat. Then came the war and, carried away by patriotic fervor, I joined the US Merchant Marine, never expecting to survive.

"Yet here I am, still in one piece. Amazing!"

"And what do you want to do now? Finish your studies and become a doctor?"

"Darned if I know!" I said. I said I felt that medicine was fine...and so was engineering. But the war had changed a lot for me—and now news work was getting heavy attention. Why? Because it put you in the middle of what's happening in the world...and maybe even provided a chance to influence the outcome. And, God save us all! did the outcome ever need improving!

Inger made a wry face at that: "Well, I only hope you're able to do more than others have over the past five thousand years."

"But Inger, here we sit at what could be a great turning point of history. The war has destroyed so much...but it's also set the stage for new approaches to everything. Last Summer, the United Nations was founded. And just this Winter, your own Trygve Lie was elected the UN's General Secretary. America has shown it has incredible productive power. And now that power can be put to use to help rebuild. We can change the world!"

"But Jim Jim Jim, what about *people*! All that's not going to change people. You Americans are so naive! If you...we...are going to change anything, we've got to be more... much more...realistic. History is one long horror-tale of war after war after war. Of man's murderous inhumanity toward man. Look at those Nazi concentration camp horrors. The latest awful chapter! People are a driven lot—driven by hate, fear, greed. Man slaughters his neighbors to get what he wants. And what he gets, he hoards—even when other neighbors are starving. Sure, people's homes and clothing and appearance have changed. They even smile a lot—Americans more than most. But don't be misled! Underneath, they remain wild beasts—the same old driven cavemen."

Taken aback, I tried to lighten the mood: "Well, I'd sure like to share my cave with you."

"That would be one *merkelig*—one strange—cave!" she shot back. (Man o man, I thought, did she ever reject that big morsel of bait I threw out! Or did she?)

I had to admit...reluctantly...that Inger's assessment of human nature dovetailed with mine, at least partly. For instance, during an enemy attack on our convoy in the Med, where one ship had been blown sky-high with a terrible loss of life, I remember thinking, God above! this isn't a theater of war; it's theater of the grotesque. Up there in those airplanes and in coffin-like submarines under what should have been the glorious sea...were young men just like me—all trying desperately to kill us before we could kill them. And here on the surface are other young men—in our Navy guncrew and escort vessels—blasting away at the attackers...trying just as desperately to kill them before they kill us. Everyone trying to cheat the Grim Reaper and the threat of violent death. And right under deck was the cause of all this havoc—lumbering merchant ships loaded with the fatal instruments of war. We Americans felt an overwhelming compulsion to deliver these to the battlefront...while the attackers felt just as strongly that they had to stop us. And, meanwhile, merchant seamen like me weren't shooting at anyone. We operated the ships and just stood here like helpless dolts—big, fat, juicy, sitting-duck targets being blasted at from all sides. It was a scene straight out of hell. *Manmade* hell. Grotesque! And making it even more grotesque was that similar horrors were being played out on all the seven seas, in the air and in a thousand other battles across the world.

Changing the subject abruptly, Inger asked where my family had come from.

"Right out of America's soil. Been in America nearly three hundred years."

"So you're a real American!"

"Yep, three hundred per cent...for better or worse. In fact, I don't think you'll be meetin' a more American American."

I said I understood that Dad's family came mostly from England and Mom's mostly from Germany, though there were absolutely no traces or memories of foreign origins among those still living. Both sides had settled along the Ohio and in eastern Kentucky...where the people were fiercely independent, as stubborn as mules, and sometimes downright mean.

"But no mean allies to have on your side in the battles of life," I hastened to add.

"Stubborn as mules, you say? And every man a king? That sounds like Norwegians!"

"You, too?"

"Try me!"

I decided I'd better not push my luck too far. I had met Norwegians before—seamen whose ships had been sunk and who had transferred to US ships. However wounded or worn out, they were not to be stopped. They were determined to keep on sailing until either they were killed or their country was finally set free.

The surprising conclusion I got out of these exchanges was that even though Inger and I had grown up worlds apart, we had much in common. We both had to toe the line in growing up. We were totally unspoiled; we were taught to work and earn our own way and *give*, not get. And we were drilled with a strict moral and ethical code. The differences (which were by no means minor): Growing up in America's Bible Belt, I had received a bigger dose of the Old Time Religion. I had nothing like the education in languages that Inger had (English, German and French in addition to the Scandinavian tongues). Nor the unique social status conferred on the daughter of an acclaimed national singer. And while I knew Stephen Foster, Irving Berlin and John Philip Sousa, Inger sang along with Verdi, Wagner and Puccini.

"But all these composers belong to you as well as me, for music is truly THE international language," Inger insisted. "What's more, our basic cultures aren't really so different. That's why Norwegian immigrants took so readily to America. And, by the way, did you know that Norway lost a bigger share of its population to America than any other land except Ireland? And that there are now more people with Norwegian blood in their veins in America than in Norway? Almost overnight our immigrants shifted from being new Americans who spoke Norwegian to being regular Americans, period. And you know who benefited from that!"

"You couldn't possibly mean America?"

"You said it!"

And so went our conversations as the *Travis* steamed westward. The days of bright sunshine made Inger as happy as a kid. She luxuriated in it! Nor did she get sunburned like most of her pals; rather, the sun lightened her hair and turned her skin into a soft tan, making her look like a model for some exotic sunlotion. Who, then, could blame me when one day in the turret I got carried away and put my arm around Inger's supple waist—hesitantly, ready to withdraw at the slightest resistance. Instead, Inger turned and faced me head-on. My arm tightened.

"Remember how you saved my life?" she whispered.

"Do I! My god, Inger, how could I ever forget?"

"Then, you ought to know about an old Norse tradition. It says that once you've saved someone's life, you become responsible for that person...ever after!"

"Howzat? Wazzat m-mean?" I mumbled in consternation.

"It means...if you want to, you can kiss me...*now!*"

Want to? I was dying to! Lips met and melted together. Arms encircled each other in a tightening embrace. The turret exploded with bygone ack-ack fire. The sea disappeared. The sun set. We soared off into space. Or were we falling?

B-O-I-N-G!

That was my head hitting the steel deckplates. Locked together in a whirl of pure joy, oblivious to the laws of gravity, we crashed—me underneath, Inger luckily on top. And what came next? Despite my throbbing head, both of us broke out laughing!

"Wowwee, isn't this a pretty sight!"

I heard the words coming in from a far, far distance. Was it a woman's voice? It came closer: ""Hey, is that all you guys got to do?"

Then, right in my ear: "How 'bout a sandwich? C'mon, Inger, straighten yourself up! See here. We went to the galley and packed a picnic. It's time to eat!"

Returning to reality, I looked up and beheld four smiling faces peering impishly over our turret. The girls waved gaily. Inger looked, too—a pained grin on her face. We shook ourselves loose, smoothed out our clothing, tried to restore our composure, and grudgingly invited the others into our hideaway—for a very untimely snack.

That evening at dinner, I discovered another side to Inger's personality—a curiously combative side that made me wonder if she harbored inside some sort of mischievous troll. Especially when it came to politics. This showed up when a rebroadcast of an early March speech by Winston Churchill crackled in over our shortwave radio and precipitated a heated discussion around the salon.

To me, Britain's wartime leader stood second only to our late President Roosevelt in my private pantheon of heroes. The President, who died less than a year before, had influenced my life deeply to date, while Churchill had offered inspiration and hope throughout the war. But now Britain's wartime Prime Minister was a "former"—recently booted out of office by what appeared to be an ungrateful electorate. Appearing in Fulton, Missouri (of all places!) he now sent his sonorous voice reverberating around the salon, triggering deep, thoughtful silence among those who had struggled and suffered so much during the past years—among us seamen on the world's ocean supply lanes and among our passengers under the heel of a merciless occupation army. He was talking about our erstwhile ally, the Soviet Union, and about securing peace in a torn world—and a sense of shock swept over us as his words poured out:

A shadow has fallen upon the scenes so lately lighted by the Allied victory.... From Stettin in the Baltic to Trieste in the Adriatic, an iron curtain has descended across the continent.

He went one to say that small Communist parties, backed up by Soviet troops, were inexorably taking over the Eastern States of Europe and imposing totalitarian control on hapless peoples. *This is certainly not the Liberated Europe we fought to build up. Nor is it one which contains the essentials of permanent peace....*

An IRON curtain! I looked at Inger to catch her reactions. But her taut expression showed she was wrestling with some tough internal thoughts. My own thoughts, in turn, got hung up on the word *iron*. As in iron fist. Iron maiden. Iron rule. Welcome, everyone, to the new Iron Age! Where East Europe would now be crucified on a Cross of Iron. Or could we take solace in Oscar Wilde's thinking...that iron curtains do not a prison make, nor iron bars a jail. For won't the human spirit still transcend all barriers, all attempts to contain and crush it...by iron weapons and iron force?

I do not believe that the Soviet Russia desires war, Churchill continued, *what they desire is the fruits of war and the indefinite expansion of their power and doctrines.*

Holy hell! I thought, we're hardly out of one war and here's Churchill warning about *another* one! Inger's face had now turned pale, her eyes narrow slivers of blue glass. And Bernie Doyle's gaze was wandering desperately all over the ceiling. He glanced at me and growled, "Those lousy commies have just thrown the world's telegraph into reverse!"

Concluding there is nothing *our Russian friends and Allies...admire so much as strength, and nothing for which they have less respect* than weakness, Churchill called for America and the British Commonwealth to form a special partnership, maintain their military power, now being rapidly demobilized, and strengthen the "Sinews of Peace" on behalf of the Free World.

The room erupted into noisy applause at this ending. But one of the passengers sat on her hands. She frowned and declared that she thought Churchill was being an alarmist. The Russians, she added, should be given a chance to show "they really aren't all that bad."

This was like throwing a hand grenade into the room. One of the mates shot back:

"Sister, you don' know what the hell you're talkin' 'bout!"

Another fairly shouted: "If you think Hitler was bad, wait till you see what Stalin's gonna do to you!"

The young women reeled visibly. Trouble was, wartime propaganda (our own, no less) had led them to believe—like the rest of the world—in the good intentions of "Uncle Joe". After all, he *was* our ally. But this particular crew had just been in Poland and seen Soviet brutality close up. Our illusions were shattered. We saw a new reign of terror being imposed at gunpoint on the Poles, who had just emerged from the long nightmare of Nazi control. This included anyone connected in any way with the Nazis, of course, but...much worse...it included anyone who looked even remotely like a supporter of democracy. Nights in Gdynia were punctuated with gunfire and distant screams. Out in the city, I was approached three times by people pleading for help in getting onto our ship and out of Poland. And when the *Travis* sailed, 40 stowaways were found in the cargo holds and under the engineroom floorplates.

A final sordid act in this tragedy was played out in Copenhagen, where we were forced to turn the weeping Poles over to their communist embassy. All of us were dismayed and burning mad, for we knew in our bones the kind of fate that awaited them back home. So now we took our frustration out on the unknowing girls.

One bright passenger, however, twisted the knife: "Okay, you see the communists as bad actors. And, like us, you also despise Norway's Quisling as the ultimate symbol of a traitor. But did you know that he based his whole case of collaborating with the Nazis on his fear of Soviet Communism? He felt that only Germany could prevent Russia from overrunning Europe...and therefore urged everyone to support Germany."

Quisling an *ally*? Unthinkable! Here was totally unwanted evidence of what bad choices politics poses—not to mention all the bad bedfellows you wind up sleeping with.

Inger at that moment shook herself and, emotion twisting her face, denounced politics in general: "It's a dirty, dirty business! It contaminates everyone it touches. It's a self-centered chase after power and prestige. It breeds conniving, calculating, superficial people. It...."

This outburst woke up Captain McPherson with a start. "Ah, yes, power corrupts," he thundered, borrowing a page from Britain's Lord Acton, "and absolute power corrupts absolutely!"

Well, everyone around the salon nodded his head at that one. We agreed...furtively, of course...that the old geezer should know that better than anyone. He had proved himself often wrong but never, never in doubt.

"But Inger," I said, "isn't that the grand thing about democracy— that it gives people a chance to get rid of bad politicians? It's when good people *don't* get involved that we get bad officials, right? Isn't that what brought Hitler to power in Germany? And wouldn't the Russian people like to get involved...if they could...and throw out a lot of their ruling S-O-Bs?"

"Posh!" came the heated rejoinder. "Politics and politicians have ruined Norway...and will probably ruin America, too. Before the war, our leaders greased up to voters by pushing big social programs...and starving defense. They virtually invited invasion. And that's what we got! Then came the Quislings. And they sacrificed everyone to grease up to the Germans."

Inger paused and caught her breath, her eyes flashing sparks. "And now, a whole flock of super-patriots are wreaking vengeance on anyone suspected of collaborating with the Nazis. What used to be a cozy, happy country is now filled with suspicion...and fear...and hatred. THAT's politics for you. Hah!"

Inger bit off the last word, leaped from her chair and bolted from the room, leaving me staring at the ceiling alongside Doyle. I was stunned. I already knew that Inger was no spineless dummy. But now she had showed...decisively...that she possessed strong convictions. All doubtlessly shaped by strong experience. And expressed with strong feelings. I concluded that while Inger might be *persuaded* to do something, she wasn't going to be *pushed* into anything.

At watch-changing time the next day, I was stopped by First Engineer Smitty, whose furrowed brow and intent look indicated he had something on his mind. He limped over to join me at the engineer's desk and said in his tentative, fatherly manner: "Been seein' a lot of that girl lately, haven't you, Jim?"

"Yessir," I answered slowly, getting the drift of his meaning. I then and there decided to beat him to the punch and seek his counsel about Inger. The long and short of it, I explained, was that while I had known other girls, and had almost married one, this time it was different. Inger was special—*very* special! I had really fallen for her. Would she even consider...could I even consider asking her to marry me?

"Marriage!" Smitty exclaimed as though I had hit him with a ballbat. "Good god, Third, you've just met the girl. You don't know one thing about her. You don't know her family. You don't know her background. You don't know how many men she's been sleepin' with. You don't know NOTHIN'!"

"But damn it all, I know enough...I know enough to know...to know I love her!" I blurted out in a flash of anger.

"Love? Yeh, yeh. What a grand thing it is! But to love or not to love, that's not the question, is it? The question is, do you really *like* her...as a person? Enough to want to spend your life with her—*all* your days. And not just the nights. Or do you just love that beautiful body?"

"I'm sorry I asked." I blurted out, turning away. "Let's forget it...."

"Now, now, Jim, I'm sorry myself. I answered without thinking. What I meant to say is that marriage is one darn serious subject. You might even say marriage is forever. You're talking about someone you're gonna live your whole life with. Let's think about it together."

Smitty shuffled his stricken feet around on the floorplates for what seemed a long time, then looked up as though he had made a major decision.

"Jim, I'll give it to you straight. You're thinking too much 'bout yourself. What about the girl...and her future? She's a...a foreigner," [He almost said *G-D furriner!*] "and you're talking about planting her somewhere in America maybe five thousand miles from home. Five thousand miles from her family and all her friends. Probably in an environment she doesn't know or understand or can't adjust to. Or give a damn about. How you gonna cope with that?"

"But, First, if we really love each other, what's all that matter? We'll find a way!"

"Again, that's great...assumin' it all pans out. But l can tell you that love can wear down to a frazzle...and finally disappear...when there's too much struggle—if things go too wrong."

Smitty's point wasn't sinking in. I guess I didn't want it to. Or my head was too hard. Or too full of Inger. He then drove it home:

"Third, up to now I had the feeling you were pretty smart...but I'm beginning to think you're a real dunderhead. Look! This girl's no dockside barmaid. She's got class. Probably comes from a good family. Might even have money. And what do you have? *Nothing!* What can you possibly offer that she's used to? *Nothing!* And what does that mean? That means nothin' but trouble ahead...for you as well as her."

He paused, cleared his throat and looked up full of sympathy: "I know this hurts, Jim, but do yourself...and her...a big favor: Let her go!"

Let Inger go? I couldn't stand the thought. Smitty had staggered me with what suddenly seemed an unbearable weight. I felt crushed. I spun on my heels and walked away as fast as I could...trying to hide my bitter disappointment.

As dusk was descending across the western sky that day, the forward lookout signaled the first sighting of the Virginia shoreline. It should have been an occasion of great joy. But I simply wasn't up to it. I had resisted Smitty's counsel mightily at first. Letting Inger go seemed almost like defying fate, which had miraculously brought us together here on the high seas, miles and miles from nowhere. Yet, his undeniable wisdom slowly began to erode my resolve. Finally, I came around to agreeing with him...for Inger's sake. And decided I must avoid her at all costs. So I had Purser Lamar spread the word that we were making major repairs in the engineroom and could not have visitors. Then, I ate in the messhall either before or after the passengers...and beat it out fast.

Right then, since I had some time before my watch began and felt a desperate need for fresh air, I walked haltingly forward toward the bow...and toward the pencil-thin strip of land that rose slowly out of the sea far ahead. High clouds drifted overhead, ingeniously painted by the vanished sun a shifting red, then gold and gray...while Venus blinked in the gaps of darkening blue sky like a guiding star over the Promised Land.

Leaning over the deck railing, I looked down where the blunt bow parted the sea and beheld a school of porpoises leaping and weaving in gay abandon as they escorted our ship homeward. I found it impossible to share in their gaiety, though. I felt empty and alone, filled with a gnawing foreboding about the future. Three and a half years had been torn out of my life by the war. I had been only too glad to contribute that to the country I love and help rid the world of a monstrous evil. Yet, after the shock of Poland and the warning by Churchill, peace now seemed as elusive as ever, and I wondered dejectedly if all the sacrifices of so many, many millions were going to be in vain. German and Japanese imperialism had been stopped, sure, but it now looked as though those evils were being replaced by one equally monstrous: Russian imperialism spearheaded by international communist subversion.

Inger maintained this could be even worse because it was so insidious in confusing the gullible, thus undermining our open societies. For instance, communism promised abundance, but in reality distributed poverty. It preached equality, but in fact set up a new aristocracy of super-bureaucrats who enriched themselves at the expense of everyone else. It extolled peace and freedom, but in practice operated as a brutal, aggressive police state. But the biggest mystery of all was that so many otherwise intelligent people in the west—especially in universities, labor unions, government and the press—swallowed whole-hog the communists' utopia line, hook and sinker, and absolutely refused to recognize the blunt facts.

How could this be? she asked me insistently.

Well, I wish I knew! I suggested, however, that the fault might well lie in ourselves—that perhaps we shouldn't expect intellectuals to be all that intelligent....

Anyway, I had experienced much during the war—maybe too much—and had grown up a lot in the process, so maybe the lost years weren't all wasted. Now, though, I knew I would have to pick up the shattered pieces and run like hell to catch up. Alone! It was a daunting challenge—almost overwhelming at that moment—and I shivered involuntarily, wondering where and how to begin. I then returned to that vagrant hope...which kept coming up though ever so vague and irrational...that Inger and I might do so together. That was one dumb, dumb hope, I now realized. I felt a strange urge to cry, then choked it off—sensing the utter incongruity of adding tears to those limitless waters below.

The clatter of footsteps behind woke me up with a jolt.

"Hei, hei! There you are!" came the lilting call. Breaking all the captain's rules, Inger came running forward, her golden hair flying in the dwindling light and bubbling over with excitement and enthusiasm.

"Well, we finally made it!" she whooped.

I kept my head down, embarrassed over my bleak mood, and mumbled: "Look, Inger. See the porpoises...."

Inger leaned over my shoulder and looked down. But the racing swimmers were nowhere to be seen; they had moved on to other games. She then turned full-face toward me, saw my glistening eyes and cried: "Hey, what's wrong?"

"Oh, damn damn damn, Inger," I blurted out. "Now you'll be leaving...and...and I'll never see you again!"

"*Oy, du toysekopp!*" (Again, a dunderhead!) "Of course, you will...if you really want to. In fact, I'd feel awful if you didn't...."

Impulsively, spontaneously, we threw our arms around each other, and kissed...and kissed. Unashamedly and openly. Clinging to each other as though afraid to let go. Much to the delight of the forward lookout, who let out a wawhoop and a piercing whistle. This snapped us back to reality. We looked up and, as Leif Ericsson must have done a thousand years before, beheld the great continental land mass of America stretching out before us as far north and south as the eye could reach, looming ever larger across the vast, beckoning western horizon. It was a deeply moving moment of insight. For there in that awesome panorama of sea and land, sunset and evening star, we caught a rare, fleeting glimpse of our future.

Chapter II

The *Travis* tied up at the B&O Marine Terminal in Baltimore to the raucous tune of unrestrained shouting by dockworkers and the frantic clatter of cranes, trucks and pierside machinery. Inger took it in with high enthusiasm. It was her first direct contact with America, and she loved it, uproar and all. It was not her first experience with the US, however. Sailing north on Chesapeake Bay, the ship had been greeted by noisy honking, and overhead we beheld an incredible sight—a whole sky-full of Canada geese winging their way along the East Coast flyway toward far-north nesting grounds. Incomparably strong long-distance flyers, they paraded by from horizon to horizon in constantly shifting, wide-arrow formations.

Inger was awestruck. She stood at the railing behind the No. 2. lifeboat, head covered by a white wool ski cap and looking like a Valkyrie preparing to invade an alien shore, her blue eyes squinting at the heavens above, the morning wind blowing blond hair all over her neck. I restrained my reaching hands, reminding myself that the 8-12 watch was only moments away.

"Never knew America was like THIS!" she exclaimed.

"You've been watching too many movies, yourself," I answered gleefully, remembering her earlier comment about Scandinavia. "Now you see with your own eyes that America is more...much more...than New York, Washington and Hollywood. We got nature, too!"

"Gee, there must be thousands up there. Where...where on earth are they going?"

"Back where they came from—back where they were born."

"But how do they know how to get there?"

"Ah, now you've asked the big one. Who knows? The Creator,

maybe! He put into each an ingenious guidance system that tells him exactly where to go and how to get there."

"Do you think He also gave that to you and me?"

"Ah, Inkie, you just never stop, do you?" I responded in exasperation.

"Well, *did* he?" she persisted.

"You really want an answer? Okay, then...you have to read a revealing poem by William Cullen Bryant, a famous American editor and supporter of Abe Lincoln during our Civil War. It's called *To a Waterfowl.* I think that'll convince you you've got a guidance system, too."

"So how does it work?"

"Ah, you rascal, now you've discovered our own little secret! For didn't it bring you and me together out of nowhere—in the far, farthest corner of the North Atlantic?"

"And where will it lead us?"

"Dear, dearest Inger, you're going to have to wait a long, long time to find that out. In fact, I'm afraid you'll never know that answer until the day we die...."

And with that, I turned on my heels and fled into the engineroom, even while I saw a new question forming on her lips.

The date was April 9, which, by coincidence, was a Red Letter Day for both of us. For Inger, it marked the sixth anniversary of the terrible shock of the Nazi invasion of Norway... while, for me, it marked the third anniversary of that wild first trip to sea when my ship almost sank in a hurricane. So we took this beginning as an unusual omen that just might signal something special in terms of the road ahead. But whether for good or bad—well, we decided to leave that to the same fate that had brought us together. Which looked pretty darn good...*so far*!

By late-afternoon, Inger and the six other passengers were cleared by immigration and customs officials and loaded with their baggage onto an open truck. They were being routed by education authorities onto an overnight train to New York, where they were to undergo briefings on their individual study plans and dispatched to various colleges across the country.

Finishing dressing in my room, I heard the truck engine start and ran frantically to the gangway, shouting all the way STOP! That the driver did, allowing me to race down and jump over the tailgate...and into the arms of seven beaming blondes. All sitting on laundry bags behind the truck cab. It was the first time they had seen me in my officer's uniform, and I got a royal reception. Inger managed to fend the others off, and we rattled and rocked over railroad tracks and pot-holed streets toward the city, all the time singing (?) at the top of our voices such current hits as *Chattanooga Choo-Choo* and *Sentimental Journey* and, in soulful tribute to Inger and me, *Let Me Call You Sweet-heart*.

"Oh, see the big houses!" Inger yelled over the din as we turned a corner and beheld the downtown jumble of stone and steel towers. Her eyes sparkled as much as the twinkling lights in the thousand windows ahead.

"Ah, er...you mean *buildings*, no?" I volunteered in what turned out to be the first of countless hints on coping with a complex new language in a confusing new world.

I talked Inger into shaking the others until train time so we could have dinner together. We then proceeded to a dimly lit supper club called the *Shangri La*. The place wasn't all that grand...but, with Inger there beside me, I considered it heaven itself. I helped her take off her coat and let out an involuntary "whew-eee!" For here before me stood my once-casually-clad shipboard comrade...amazingly transformed into a statuesque star by high heels and a plain dark dress, its shimmering thinness revealing a tantalizing pattern of smooth-flowing curves. She was the most stunning woman I had ever seen.

"Inger, you're beautiful!" I gasped.

"You mean you hadn't noticed before?" she teased.

My "Vonderful Valkyrie," as I had jokingly called her, now came up nearly to my height. And when we danced, she surrendered herself lithely to my embrace, holding the back of my head in her left hand so that our lips almost met. We burrowed into each other, swinging and swaying to the soft music. It was enchanting. *Inger* was enchanting! If I had any doubts before, they now ganged aft a-glee. I knew I would henceforward hang on to Inger, come what may.

We took a cab to the B&O station where we reluctantly parted. I waited until the train clanked off down the switching yard and, feeling a vast emptiness inside, returned to the ship. I don't think I ever felt so lonely. After two more days of chafing at the bit, I finally managed to sign off ship articles and bid both ship and sea farewell. Then, shirt-tails flying, literally, I made a beeline back to the B&O station and took the first train to New York City. And there I found Inger again...holed up in a student reception center/inn on the near East Side.

Completely captivated by THE metropolis, Inger had already walked from the Battery in lower Manhattan to Central Park, taking in every block's contribution to the matchless variety and richness of the city...and humming all the way "East side, west side, all around the town...." She had also managed, somehow, to walk along 42nd Street from the East River to Broadway and Times Square and on to the Hudson (which seamen called the North River since it led north, even though it lay to the west and flowed south). With me barely keeping up with this perpetual-motion dynamo, there then followed a whirlwind tour of wonders like the Empire State Building, with its breathtaking views, Rockefeller Center and the Radio City Music Hall and the fabled Statue of Liberty. Here Inger cautioned that I could jolly well forget taking her as one of "the wretched refuse from [Europe's] teeming shores" or one of "the huddled masses yearning to be free." *Free*, I could personally guarantee anyone, this lineal descendant of the Vikings already was...in no uncertain terms!

Inger also took in a couple landmarks that were extra important personally: Carnegie Hall and the Metropolitan Opera building. And Macy's department store. Macy's? That's right! In Scotland, the girls had been treated to a re-run of the film classic, *Miracle on 34th Street*, and it made Inger as happy as a kid at Christmastime. So now she toured the whole store, eyes bulging at the mountains of goods and goodies. And at such low prices! Prices Europe had never even heard of. It wasn't as if Inger could buy anything, however. Emergency currency restrictions enforced by Norway meant she could take only a handful of dollars out of the country, so now all she could do was look...and dream.

Since Inger was going to Kalamazoo, and I to Pittsburgh to visit my mother, we decided to take the train together at least part of the way. Which gave me the chance, full of apprehension, to introduce my special new friend to Mom. Not that showing her Pittsburgh was such a hot idea (even though I had spent the first 10 years of my life playing on its steep streets as a regular urban urchin—all the time thinking it pretty grand). The streetcar ride from the downtown train station to Glenwood proved a shocker, especially as we rattled past the immense J&L steelmill complex sprawling along the Monongahela River and saw a century of industrial grime coloring the houses and hillsides an immeasurably sad, unerasceable gray. *Redselsfullt!* [Terrible!] moaned Inger. She shook her head in abject sorrow, not so much over the distressing landscape as at how this mess was coloring the lives of the people caught up in it.

Well, she need not have worried about Mom. I had telephoned beforehand, and now she stood smiling radiantly at the entrance to our apartment on Almeda Street, ready for us with my favorite dinner—chuck roast with all the trimmings—and one of her magnificent apple pies.

It had been over a year since my last visit, and I noticed that Mom, now in her mid-50s, was getting heavier and her hair, grayer. Even so, she still retained much of her earlier dark-haired beauty, highlighted by eyes that alternated between soft and flashing, plus an equally soft southern drawl. Yet, this softness, I knew, was wholly misleading. For she also had a razor-sharp brain and a tongue to match, and she never hesitated to use the latter to cut down the more troublesome members of our wildly mixed ethnic neighborhood.

Now, however, Mom was the sole of hospitality—*Kentucky* hospitality. And no one, and certainly not the warmly receptive Inger, could resist that! So, contrary to my misgivings, they hit it off right off the bat. In fact, Mom was bowled over by Inger's derring-do and total lack of affectation and "feminine wiles." When the two went shopping along Second Avenue, Inger carried two bags full of groceries straight up our skijump-steep street, pausing only to help Mom catch up. And in the apartment, she turned with ferocious energy to washing all the windows. Incredible! Why'd she do it? Because she had one huge phobia: She couldn't stand dirt, and least of all dirty windows....

"At home we keep our windows gleaming like crystal," Inger proudly announced, finally a bit out of breath.

"And I betcha they open out onto better views, too," I added. (What I didn't mention was that I couldn't remember when our windows had ever been washed—ever!)

Inger's attack on the windows did the trick for Mom. She took me aside and said, "Son, if you let that girl go, you better have your head examined."

Yet Inger had to go, nevertheless—to Kalamazoo, that is. For it was getting late in the semester for the school to admit a new student, even one justifiably delayed by shipwreck. So we again beat it to the train station and bid each other another sad farewell. I myself intended to travel soon to Detroit to visit my father.

Yes, Inger, they're divorced, I had to tell her. Well, she didn't like that at all. No matter how many Norwegians might now consider that the modern thing to do, she wasn't buying it.

"A disgusting, cowardly admission of personal failure—the easy way out," she called it.

"So how do *you* feel about divorce, Jimmy?" she asked ever-so-diffidently.

Watchit! blared my inner warning system. Alerted, I saw that curve-ball coming all the way from Inger's tonsils. So I stepped up to the plate and batted the sucker clear out of the ballpark:

"Why, I agree with you, honey...absolutely. Wholeheartedly!" (What's more, I did!)

After what seemed an eternity, I arrived in Kalamazoo and hurried to the college campus to see Inger. We met outside the girls dormitory and, right in front of a crowd of ooh-ing, ah-ing coeds, threw our arms around each other...triggering a big round of boisterous applause. Inger put her mouth close to my ear and said something in Norwegian.

"Hey, I've heard that before...on the ship," I said. "Isn't that the title of a song? What's it mean?"

"Jeg elsker deg! And, yes, it's by Grieg...but I meant much more than that."

And when I still looked puzzled, she added: "I love you! Didn't you know, dummy?"

Well, dummy was alert enough to discover that Inger had already managed to become famous on campus. Or perhaps *infamous* would be the better word. We found a secluded bench under a wide-spreading oak tree, and Inger related that, first off, there had been "that unfortunate news story." Her proud hosts, it seemed, had arranged for her to be interviewed by the local newspaper...and, right off the bat, the reporter asked what the honored foreign student thought of America. And the American way of life.

And Inger told him, but good (bad!). In her straight-forward, honest way, she replied that the reality simply didn't fit the image. She said she had grown up as a fervent admirer of America, believing that here, as nowhere else, dreams came true. But now she found herself shocked by the dirt and trash in the streets, the city-slum eyesores, the poverty among so many, the surprisingly many alcoholics downtown (almost as many as in Norway!), the garishly lit bars and commercial strips and the billboard-cluttered highways. She wondered out loud: "Have I landed in the wrong country?"

And that's exactly what became the story's headline:

Foreign Student Asks: *Did I Land in the Wrong Country?*

"But, dear Inger, did you have to be so blunt?" I asked, plenty peeved myself.

"Well, he wanted to know the truth. And how could I say something that isn't so? Or that I don't feel?"

"But didn't you have anything *good* to say?"

"*Selvfoegelig!* Of course! I said I was struck...truly...by all the food in the supermarkets, by your amazing drugstores, by all the clothes at such low prices, by the miles and miles of private houses and their well-tended lawns. By the millions of cars. And the great open spaces. And the beautiful trees. And how interested, kind and helpful everyone has been.

"But, Jimmy," she moaned, "I found the reporter wasn't even listening. He must have thought all that wasn't news. He...he...he didn't use a word of it!"

Inger almost broke down crying, so we changed the subject. Which turned out to be almost as bad. Seems there were several ongoing controversies at the college, and Inger in all innocence was displaying an uncanny penchant for supporting the unpopular side. For instance, her fellow students had proclaimed a hunger strike in protest against "the inedible food" being served in the cafeteria. Inger, however, still reeling from years of subsisting on the leanest of diets, thought the food was darn good. Worse, she said so...loudly. And (horrors!) that the protesters "were behaving like spoiled brats."

Then there was a more personal problem: The unknowing, unthinking Dean of Women had assigned the survivor of five years of Europe's worst-ever war to live in a dormitory with 18/19-year-old innocents from the Midwest—and (more horrors!) to observe a 9:p.m. curfew.

"They're wonderful, Jimmy...*virkelig*...really! But they spend all their time washing their hair and underclothes and talking about Hollywood stars and giggling about boys. And *hva i helvete* are you and I going to do with a nine o'clock curfew!"

She got my attention with that one. I had no ready answer, but suddenly a vision flashed through my head...and there I was scaling the dormitory walls like Romeo pursuing his Juliet.

I related this to Inger, who picked up on the drama in mid-act. She felt the college's wound was actually "not as deep as a well nor wide as a church door"—and that she hoped... fervently...that our story's ending would have far less woe than Juliet's and her Romeo.

Finally came the most serious problem of all. Looking at Inger's academic record, the admissions office had displayed a total ignorance of comparable US-European standards. What in the world is this thing called *artium?* they plaintively asked, as though Inger was trying to deceive them. So they placed her in basic undergraduate studies with all the giggling teenagers instead of at work on her Master's Degree.

"Now I'll never, ever finish school!" she wailed.

I went to bat with the Dean of Admissions, who received my explanations with studied disdain. It was like talking to a tree stump—a very deaf tree stump. So Inger and I wrestled long over what to do. Acquiescing was out. That she could not, would not do. Yet, she was almost penniless. If she gave up her scholarship at "K" and transferred to, say, the University of Michigan, where she could get a realistic evaluation of her credits, how would she pay her way?

Ah, there *was* a solution, though! One I had been working on since Pittsburgh. This meant that I had to rid myself of the lurking specter of First Engineer Smitty's admonition and ask Inger straight-out to marry me. I wasn't sure I should, and I wasn't sure she would. But I felt I simply had to take that chance...for I knew now beyond all question that nowhere on earth was I ever going to find anyone else like her.

On a smiling June day we rented bicycles and peddled for a couple of hours around the campus and the city and beyond into the outskirts, finally plopping down onto thick grass under a maple tree beside a little stream. A gentle wind sighed through the leaves. The water splashed and gurgled over rocks. A big bluejay chirped overhead, and a cardinal trilled lustily nearby. Inger leaned back against the tree while I maneuvered my head onto her lap. Then, filled with nervous hesitation, I gazed up at her relaxed, smiling face. NOW was the moment to do it! I thought. And the key to success? This would be a gradual, tactful approach. At least, that's what I had decided. Instead, completely distracted by Inger's nearness and warmth, I heard myself blurting out:

"Inger, let's get married!!!"

"*Hva sier du?*" she exclaimed. "*Du*...you can't mean that!"

"Yes, I can. And do. And will. Let's get married...*right now*!"

"Oh, Jimmy...," she murmured happily. Happily! She leaned over to hug me, lost her balance, then playfully threw herself over me and away from the tree. Laughing like kids, we rolled through the grass, with Inger emerging on top, showering my face with kisses. Then, to my utter dismay, she stopped...and a disturbed look clouded her eyes.

"But how *can* we marry, Jimmy? You know how I feel about you— you've just seen that. But what about my family? And Norway? You're the one friend I have in all of America. And when we're apart, I die of loneliness. And homesickness. How could I ever leave my home, Mamma *og* Pappa, and my...my country...for good?"

"But damn it, Inger, it's not as though you're leaving for good. You can always go back for a visit. In fact, one day we'll go together...."

"*Ja, Ja*...but that's not the point. How would *you* feel if you had to move to Norway... and live there? And work there...and cope with a new language...and all the new customs? Well, that's how I feel about staying in America. I belong *there*, not here! Here I feel like a grounded bird. I can't fly! America is one big, confusing new world. It's scary! I'm not sure I could ever adjust to it...."

"Hey, Val...Valkyrie!" I said, moved to laughter. "Where's that old bravado? Was that just a put-on? If anyone can make it here, it's you!"

"But back home I never once worried about what's right or wrong...."

"*Right*! Tell me, dear Inger, who really knows what's right?"

"Pappa!" she trumpeted. [I should have seen this coming, for Inger had already shown she admired her father over and above everything on earth. So if it's true that a man should seek out a wife who loves her father, then I was going to be lucky, indeed. IF true!]

Inger continued without stop: "...And Mamma...and my friends back home. The way they thought, and felt, and acted—their work and study habits, their social manners, their approach to sex and marriage. I took it all for granted. That was the natural way to live. The *right* way!"

She stopped and looked at me with those big blue eyes, now pensive, troubled, probing:

"Your America's a wild, crazy jumble. I don't even know where to begin on it."

"Darn it, Inger! Why even worry about such things. Here everyone thinks *his* way is the right way. That makes a hundred million ways to do anything. And your way's got to be as good as anyone's."

I wrapped my arms around her and held her close...a long time...then said: "You know, Inger, I thought you would worry much more that I have nothing to give you—nothing! No money. No real prospects for the future. No...."

"Ah, but you are enough—just you." she replied softly. "*You* are enough! And as for the future—well, we're both young and strong...."

"And you're glorious!" I shouted.

She did say *yes*, didn't she? Of course! It was included in her answer so naturally I almost missed it. Or did I?

Inger turned her eyes away and looked out to where the rolling green meadows met the sky, then back to me, repeatedly, as though she was capturing some hidden message far out there beyond the sky and sharing it with me. And talked as much to herself as to me:

"Let's always remember this moment, Jimmy. Let's always remember the love we feel for each other *this moment*, no matter what happens in years to come. Let's remember how much fun we have together. And how grand it is to be alive. And be able to *feel* and experience living—these moments, these hours, these days. And the wonder of having each other to share our lives with. And being able to do wonderful things for each other. And let's thank God every day that He brought us together...and has given you to me...and me to you. Let's make this moment live *forever!*"

Inger shook herself, as though returning to earth from a distant planet, while I myself tried to return from a host of thoughts triggered by her unexpected, deeply felt stream of words.

I thought it idle, meaningless even to attempt a response. Instead, I pressed her hand...hard.

We thereby agreed that this moment would become known as The Moment—a wondrous interval when nature clothed herself in her finest garments to witness and bless our promise. *Promise.* [Interestingly, the Norsk verb *love*—two syllables, as in lo-ve—means both *law* and *promise*, but it migrated into English as the single-syllable *love*...and you know what that means!]

Now fully back in the pragmatic present, Inger paused, then said that as far as marriage was concerned, she had to resort to one condition: "You've *got* to finish college. Regardless of how long it takes. Or how tough the going gets."

She then added the magical message: "We can get married as soon as you firm up your education plans."

Hooray! I hollered...though I wasn't sure the exclamation sounded within me or outside. Frankly, I didn't find the condition either surprising or onerous. It fit in with Inger's firm belief in order, purpose and effort in life. Which she summed up in the assertion—much to the dismay of many—that the pursuit of happiness embraces not the pursuit of property and pleasure BUT of quality and achievement. She contended that man is endowed by his creator not so much with certain inalienable rights as with certain inalienable *duties*. And that chief among these is the obligation to develop one's knowledge, capabilities and understanding to the fullest. For how else could you really contribute to either yourself or others? Or participate fully...and responsibly...in a democratic society?

So I promised to pick up on my war-aborted college studies the soonest.

Tearing myself away and returning to Detroit, I checked in at my father's house. Then, noting that my *Travis* payoff was dwindling fast, I visited the Hudson Motor Car Company, where I had worked briefly in 1942 as an aircraft riveter (so I had re-employment rights). I got a job all right, on the auto engine assembly line. [Ever work on a factory assembly line? Don't rush to try it out. It's awful! As stultifying and deadening as Charley Chaplin portrayed it in his classic movie, *Modern Times*.] For eight hours daily for a month I struggled on my flat feet to drive eight bolts into the oil pan as the engine blocks moved by, upside-down, in endless, exhausting procession. By shift's end, my feet ached all the way past my spine. Finally, one day at lunch-break the sympathetic Polish worker who had helped break me in on the job took me aside and said,

"Look, Jim-boy, I've been here 20 years. And it's pure hell. What a fate! You want that? Course not! You'd be nuts if you did. *So get the hell out of here!*"

And that I did. The next day I took off from work, visited Detroit's licensing bureau and, using my marine experience, applied for a stationary engineer's license. Somehow, I passed the exams (with a friendly assist from the Navy-veteran examiner) and was assigned to running the midnight shift at a powerplant serving a westside City of Detroit housing project called Herman Gardens. Later, I took a bus to Wayne University, where my indecision about career choices was resolved when I came upon a building bearing a new sign: *Journalism Department*. Standing on the sidewalk wondering whether to go in, I was greeted by a stocky man with tousled gray hair and a keen expression, who introduced himself as Bill Holden, lately of the *Detroit Free Press* editorial page and now dean of Wayne's brand-new journalism program.

"Hi! I was just wondering whether to get into news work," I volunteered.

"Great!" he said. "I've just finished wondering whether to teach it. Come on in and we'll try it together...."

So I signed up, paying out the unbelievably low sum of $75. for a semester's tuition and selecting the biggest study load Wayne would permit—a catch-up schedule of 18 credit hours. Dean Holden also took a surprisingly liberal tack regarding my academic standing, fully crediting my previous year at Marshall College and allowing a half-year of science credits for my US Maritime Service schooling. This meant I still had 2 1/2 years of full-time study to go.

How would Inger react to this tough new reality? I wondered. And especially to the fact that I would have to both study full-time and work full-time? All this because of some devastating news I had picked up—that the US Government was not recognizing merchant seamen as WWII veterans and, therefore, was not allowing them education and family support benefits under the new GI Bill of Rights. This despite the fact that the US had lost more than 800 merchant ships during the war, with thousands of my shipmates being blown apart, drowned or burned alive, dying of exposure in open lifeboats and starving in prisoner-of-war camps. With many more thousands maimed and crippled. In fact, merchant seamen had compiled a higher fatality rate than all the Armed Services except the US Marines. But, no, we were being considered civilians, not military. And while nations like Great Britain and Norway hailed their merchant seamen as war heroes right alongside their fightingmen, and treated them the same, the US Government was treating us like a bunch of bums.

Inger was dumbfounded. She frowned and finally asked, but were merchant seamen better paid during the war?

Yes, in some cases, but not in general—and certainly not in my case, I answered. During the 11 months I spent in three different USMS training schools, I drew the same pay as US Navy personnel. And nothing at all when not in training or when on leave between my seven ships. So, my pay averaged out the same as Navy people with similar rank.

Well, Inger simply refused to believe that such a monstrous miscarriage of justice could happen—and in fair-and-square America of all places!

My own reaction? Well, I had gone to sea to serve America in its hour of need and never, at no time, not once, expected any reward. And now it was clear I wasn't going to get any—that I wasn't even going to be treated like other WWII veteran-survivors sitting right beside me in the same classroom. So it was obvious that Inger and I would have to manage solely on our own. And we *would*, regardless.

Yet, I felt strangely bereft and immeasurably sad about it all...not so much for Inger and myself as for the many other merchant marine survivors and their dependents—the really needy—who might not manage at all.

[A postscript should be added here: In 1988, the US Congress passed a bill recognizing WWII merchant seamen as WWII veterans. By then— over 40 years too late—90 per cent of my shipmates had sailed on across a wide, wide sea and would never know they were being so honored...finally.]

Inger's own education dilemma was met head-on, in her own inimitable way. She decided to work all Summer and save enough to enroll at the UofM in the Fall. And as for accepting help from me or anyone else, that was unthinkable. Forget it! She picked up copies of the Detroit newspapers and pored over the "Help Wanted" ads. She was dubious about handling work-world English, and she couldn't type. What, then, was left? Ah, *there* was something! Grace Hospital needed a receptionist in its Admissions Office. So Inger got a Greyhound to Motor City and hoofed it to the hospital...and one look must have done it, for she was hired on the spot and assigned to afternoon hours (3- 11:p.m.). She was also offered quarters in the hospital's nurses home. What a break! she thought—now she could begin to save money for that one-day-far-off-in-the-future, constantly-dreamed-about voyage home to Norway.

Inger found, however, that those savings came at a high price. She had just begun to get a grip on her receptionist job when her smooth, tender skin erupted in an angry red rash. Alarmed, she consulted the resident doctors. No less alarmed, they stroked their chins and came up with myriad unsettling diagnoses, guessing that her problem was due to all sorts of mysterious causes, from nervous tension to genetic defects. Meanwhile, the rash worsened, and so did Inger. She kept suggesting, to no avail, that the condition might be related to allergic reactions she had always had to insect stings.

Insects! Here in our hospital? Clearly, only a foreigner could suggest such a thing—probably a G-D one, at that....

Meanwhile, Inger became friends with the chief nurse—the friendly, capable, attractive Gladys McIntyre, an American of Norwegian descent. Gladys went with Inger to the nurses home and found the answer: Bedbugs. The place—the *nurses* home!—was crawling with them, and they had been feasting ravenously on the inmates. The building was fumigated, and Inger began shortly to look her lovely self again. But the housekeeper, exposed before everyone as an indolent slob, became furious with "that gawdam furriner." She accused Inger— who had a passionate aversion to dirt and corruption of all kinds—of bringing in the bugs *in her clothing*. And what's more, of bringing them into the USA from "that dirty hole over there."

Could she possibly mean that as a description of *Norway*? I asked, utterly perplexed.

Inger wept. She knew it was time to move on.

Our wedding took place on a hot, muggy day in July. Detroit at its best, I thought, mopping my forehead. I was glad no reporter had asked Inger what she thought of *this* town. Smarter than me, as usual, she came down the stairs at the hospital to meet me dressed in a light blue summer suit, looking cool as a Norwegian summer and more radiant than ever.

The ceremony itself was low key—*very* low key. My tall, thin, always interested, always helpful sister Betty was the only one from my family who cared to attend. Dad's new wife, Ellen, loudly proclaimed that she couldn't stomach my marrying a foreigner and wanted no part of such an outrage. Inger had met both at their house on Devonshire Drive on Detroit's eastside and at least liked Dad, who was built like an athlete (and was a veteran of both War I and II). He also had a good sense of humor and called Inger variously Duchess, Ink, Norgie or Icebox, depending on the situation—or, more to the point, the provocation. Yet, he was incredibly self-centered and macho, which made it all the weirder that he had married Ellen, who was cold and remote and spent all her free time reading Christian Science literature. A real odd couple! And as for Dad's vision of the future... well, his ideas for me centered on one insistently repeated call: "Come to Detroit and get a good job in a factory." He couldn't quite grasp what good lay in "all that college bunk."

The marriage site we selected was the stone-still, refreshingly cool downtown Presbyterian Church—or, more precisely, the Minister's

Office. (Like most Norwegians, Inger was Lutheran while I had been raised as a Methodist, but we both despised sectarianism.) Since we needed a second witness to make the proceedings lawful, I went out onto the sidewalk and asked a buxom, middle-aged lady to help out. She said she would be glad to...and did.

Where was Inger's Norwegian family on this banner occasion? The parents didn't even know their daughter was getting married! Inger didn't dare tell them, fearing they would conclude that she had fallen in with the first sailor she met (which happened to be close to the truth!). She decided, instead, that once we got settled, she would tell them she had met me at college, and that, while I was poor, I was promising (I was sure glad to hear that!).

But *poor*? In *rich America*? She feared they wouldn't believe that, either.

Plans for our honeymoon also went amiss. Just like the wealthy, we saw this as being spent in an exotic foreign country. That is, it was to take place right across the river, in Canada. And it was to last one whole day, since both of us had to get back to our jobs the day after. I remembered Windsor as being somewhat less enticing than Paris, Rome and Rio...but who cared! Inger and I were scarcely conscious of where we were—only of each other.

Then, completely unexpectantly, our honeymoon got extended. Coming home, we were stopped at the International Bridge by US Immigration officers. They wouldn't let Inger back into the country! The problem, it seemed, was that the foreigner had entered the USA on a student visa and, lovely though she was, could not—NOT, sir!—use it to re-enter once she had left. It took two days of wrangling to cut through the red tape, with me having visions of having to emigrate to be with my beautiful new bride. But then—oh, what a relief!—they let her back in.

Another crisis struck in terms of where to live. I had been looking for an apartment for a month, at a time when postwar housing short-ages made rentals almost non-existent. Then, one day after our "trip abroad," Inger found an ad in *The Detroit News*, and we responded, along with a score of others. It looked like a waste of time until I pushed Inger forward. Then, lo! she so charmed the caretaker and her husband (?)

into believing we would make ideal tenants that we got the nod. However, noting the lean and hungry look the husband (?) cast upon Inger, I concluded he was far more interested in her figure than her credentials...and resolved to watch him like a Secret Service agent shadowing an assassin.

Lean&Hungry touted the apartment as "furnished." And, indeed, it did have a couple sticks of beat-up furniture. But it crawled with dirt and assorted varmints, and hadn't been painted for years; landlords evidently refused to do such costly work under city rent controls. Worse, it was on the top floor of a three-floor building and, in Detroit's summer clime, heated up like a ship's engineroom in the tropics. More, it was located on Charlotte Avenue in a seedy, rundown neighborhood of workers and transients—a far, far cry from the fjords and fjells, forests and lakes and fresh breezes of Inger's homeland.

Foremost among the varmints the apartment provided home to were swarms of cockroaches. When the light was turned on at night in the kitchen or bath, they scurried for cover like a stampeding herd running from gunfire. The sight almost drove Inger into taking the next ship home. Instead, she served them generous doses of *Black Flag*. And while this didn't end them, it did shunt them around to other apartments...temporarily.

As for getting help in furnishing the place from Dad and his wife, this consisted of the loan of one pillow to lay our heads on. However, after one week Ellen asked for it back. Apparently, in all her biblical readings, she had missed the story of the Good Samaritan.

Despite the drawbacks, we considered ourselves lucky to get any kind of living quarters. And in a couple of weeks, under an all-out assault with paint and soap and water, we converted the place into our first home. "Downright *hyggelig!*" said Inger, bestowing the ultimate Scandinavian accolade of coziness on the former coal mine.

Then came a shocker: *Inger couldn't cook!* In Norway before the war, she offered in apology, there had always been "a maid from the valley" to do such things. Besides, Mamma was a fanatic on cleanliness and wouldn't think of letting her children mess up the kitchen. So Inger spent eons, and shed much blood, trying to open canned foods. Also, being used to electric ranges, she was terrified by our gas stove.

Surely, she predicted, we would suffocate in our sleep—or blow sky-high. And one day she forget to turn off the gas...and we almost did!

A strange thing that looked like solid peanut butter appeared in the refrigerator one day. This, Inger devoured with gusto, much to my alarm. It turned out to be *geitost*—goat cheese.

And what was this even stranger thing, this fluid, this firewater called *aquavit*? The answer came at Christmastime when Inger, finally hitting stride in the kitchen, served up a traditional Norsk dinner of country spare-ribs and red cabbage, together with ice-cold aquavit and beer as a chaser. It was delicious...and I never knew what hit me until the morning after.

I blundered onto another landmine of sorts when I came home with my first post-marriage paycheck and, like others I had seen, proudly presented it to my wife. Inger, however, unceremoniously flung it back with a sharp...

"*Nei, takk!*...no, no, no! That's no job for a woman. *Vaer en mann!* Be a man! *You* handle the finances."

But what about women's rights? Inger shrugged her shoulders at that one. Not that she didn't believe in sexual equality in the work place and the social/political world. But she was impatient with the whole subject, and with those who pushed it. She felt she *was* equal, to anyone and everyone—male, female, whatever. But she wore her equality with easy grace, born of a long tradition of self-reliance in a notoriously harsh environment. In the home, however, she felt the man should be the strong, capable party the whole family could look to for support, security and guidance. And she violently opposed anything that detracted from that. The paycheck incident was her way of letting me know that she wanted me to fill that role to the hilt...if I could.

As Autumn began, the stage was set for a great leap forward. Right on our faces!

Inger believed that you really appreciate things only in direct ratio to the effort you put into achieving them, and that human character is shaped through hardship and struggle. And how much character, she wanted to know, is developed among the current young who are catered to in every way and given everything they demand...by foolish parents? Well, I didn't know the answer to that, but I did know a bit about hardship and suffering. I also feared that our plans were founded on almost inhuman demands, and worried over how much battering our nerves could take. We shortly found out.

I usually got off the midnight shift at the powerplant at 8:a.m. and went straight on to Wayne for a long day of classwork and study. This meant that as I came crawling home in the afternoon, Inger, after two daytime courses at the UofM extension school, was departing for her evening tour at the hospital. So, while I worked, Inger slept; and while Inger worked, I slept. Not only did we thereby seldom see each other except on weekends but, when we did, our nerves were so frazzled that we fell to quarreling over the most petty things, much to our neighbors' discomfort...and sometimes alarm. Respective nations, families, friends, customs all came in for a regular, rough working over.

These set-tos fell into a familiar pattern. Some aimless spark would ignite our charged-up emotions; the conflagration would grow and throw out billowing clouds of smoke; the rocketing debate would gather speed, and off we soared into fiery orbit. One particularly sensational flight came on a Saturday morning when I came staggering up the stairs to our third-floor apartment with my arms loaded with books.

Looking out of our kitchen window, Inger saw me coming from Cass Avenue and, appearing fresh as a Spring morning, met me in the hallway with a smile. This turned to a frown when she saw the books. "What in the world is *those?*" she demanded.

"Novels," I replied, out of breath. I had stopped by the library on the way home from work, then walked the 11 blocks to avoid paying out another bus fare...and felt dead-tired.

"Novels! You've got a lot of nerve dragging home a pack of novels."

"Oh damn it, Inger, these aren't ordinary novels. They're by Hemingway, Faulkner, Dos Passos, Dreiser, Steinbeck...."

"Well, I don't care who they're by. You promised to wash the windows today. And here you come home hauling all that trash!"

"But...but...but these aren't trash! They're for my class in the modern novel...."

I saw with sinking heart that Inger had lapsed into one of her Ornery Troll moods. This meant that the mythical little creature from the farthest fjord—normally just mischievous but now downright wicked—

had taken over inside her skin and was running the show. I myself felt angrier by the second and feared that, like Dr. Jekyll, I would shortly turn into the very scoundrel—Mr. Hyde himself—she occasionally accused me of being.

Our yelling began to attract an audience, as one neighbor after another stuck his/her head out of the hallway doorways. Inger, mortified at creating a public spectacle, pulled me in through the door...jerking my arm so that all my books tumbled down all over the floor.

"Pick them up! Pick them up!" I shouted. I grabbed Inger by the shoulders and tried to force her down to get the books. She twisted away.

"*Jada!* Now show how strong you are, you brute. Show how you can manhandle a helpless woman. You wouldn't dare do that to another man. You're a savage! All you Americans are savages...."

"And you, you Viking butcher — look who's talkin'! Your hands are red with blood—blood from all the murders your ancestors committed all over Europe...."

"And where's *your* culture?" Inger shot back. "The only thing you Americans think about is making money—money, money, money! Eating, drinking, sex! Big cars, big houses, big bellies, big talk! Where's the good music, the art, the fine literature? You haven't built a nation. You've built a cultural wasteland!"

"Culture, culture, culture," I mimicked. "You sound like a big, fat cacklin' hen who's just laid an egg. Okay, Big Mouth, who do you think wrote all these outstanding books—Fu Manchu?"

"Now you're shouting. Which show's you've lost the argument. Ha, ha, ha!"

"Oh you devil! You vicious devil!"

"Ah, so now you're also going to show how vulgar you are. Your father taught you well, didn't he? He's the crudest man I ever met. Common, common! And that sister of yours...."

About this time, everything turned red. I lunged for Inger but she deftly darted beyond my grasp into the livingroom behind the overstuffed chair with the new slipcovers she had so painstakingly sewn into place.

"Vulgar, vulgar...a common sailor!" she taunted, unabashed by my growing fury. "What's the use of your going to school? You'll still be a caveman, no matter what you learn."

Moaning like a wounded beast, I lurched across the chair and caught Inger on the run. Our momentum pulled the chair over and the three of us crashed to the floor in a cloud of dust. We thrashed around furiously, with Inger showing amazing strength. Our scarred diningtable, empty fruit bowl and candlesticks tumbled down on our heads. I finally managed to claw my way on top and clamped my hand onto Inger's mouth.

"Stop it! Stop it!" I cried. "I can't take any more. You're killing me...."

"And you're chok...chok...choking me to death," Inger gasped through my hand.

That came through as though from a great, great distance. With a start, I saw Inger's face turning red, her gasps growing fainter. I tore my hand loose, and a rush of tears—mine!—poured over her face. I bent down and kissed her...frantically, desperately.

"Oh, Inger, I love you, love you!"

"The Moment!" she answered softly. "We forgot The Moment, Jimmy. And all our promises. Remember?"

Panting, sweating, weeping, we wound our arms around each other, embracing with all the fervor the doomed feel when granted reprieve from damnation.

Bang! Bang! The jarring sound broke through our consciousness. Followed by voices:

"Open up in there!"

"Somethin' wrong?"

"Why's it so quiet?"

I finally realized what the commotion was about. Several people were outside our door. I kissed Inger again and brushed the tears from her cheeks. I then cracked open the door and there beheld the caretaker's husband (?) with several neighbors. A sudden vision flashed through my head of my being led away in handcuffs by the police, with Lean&Hungry chortling with glee as he closed in on Inger.

"And where's Inger? She okay?" he said, pressing forward to see through the opening.

"Nothing wrong at all...not at all," I answered. "We were just doing some cleaning, and overturned the big chair."

"Well, now, you know how much we wanna help...."

"Yeah, I know," I said, adding to myself "all too well." I eased the
door shut again. "But everything's just fine here. Sorry we bothered
y'all. And thanks, thanks...."

The door shut with a decisive click, and I leaned against it, letting
out a deep breath. I looked around for Inger, and there she sat in the
same place on the floor. And then, as if my sheer magic, she smiled...one
of her most brilliant smiles...and the whole dreary place lit up like a
neon sign.

"You know, you Americans aren't really so bad after all."

"Nor you either, sweetheart," I answered, wrapping my arms around
her...real tight...to make sure neither of us could ever get away from
the other.

Toward mid-Winter, Inger disclosed she was pregnant, and much
of the old tenderness returned to our relationship. However, the work
overload inevitably blew a fuse. There was a painful miscarriage, and
recriminations again filled the air. It was a terrible blow for Inger. She
had looked to the baby to fill a void she could hardly explain, even to
me. While she had kept up a brave front and busied herself in a whir of
frenetic activity, she was intensely homesick at heart, bereft at the loss
of family and friends and the natural grandeur she had grown up with.

"Here, I feel like a zombie, walking around looking normal outside but with nothing but emptiness inside," she said. "My body's here,
but not my heart. That's in Norway. I'm afraid, Jimmy, you've married
half a person. And what good is half a wife?"

How could you answer that? I couldn't. But I could hope — hope
time would work some kind of magic and change things.

The past continued to haunt us, nevertheless. Compulsions born of
wartime deprivation triggered wild eating sprees. One day Inger emp-
tied a whole bowl of whipping cream intended for a cake she was
making for a neighbor's birthday. Another time a big jar of peanut
butter disappeared in one sitting. Then a precious slice of smoked ham
went down the hatch. Then a whole bowl of hard green apples. Each
with sickening results.

Underlying memories of her shipwreck also took their toll. Inger would often wake up from nightmares shaking and screaming, "The ship! The ship is sinking! We're drowning! Help, help!" And there would go another night's sleep.

The state of my wife's emotions showed up stark-clear one day when her father came through town for a brief visit during a singing tour of the upper-Midwest. Inger, a full year of America now behind her, met him at the train station on Michigan Avenue, filled with resolve to demonstrate how well she was handling her American experience. Yet, the moment he stepped off the train, all resolve fled...and Inger broke down in wild sobbing!

Well, right then and there, Pappa got our whole story...without a word being said. He had incredible *teft* or feel for people and situations, developed in a lifetime in the topsy-turvy world of entertainment. Nor was he about to get involved in other people's problems— even his own daughter's; at age 60 a professional singer has enough to worry about just keeping his voice going. He also felt that too much sympathy or help for others only weakened their will and ability to cope with life.

That awful day, these attitudes proved tough going for Inger, but it also increased her respect for him (IF such a thing were possible). Mine, too....

I later got a chance to hear Pappa sing, and have never quite gotten over the experience. Inger arranged a concert at a northwest church, and from the first note, I was captivated, no less than the audience itself. The program wasn't much—a hymn, a couple light operatic arias, a few popular melodies and Norwegian folk songs. What made it so memorable was the *intensity* Pappa brought to his performance. His rich tenor sprang from an enormous chest and large lower jaw. He had singular stage presence, and put everything into every song he sang. I glanced at Inger and saw she was spellbound...and began to understand what it must have meant for her to grow up in a home centered on music.

By coincidence, Henry Ford died just before Pappa's visit, and all of Detroit joined in celebrating the man who did so much to put the world on wheels. Pappa turned out to be a fan. The reason, he said as we watched the funeral procession on Woodward Avenue, was that Ford not only pioneered mass production methods and thereby cut the price of his Model T's to the bone but he also paid his workers a then-unheard-of $15. per day...and thus enabled them to buy the very cars they were building. He was thus a father of mass marketing, as well. So, while political and military leaders think *they* change the world, they're really pikers alongside people like Ford, Edison, Bell and Einstein, said Pappa — for these pioneers' work has changed the whole pattern of life for everyone.

When Wayne's Spring semester ended, Inger and I took a long look at each other and our situation and decided that some drastic changes would have to be made...if either we or our marriage was to survive. Inger, like me, had no intention of giving up, and I knew by now what *that* meant.

The last of my sea-service earnings had been invested in a used car—a 1941 Olds. Christened the Gray Ghost, it *looked* good...but, alas, was later discovered to have been rear-ended by a truck, which knocked the driveshaft out of line with the engine. So, to our horror, it leaked a trail of oil all over Detroit and needed new infusions daily. Nevertheless, we packed in some food and our few clothes and headed north to Lake Huron. At East Tawas, along a sparkling shore of sky-blue water, we found a small cottage in a pine wood and finally had a real honeymoon—beachcombing, biking, reading, warming each other on gloriously cool nights and healing the wounds of a grueling year.

Our new approach called for me to quit the powerplant and its impossible midnight shift, get a "decent" day job and attend evening classes under a sharply reduced study load. As Inger said, we had to recognize we weren't going to change either ourselves or the world overnight, anyway...so why knock ourselves out trying? She, in turn, would try to shift to day work and evening classes. Then, lo and behold, we might actually get to *see* each other once in a while...

Inger's work was contributing much to her feel for America. Along with the normal flow of patients being admitted to Grace Hospital were some grim emergency cases, and Inger would have to get their personal information—and, above all, data on their insurance coverage and ability to pay—under often frightening conditions. No-money-no-treatment was the rule.

Then, one evening a black man, wide-eyed with distress, half-carried in his pregnant wife, now in the last throes of child-labor. Inger watched in disbelief as they were turned away. The reason: No blacks were then allowed in the obstetrics section. The two staggered out onto the entrance landing and collapsed. And Inger ran out and helped the moaning mother deliver her baby...right outside the hospital door!

This could never have happened in Norway, a shaken Inger declared. [She failed to add that there were hardly any blacks in that northern realm anyway...though there were plenty of *Same* or Eskimotype peoples, who often got short-shrift, too.] Even so, such incidents led to my becoming a champion of racial equality and some form of government health insurance—much to the annoyance of just about everyone we met. Inger wisely held her tongue in this regard; she knew instinctively that foreigners' views were not welcomed on such sensitive social issues.

Comic word problems punctuated Inger's work as she typed along by the hunt-and-peck system. For instance, there was the patient who said he was a tool-and-die worker at a GM plant. Well, Inger interpreted that as "toil and die" and felt it was pretty sporty of him to take such a detached view of his grisly work-life fate (which, for such a highly paid skilled worker, was hardly all that grisly).

Also, when and if a hospital patient died, Inger had to call the City coroner's office. Where a gruff voice would bark "cor'ner's office". For a long time, Inger wondered what kind of building had such a strange corner. There were also troubles with "v" and "w". Wayne often came out as *Vain Uniwersity* [there was nothing vain about that school!] and my wristwatch became a *waluable vatch*.

The hospital staff enthusiastically embraced Inger (figuratively speaking), with my getting no little agitated at one doctor's extra attention to my Valkyrie. Even so, she felt she should be doing something "more professional"—making more use of her education and unique fluency in foreign languages. But what? And how?

The answer came during one of her frequent trips to the Detroit Library's foreign language department. Why not right here? she wondered. Why not be a librarian?

I suppose more cautious souls would have drawn back from such a challenge. But not Inger. To her, America's greatest gift to the world lay in its opportunities. It overflowed with them. The trick was to be alert enough to discover and grasp those that fit your capabilities. And, then, through all-out effort, you *would* succeed. Luckily, I had worked in the library at Marshall College before the war, even if my role was only filing, dusting and running for books. Couldn't I teach my wife *something* about library work? Well, why not try? So Inger and I spent many days wading through the card catalog and musty book shelves at Wayne...until, at last, she began spouting information on the Dewey Classification System and assorted reference works like a professional.

All this was, of course, meant to prepare Inger for a job interview...but the huge Dewey volume was also put to spectacular use in an ugly street incident.

The 15 blocks from Grace Hospital home ran through a black neighborhood, then a rundown poor-white area...and Inger walked this risky stretch every workday toward midnight. But she didn't just saunter along; she skimmed over the pavement like a stone skipping over a pond—blond hair tucked in under her hat to avoid attracting undue attention. The hope was that potential molesters simply wouldn't care to catch up with her—or be able to. (I could barely do so myself.)

Yet, one evening as she sped homeward down Woodward Avenue, she heard a car slowing behind her. Her stomach knotted as it failed to pass. She walked faster, clutching tighter her handbag, which included the heavy Dewey tome. Suddenly, on her left, she heard a growly voice call out:

"Hi, beautiful! How 'bout havin' a little fun?"

"Oh baby, where *did* you get them knockers?" croaked another.

The car, a battered black sedan, drew alongside and was now matching Inger's pace.

Out of the corner of her eye, she saw vaguely two men. The nearest—unshaven, dressed in a dirty pullover, obviously drunk—leaned out:

"Man-o-man, baby, you're one livin' doll! C'mon, slow down. Get in d' car. We'll give ya a lift home...."

Inger picked up her pace, turned and looked directly at the nearest man a long moment—unsmiling, unflinching, silently warning: "Careful, mister! Don't tread on me...."

As they reached an intersection, Inger flew across, the car continuing beside her. She then turned abruptly right into a one-way street, leaving the car pointing down Woodward. *Gud i himmelen!* she breathed in exasperation. It was a one-way street all right—the *wrong* way. And for the first time, she felt a bolt of fear knife through her. Behind she heard loud curses as the car screeched to a stop. Gears clashed as it backed up across the intersection, then screeched into a turn and shot toward her. And again came the raucous voice...now enraged:

"Okay, ya smart bitch, ya wanna play games? We'll show you how!"

Jesu, hjelp meg! Inger breathed in desperation.

The car stopped and the driver staggered out. Unconsciously figuring her only defense lay in a frontal attack, Inger spun toward him and swung the bag of books with all her strength [which wasn't little, as our wrestling matches had shown]. Taken by surprise, the hoodlum didn't even get his hands up to ward off the blow. The bag landed under his chin and sent him sprawling over the car's hood and into the gutter.

His pal then came lurching around the car after Inger. But she took off like an antelope. The race was strictly no-contest. A block away, she glanced back. And there was the driver, holding his head. With his pal stuffing him back into the car.

Inger raced on to Charlotte and Cass and, at the corner, ran right into my arms. It was my night off, and I was on my way to meet her. Trembling as much from excitement as from fright, she gasped out the story, finally shaking with laughter as she told of the driver getting a face-full of books.

"But the *books*!" she cried. "We gotta get the books...."

So we retraced Inger's flight-path back to the assault area and there, in the quiet of midnight, found the books in the middle of the sidewalk, still intact in the handbag. And never, never, we agreed, had the Dewey Classification System ever been put to such sterling use.

When Inger went in to the Detroit Public Library for the crucial job interview, she impressed everyone with her knowledge, was promptly hired and assigned to the downtown branch's Foreign Language Department, behind J. L. Hudson's department store. After all, as her bosses soon came to acknowledge, it wasn't every day you got *that* kind of a librarian. And not just because of her language skills. No one proved more sympathetic when "war brides" came in and silently wept as they leafed through books and newspapers in their native language. Or skid-row characters fell off chairs as they dozed off into dreams of full bottles and better days. And no one was more persuasive with policemen when they threatened me with tickets for illegally parking on busy streets when picking Inger up after work.

A colleague from the library also came running to the rescue regarding shopping, cooking, medical and repair services and myriad everyday matters. Frances Smith, an immensely capable, very Swedish-looking Swedish descendant from Minnesota, joined hands with Inger and helped her cope with a multitude of vexing problems in a strange land. So did her husband, the kindly, highly informed Reverend Victor J. Brabner Smith. Something of a perpetual student, Brad was working on an advanced degree at Wayne and, oddly enough, never discussed religion with friends. And friends is exactly what Inger and I became with both [through many parishes and experiences, for a lifetime].

As for my own quest for that decent day job...well, that proved a lot more difficult than I had imagined. For half a year I struggled at trying to be a Fidelity Mutual life insurance salesman. The firm called it "underwriting." It was hopeless. I had two grand supervisors, but was simply unable to talk hard-up workers into buying insurance when they needed every cent of their income to support their families. Even though their families needed the extra security. Meanwhile, I myself was getting hungrier by the day.

Journalism Dean Holden came to the rescue. One day I was hauled into his office, wondering what I had done wrong. But the Dean wanted to know only if I would be interested in a reporting job opening up at the *Chrysler Motors Magazine*. Would I, indeed! Everyone at school *knew* that a journalism student couldn't get such a job; there weren't that many slots around town even for experienced writers. So happy day! The Dean went on to say he had been watching my performance under trying circumstances, and would be glad to recommend me to the editor. Recovering, I blurted out thanks and left in a blur of motion—first, to tell Inger and then to talk to the editor, Jack Meagher. We hit it off and I was supposedly launched on my chosen career at the princely salary of $300. a month. Just in time, too—for Inger announced that a new heir was on the way.

Yes, *supposedly.* Something shocking happened on my way to employment.

When I went to the company doctor for the required physical, I failed the test. *Failed!* Palpitation—runaway heartbeat, he said. A War I veteran himself, he said that the prolonged tensions of wartime service had wrought deep psychological damage and left me a "walking wounded." Moreover, that I could expect to have a "nervous heart" for the rest of my life. Thinking of Inger and her struggles with America, I almost collapsed from grief and anger: My Merchant Marine service was again proving a grim albatross around my neck. I protested that I simply *had* to work to pay both the rent and my way through college. He thereupon asked to hear about my 3 1/2 years at sea. He shook his head in sympathy, reached over and took my pulse again, then declared with a smile:

"My boy, you've passed the test." [What a doctor!]

But how in the world, I asked Inger, could we afford a baby? She pooh-poohed such worries. She said that where you *are* scarcely matters; it's *where you're going* that counts. However dismal our surroundings and life today, given all-out effort, we could look forward to a better tomorrow. And now, to a bigger family....

Inger broke off at the UofM and began taking correspondence courses in library science from the University of Iowa, with the aim of moving into book cataloguing. I thought it pretty far-out that such an outgoing and likable person would want to bury her nose in analyzing books instead of dealing with people. But I was now too buried to protest—in my own efforts to become a journalist. Or, rather, a *reporter*, as Dean Holden would have insisted. He viewed the former label as pretentious, defining a journalist as "a reporter looking for a job." And I had had enough of that!

Meanwhile, I suffered through nightschool English and the basic news studies—straight reporting, feature and editorial writing—all of which Inger found equally interesting, demanding second-hand instruction for herself at home. She showed an amazing flair at generating story ideas, at fact-finding and even at writing...*in English*...and joined excitedly in helping me put together practice news features. Together, then, we developed considerable proficiency at this game, especially since I could apply our joint ideas to my work at the magazine. Much to the editor's surprise and satisfaction.

Even so, my real love at Wayne was the social sciences...and, like a sponge, I absorbed reams of books and discussions on history, politics, sociology and economics, including an esoteric-seeming class in government financing. [This seemed quite useless at the time—but you never know what the future can bring: Stay tuned!] These subjects led to daily debates with Inger, who, I discovered to my chagrin, obstinately disputed virtually every viewpoint I picked up at college.

The views most prevalent around the sidewalk campus was that *the* answer to society's problems of poverty, ignorance, discrimination, wars and the ravages of business cycles lay in new government programs and tighter government controls—plus higher taxes on the rich to fund massive Federal income redistribution schemes. Inger, however, refused to buy this view. Fact is, she objected violently. She would have nothing—NOTHING!—to do with any system based on bigger government bureaucracies and red tape and distant bureaucrats telling *her* what to think and what to do.

Yet, drawing on my painful Depression-era experiences and dockside view of the world, I argued just as fervently that only big government could cope with the world's big problems. I also contended that it was morally right to take these positions. My teachers and fellow students, all self-proclaimed liberals, had preempted the high ground, I felt: They gave the impression they *cared*. People like "my benighted wife" who argued that big new government programs were impractical or unworkable or simply too expensive in terms of results...didn't seem to care.

Well, Inger almost bit my head off on that one: "Show me one of your ivory-tower teachers or liberal pals who's willing to pay one cent for these cockeyed schemes out of his own pocket—instead of someone else's—and I might...just might...believe him. And you!"

A more universal issue was raised for both of us with the publication of George Orwell's disturbing book, *1984*. All the more disturbing since it followed his *Animal Farm*, Aldous Huxley's *Brave New World* and Arthur Koestler's *Darkness at Noon*. To Inger, these were clear foreshadows of a disastrous future—of government takeover of virtually all private functions and of Big Brother domination of the ways we think, work and live. But not to worry! my campus pals said, 1984 was decades away. And besides, wasn't Orwell's dreadful picture a bit overdrawn—literally "too far out"?

Well, not for Inger. She chortled over the book as confirmation of her worst fears. And as for myself, I slowly came around to admitting that the books mentioned above provided an exclamation point to my experiences with communist rule in Poland. So through endless pulling and hauling at the issues, Inger and I finally found common ground, agreeing there is really one overriding challenge of our time: The survival of the individual and individual freedom in face of the ominously growing power and tyranny of the state. And that people who are able to recognize this had one overriding mission: To fight with all their might to hold back this tide of darkness as long as possible.

I also learned there were times to keep my mouth shut on politics. During the tumultuous Truman-Dewey campaign, I came out four-square for the Man from Missouri—which didn't sit at all well with my magazine editor. In fact, I came within an inch of being fired. Especially when I went around the office with that smirky smile after Truman's razor-thin victory.

The *Chrysler Motors Magazine?* This turned out to be a well-illustrated, soft-sell, good-labor-relations instrument designed for Chrysler's 100,000-plus employees at its score of plants around Detroit and elsewhere. And Meagher was the head of its 6-man staff—a gruff and tough, unsmiling editor who Inger said looked more like a labor boss than a management man. Especially in the morning when he came shuffling by my desk in the open office "slave quarters" with his topcoat collar pulled up and his hat pulled all the way down to his bushy eyebrows...scowling all the way into his inner sanctum.

Even so, he knew well how to put out a quality magazine. Above all, he put great store on staff initiative in coming up with and developing good story ideas. This meant I had to do stories on employees' activities ranging from stamp collecting to chicken farming, and cover every manufacturing activity from the auto assembly line at Chrysler on East Jefferson to the machine shop at DeSoto on the west wide, to the foundry at Dodge Main in all-Polish Hamtramck, to the corporate offices in Highland Park. Working with photographers all the time—which proved a lot of fun.

Also, I had to drive the Gray Ghost Olsmobile to all these locations. That is, until complaints came in the I was driving a *GM* product, of all things. So Chrysler arranged for me to buy a Plymouth right away (instead of waiting the many months usual during those postwar days of acute shortages). It was thus good-bye Gray Ghost, hello Blue Streak! Hello, too, to a $50. monthly car payment which we didn't have.

When Meagher had us staffers and spouses out to his house for dinner one day, my dearest wife got possessed by the Ornery Troll and kept asking him unsettling questions, such as: Do you and management *really* care about the worker and his welfare? Or is the magazine intended as an instrument for exploiting the worker? Aren't all your glossy stories *actually* chocolate coating over a bitter pill? And you, Mr. Meagher [she never addressed anyone accept old friends by the first name], you're more a propagandist than a newsman...*ikke sant?*

Jack looked long and hard out the window on that one. While I almost choked, then grinned...feebly...and tried to bear it. This had happened before with others. Inger seemed to take devilish delight in needling people in authority and in pricking inflated egos. I regretted now telling her what one of the workers I interviewed said— or growled—about the Magazine:

"Sure, I glance t'rough it. And den I t'row it in da wastecan along wit da union rag."

Back at the office, I got the silent treatment for a week. Things looked bad, especially when my special pal, Bob Booth, the art director, told me that Meagher made a regular habit of cleaning out the newest reporter every year or so in order to bring in fresh ideas. And, alas, there I stood at the bottom of the heap as the latest hireling. But then I turned in a thought piece based on Inger's views on freedom-vs.-the-state. Which Meagher ran, with some minor tinkering, as our lead editorial. That saved my hide! He even announced the following week that I would be named Assistant Editor. Since two others bore the same title, Inger concluded this was being bestowed in lieu of a salary increase. Sad to say, she was right!

Inger's special problems and needs as a newcomer to America—of trying to fit in with a new society—began to become clearer through my studies. Despite an infectious friendliness, she often experienced the cold reality of being "frozen out" by a person or group, of being "put in her place" as a foreigner. And all too often she heard it said (by my family, too): "Sister, if you don't like it here, go back where you came from!"

Oddly enough, Inger found little solace among other Norwegians and their descendants in the New World. They simply didn't speak the same language. The big wave of immigrants from Norway hit America in the late 1800s. And while Scandinavia had changed enormously since (not always for the good), with all these changes ingeniously distilled in Inger, the perceptions handed down to children and grandchildren in the USA stayed rooted in the past, reflected as in funhouse mirrors in oddly distorted images. And how many do you suppose shared her magnificent obsession for classical music and grand opera?

This heightened awareness launched me on a research project that culminated in such a long and tedious report that it earned me an A in Sociology. Inger's most wracking problem, I concluded, lay in loss of status. She had been born and raised with that in her homeland—getting it naturally from her renowned father and the extended Krogh family of professionals and businessmen. In coming to America, however, she had inherited my status [poor wretch!] and dropped several rungs on the social ladder. Settling in the bleak surroundings of the inner city had ballooned her tough adjustment problems. It was also taking a telling toll on our relationship. All this moved me to pen a poem as both a tribute to my wife and a slap at my own myopia, which I read aloud to Inger:

The Strangers

> Strange it is, the way they act
> Strange their ways—and that's a fact.
> How they laugh and love and cry:
> Strangely, strangely—not as I!
> > This may seem gloom,
> > this hint of doom...
> > but who is strange?
> > Strange to whom?

> Natives, natives, I say they are.
> (Calling them that makes me better by far.)
> Backward races—lost in stupidity—
> Simple, naive (without my cupidity!).
> > None should rue
> > this cue so true:
> > But backward from where?
> > Backward? Who?

> Pagan their God, their rites are strange.
> They'll go to hell if they don't change!
> Hell? That's here! They've got it while breathin'!
> I've fired it myself with words like heathen.
> > By now, I guess
> > you know the rest.
> > Just for a jest:
> > WHO's heathen-est?

Since poetry, like jokes, was proving the toughest thing for Inger to grasp in English, she had me read the poem once more. She then read it herself, nodding vigorously...and lowered the paper slowly into her lap. By the light in her eyes, I could see one of those penetrating series of disingenuous questions coming on:

"Jimmy, do you think everyone is doomed to stumble through life with blinders on?"

"Yeh, seems so. *Probably* so."

"Why's it so hard for most of us to put ourselves in the other guy's shoes—to see ourselves as others see us?"

"You've put your finger on it: It's our blinders. We each got a unique pair growing up...*wherever* we grew up. We're also made so self-centered and self-absorbed that others' problems simply don't penetrate our alligator hide. Except, of course, when we think others can somehow benefit us."

"Then does anyone ever come to understand others...*really?*"

"Maybe...if you've got a lot of empathy. But, then, how many have that in depth? In the depth it takes? Or maybe you can do it through an enormous effort of will. But, then, how many care enough to put out all that effort?"

"So you probably have to *want* to do that, *ikke sant?*"

"Absolutely."

"And what does that take? How do people come to *want* to do that?"

"By the grace of God!"

It's not that I wanted to shut off Inger and her questions with that reply; I simply didn't know any other answer. Or even if there were another answer.

Similar results came in most of the countless such cases she served up daily. Like a latter-day Socrates, she never stopped posing questions about America and life itself—many irritating, some infuriating. But, boy, was she catching on! While I was being forced to re-examine everything I had ever learned....

A husky, round-faced, blue-eyed baby boy was born to us that Fall. And just in time a friend at Wayne told me that his father's real estate firm had a larger apartment available in a four-unit building on Blaine Avenue, in an all-Jewish neighborhood off 12th Street. So we toiled through another clean-up, paint-up session, and moved away from Charlotte (hurray!).

One look at Inger as a mother convinced me that life could never again be the same for her. She had accomplished what she considered a woman's biological imperative. [A man's is quite different, no?] She had found absolute fulfillment. She saw in her baby another pilgrim beginning the great journey of discovery that is life. He would behold the world with fresh new eyes. And his parents, if wise enough, could use his vision to see the world afresh, as well. Of one thing I soon became certain, too, and that was that no parent anywhere was going to dedicate herself to that challenge like Inger.

But what in the world do you *do* with a baby, she wondered, truly perplexed. It was like cooking; Mamma hadn't told or shown her anything. Baby care was mysterious—plain scary!

And there we stood with no one to turn to for advice.

When we got home from the maternity ward with James Philip, as Inger christened him, we were certain that such a fragile creature wouldn't survive the night. It was a cold, rainy September...and we just knew he would freeze to death in the chilly apartment! Having no crib and none of the loot that American mothers collect at baby showers, we bundled him into an open suitcase on the kitchen table, turned on the stove burners, and sat up with him all night. Inger repeatedly held a mirror up to his mouth to test whether he was still breathing. Then, when she changed the baby's shirt, she trembled with fear that she would pull off an arm. And breast-feeding didn't go at all, as the new arrival told us in a very loud voice.

Yet, despite all our efforts to stymie his development, the little one soon beamed with Inger's engaging smile...and grew and grew as he ate and ate. Pablum and other totally tasteless baby foods went down with remarkable relish. And I became a past master at...ugh!...changing diapers. The baby even took on a couple nicknames—Mimbo and Paasan. Inger said the latter was the moniker of a playful character in a Norwegian comic-strip. [I later discovered it also means *bag* or *sack* and wasn't at all sure how appropriate that was...?!?]

Now, Inger decided, it was time to begin saving seriously for the long-dreamed-of, long-longed-for trip back to her homeland. For now she had something BIG to show for her American experience besides insect bites and bruises. So even though she soon went back to work and hired an elderly lady to attend to Paasan, the pantry became ever more bare...and the diet leaner.

This spurred me into a furious flurry of activity at the Magazine which, believe it or not, was capped by a tiny raise. Casting our laughing Paasan in the star role, Inger and I put together a photo feature on adopting a baby, called "Master X Finds a Home." Then came another feature on the Detroit library system and its inviting trove of "buried treasures." Borrowing from my seagoing days, next came an article on shipping on the Great Lakes. Then one on urban planning and the proposed network of expressways that would one day crisscross (and tear up) Detroit. Inger's dreams led to an unusual story on their veiled meaning, "Got Nemeses on Your Premises?" And I even snuck into print a short story on intrigue in outer space, which took off from a course at Wayne on the United Nations and was actually a subtle plea for stronger international cooperation to head off disastrous new outbursts of nationalism.

Art Director Booth worked wonders on these stories with layouts that magically changed the mundane into the visually extraordinary. Tall and industrious, patient and pleasant, Bob tirelessly taught me lessons I would never forget on how to crop and arrange photos and use different print fonts and sizes, and even white space, to create layouts with flair and punch. One such collaboration came on a story I did (with Inger's backstage help) on the horrors of drug addiction. This was set off by a double-page photo showing a derelict walking through a wintry Grand Circus Park. An ordinary photo to begin with, this was altered in the darkroom (by placing a pin in his back on the print-paper and turning it slightly while printing) to show him plunging into a whirling world of ice and snow. The result so impressed *Look Magazine* that its editor requested permission to run the picture in an article of its own...on narcotics.

Inger, meanwhile, shifted from the library's Downtown Branch to the Music and Drama Department at the stately Main Library building on Woodward Avenue near Wayne U. Languages were fine, but, for her, only a means toward another end. Music was her real love. And now she could work in familiar surroundings with familiar symphonic and operatic works, folk music and popular songs...and with the singular people who found all of this absorbing.

I myself wasn't quite one of those yet, but was getting there...if ever so slowly. *How* slowly was revealed when Inger dragged me to a production of the opera, *Tristan und Isolde,* at the Masonic Temple. I guess I wasn't ready for Wagner, for I simply never found out what was going on. [And am still trying!] Actually, I felt more at home then with songs like "As Time Goes By" {which was still enthralling the nation as the theme of the recent movie, *Casablanca,* starring the matchless Ingrid Bergman and Humphrey Bogart}, Edith Piaf's lovely "La Vie en Rose," and the catchy melodies from the remarkable recent Broadway hits, *Annie Get Your Gun* and *South Pacific.* Not surprisingly, Inger was especially taken with Ezio Pinza and his moving "Some Enchanted Evening."

In music Inger found a special alchemy that played on the heartstrings, set wondrous moods and transported the soul far beyond even the most somber surroundings. Her spirit took wings with the hauntingly beautiful Adagio Movement from Beethoven's *Ninth Symphony*, the Intermezzo from *Cavalleria Rusticana*, Mozart's *21st Piano Concerto* and the wondrous harmonics of the quartet in *Rigoletto.* And soared with the love duets from *La Boheme* and *Madame Butterfly.* Or thrilled to the call to greatness in the *Ninth's* stirring massed choral proclamation, "Alle menschen werden brueder." At the same time she resolutely avoided Grieg's compositions and the "going home" Largo from Dvorak's *New World Symphony.*

Inger early on discovered Texaco's Saturday afternoon broadcasts of opera performances from the Met. She never, never failed to tune in weekly, and clung to them like a drowning man grasping a life preserver. For here was living, vibrating proof that America was not just a funnyland of jazz, rock, rap, roll and pop entertainment aimed at the lowest common denominator of taste—but that we also achieved and offered the best, at the highest standards. [O Texaco, why...*why*...did you stop such a grand contribution to the nation's life!]

"But why do so few people go in for opera," I asked Inger.

"*Exposure*—that's the key!" was her enthusiastic response. "The more you hear it, the better you like it. Look at the Italians. They're exposed to opera from the cradle up. And they love it! But how often do our own broadcasters and advertisers air classical music? All too seldom...because the audience is so small. And getting smaller...because they're helping make it smaller, through neglect. So opera in America is caught in a downward death spiral."

"Is that reversible?"

"Maybe—if people ever come to realize that opera's the ultimate in show biz. It has flash and dash, wonderful stories to tell, a rich history, colorful composers and Big Name singers. But to appreciate all that requires effort, real concentration. And I'm afraid most people would prefer their music spoon-fed—the kind of raw stuff that appeals to the senses, *not* the spirit."

"Think I'll ever manage to join your select circle?"

"Just follow me! And you'll become one of us few. We few...we happy few...we band of lovers—of opera, that is."

"Ah, now you sound like King Henry the Fifth...at Agincourt."

"Think he'll ever star in an opera?"

"Sure, if you'll compose it. But Shakespeare's already given him immortality in a great drama. That's enough!"

The year of the founding of the North Atlantic Treaty Organization in response to mounting Russian breast-beating, followed by the cruel communist blockade of Berlin and the allies' response with the incredible Berlin Airlift, found Inger finally going home with Paasan on the Swedish-America Line's *Gripsholm*, wondering all the journey if the world would suddenly erupt in a new world war...and we might never see each other again. It was truly a time that tried men's souls [which, unbeknownst to all, would last a half-century as the "Cold War"]. And nowhere were these trials more pronounced than in Norway. For here was the only NATO member with a common frontier with the Soviet Union—a member whose scant population of 4 million was supposed to protect NATO's whole northern flank with its 1200-mile reach from the North Sea into the Arctic. The nation also harbored a radical fringe whose members kept things stirred up internally. They didn't like NATO or any defense commitment that might anger their big communist neighbor. And they only grudgingly accepted the grand Marshall Plan, which one of the heroes of WWII, George C. Marshall, had recently proposed in an address at Harvard.

Even so, Inger got her spirits recharged without incident back in her home stomping grounds. She found Norway *opp i stry* about such exciting things as Thor Heyerdahl's bold 101-day voyage in a balsam raft west from Peru to the South Seas, Olympic star Sonja Henie and her Hollywood doings, and the war-related problems surrounding opera diva Kirsten Flagstad (who had sung with Pappa) and the renowned author, Knut Hamsun. She then returned to the USA with a grand surprise—her two-years-older sister, Grete. And what a pearl *she* was! Quiet, good-humored and helpful, Grete was assigned the job of taking care of Paasan while Inger worked. And this she did well except that the former "little one" had now become so big it took a crane to pick him up, as was attested to by Grete's aching back.

Meanwhile, I finally completed my classwork at Wayne and received my BA in Journalism—*nine years* after that first year at Marshall College. It was a banner occasion for Inger, too: Hadn't she worked equally hard to make it happen? Best of all, perhaps, was the fine print she noted on the sheepskin (which bore no relationship to any sheep I knew) which said "With High Distinction." This was no particular testament to brilliance. Since I had little time for homework, Inger long before had taught me the system she worked out at the University of Oslo: Like a reporter, you take careful notes of the key points made at class lectures, discuss these with someone close (Inger!) to fix them in your mind, then play them straight back to the teacher at exam time. And because academics love to hear echoes of their own words above all else, it worked!

Okay, you've passed the school tests, Inger cautioned, but now the *real* tests begin...out in the demanding, unforgiving, rawly competitive career world. So how are you going to stand up to that challenge?

Well, neither of us was exactly a stranger to tests, inside school or without, and a new one immediately came along. An ad appeared in *The Detroit News* indicating that McGraw-Hill Publishing's local bureau was seeking a reporter. And that's how I came to meet Stan Brams, bureau chief, one of the sharpest minds and most capable journalists the field has produced. Trouble was, I explained to Inger, I would have to take a $50.-per-month pay cut—the exact amount I had gotten in raises after two years of struggling up from the cellar at the *Chrysler Motors Magazine.*

"I simply can't do that to you and Paasan," I protested.

"Absolute nonsense!" she shot back. "Tell me, do you really want this job?"

"Sure, I've got to get some general reporting under my belt...if I'm ever going to understand what news people go through. And the sooner, the better."

"Well, forget the money," she said, adding words I was to hear many times later:

"Jim, you've got one life in which to do all the things you want to do—ONE life. So, even if it hurts, *do* it!"

The result: On to new offices in the Penobscot Building!

As Inger and I had long since found out, there was one over-all story in Detroit's unrelieved jumble of factories, corner bars and blue-collar neighborhoods, and that was the auto industry. With the new job, I began to work at its very heart...and Detroit became magically transformed. Downright interesting! About a third of the bureau's work was for *Business Week*, a third for the company's 40 or so other magazines, and a third for Stan Brams' own special newsletter, *Detroit Labor Trends*. So now I found myself reporting on new car models, industry expansion plans, automation, market trends and the endless management game of musical chairs. There were also endless labor problems that commanded attention—as well as an articulate, hard-fighting, redheaded United Auto Workers leader named Walter Reuther, who was proving a sharp thorn in management's side.

"Boy, *there's* the kind of guy I'd like to meet," I said one day to Inger.

"Well, why don't you?" she responded.

"Oh, he would never talk with me."

"Posh!" she said. "Who ever heard of a labor leader who wouldn't like to get some ink in a major magazine. That's the kind of meat they feed on...and get re-elected by. Go to it!"

So I arranged an interview (as Inger indicated, it wasn't hard at all) and found that unlike other labor leaders, Reuther spoke not just to the pocketbook issues of his members but also to the concerns of all working people—indeed, of all society. What a rarity!

Another rarity I interviewed was George Romney, president of

American Motors (and later governor of Michigan, etc), who was betting big stakes on the future of the small car in America. Strangely enough, he was right...as the future would prove...but, unfortunately, he was also many years ahead of his time. The visit also gave me the chance to meet Romney's PR director, Bill McGaughey ("pronounced McGoy, if you please, Jim"). This kicked off another lifelong friendship [plus a special job connection many years later].

With his fringe of gray hair, penetrating eyes and low-tone approaches, Stan Brams looked and acted as intelligent as he was. He also proved to be a great teacher—who now was faced with one eager learner. Actually, *two*, if we include the equally eager Inger, backstage. Stan was almost a fanatic in demanding the utmost accuracy in reporting, together with the closest checking and rechecking of facts. [Yes, there *are* some newsmen like that left!] He was also an expert on taking a given body of information and rewriting and directing relevant segments of it to the interests of specific readerships. For instance, on a major auto design change-over, we would do an over-all story for *BW,* then pick up and slant the construction aspects for *Engineering News-Record,* the machine-tool needs for *American Machinist* and the supply-side orders for *Purchasing Week.* Labor aspects would get sharply condensed and go into our *Labor Trends* newsletter.

I also quickly found out that writing tight copy for a newsletter involves not only sharply focused thinking but a wholly different, right-to-the-point writing style. A page of copy for *BW,* for instance, could wind up as a tight paragraph in *Trends.*

Inger, like me, was having trouble organizing a large body of information during her writing chores, and asked me how Stan might approach such a challenge. It's simple, he said. (I was glad to hear that!) The trick, he continued, is to make a list of the various points you want to cover, then grade each in terms of its importance priority. Thereafter, divide your raw material according to your grading system and follow the ascending numerical order as you write. And, lo and behold, you've got your story. Simple, right? Yeah...just try it!

And how do you put together a really solid, interesting feature article? Oh, that's also simple, Stan said. First, you come up with a catchy, timely lead which, hopefully, is so compelling it makes readers feel they *must* read your piece. Then, you make a point—generally the most important—and immediately prove it with a pointed example, a revealing fact, a quote, a colorful anecdote, etc. Then you make another point...and prove it the same way. And on and on to the end. Simple? Yeah, yeah...!

Inger watched me plunge into my new job with genuine interest but, obviously, could not participate in it directly. So she continued to perceive the world of Detroit mainly in its outward manifestations: It was cold, rainy, flat and gray in Winter, muggy, flat and gray in Summer. And people's moods corresponded. Their vision struck Inger as extending about as far as the nearest bar, pretzels and pizzas, the Tigers, Lions and Red Wings, and the endless inanities appearing on that new entertainment abomination—television.

Not that she didn't find many entertainment bright spots on TV. For instance, there was Arthur Godfrey and his folksy banter, "Howdie Doodie" for Mimbo, and the amazing Billy Graham saving countless souls. Aside from TV, there were also top movies like "The Best Years of Our Lives"—a mirror image of the adjustment problems all of us WWII survivors were going through, not to mention our folks at home. And prize-winning dramas like "Death of a Salesman" and "A Streetcar Named Desire." And the Kinsey Report on sexual behavior in the human male—which seemed to shock everyone except our Scandinavian friends, who were surprised it took so long to make such "common knowledge" public.

Into this situation a blow fell one day from a totally unexpected direction. My friend from Wayne phoned (the same one who had steered us into our current apartment) and said in a low voice that his father was selling our building...*to blacks*. It was straight-out "block busting," he confessed. An offer had been made that could not be turned down. And my friend wanted to let me know in advance...just in case.

In case of what? I wondered out loud. Inger and I had no problem with such a development. We knew that one of our building's four apartments had recently been vacated, so I replied that we would simply welcome the newcomers like anyone else, whether black, white, red, yellow or whatever. And as for blockbusting, the only form of that I knew was from the war, when my Liberty ship had managed to dodge and twist its way through the Med with 10,000 tons of blockbuster bombs—all bound for the Persian Gulf and, beyond, for the USSR. One little firecracker would have blown us to Kingdom Come.

Our neighbors seemed to fear exactly that kind of a blow-up now. Blacks from the South had flooded Detroit as production workers during the war and, in terms of housing, had been largely confined to the worst areas of the city. As a result, a deadly race riot had broken out in 1943. And now their ballooning numbers were forcing them to expand to areas like ours. Our Jewish friends weren't quite sure how to react. They had treated the only Gentiles on the block with boundless warmth and generous servings of apple strudel...and had lavished an almost overwhelming affection on the street's standout blonde, as well as on Mimbo. They had also extolled equal rights and racial integration. But now that the reality was close at hand—right next door, in fact—they suddenly stopped talking.

The day came when our new neighbors moved in. And moved in. And kept moving in. A dozen blacks must have moved into the vacant first-floor apartment. Nor did the newcomers stop there. The attic came next. Huge sheets of plywood were scraped through the hallways, then hammered onto the upstairs rafters. And another half-dozen people moved in overhead, stomping with joy over their new quarters. (Luckily, it wasn't Summer: The heat would definitely have moderated the stomping.)

"Improvements" in landscaping were undertaken next. All the friendly old bushes that graced both sides of the entrance stairway were chopped down, their axed trunks left protruding forlornly in the denuded air. Evidently the newcomers wanted unobstructed views of street doings from the steps and porch.

I guess the rape of the bushes did it for Inger, who grew up loving nature right next to Godliness. It hit her as an unspeakable affront to her sense of beauty, harmony and order. It was the straw that broke the back of her determination to tough it out in America...regardless. Grete wasn't helpful, either. She had been having a hard time coping with English, even along the 12th Street shopping corridor that resembled nothing so much as an East Europe ghetto. There was also that trip into the back alley to the garbage cans: She ran straight into some feasting rats so big *they* chased the cats. Well, her garbage bag went straight up and Grete cleared straight out, and her screams might still be reverberating around the neighborhood. So, after a brief surge of excitement about all the new things she beheld in this new world, she lapsed into her own bouts of homesickness. And her gloom infected Inger.

Shortly after the newcomers moved in, Stan Brams and I had to work late one evening to meet a *BW* deadline...and when I finally got home, tired and trudging heavily through a cold Autumn rain, I found Inger in tears and Grete in hysterics. Clothes and...my God!...suitcases were scattered all around the apartment.

"We can't go on like this!" Inger sobbed. "You can talk all you want about equality... but it's insane to pretend that people aren't different. Insane!"

"Never said they weren't," I mumbled lamely, trying to figure out what was going on.

"Well, they are! Your jackass friends at college go on and on about the glories of different religions...and races...and nationalities. And how everyone's created equal. But no one dares talk about what really counts—about a person's development level—how far he's emerged from the cave...the jungle. About his standards...his behavior. If some people—white, black, red, green or whatever—want to live like pigs, they can do so. But not around me. And not Paasan. I'm getting out of this dirty hole...right now. *Forever!"*

More clothes were pulled out of the dresser and thrown into the suitcases.

"We're leaving for Norway!" Inger shouted in a no-compromise tone. "I'm sick of dirt and disorder. SICK! I'm sick of bites and bruises. Of sleights and slaps. Of working myself ragged. Of struggling uphill and getting nowhere. Of four years of hell! I'm sick and tired of it all. I'm finished, Jim. *Ferdig!* I'm going home. And I'm taking Paasan."

"But Inger, what about The Moment?" I pleaded. "Have you forgotten our promises?"

"Not at all! But let's remember them somewhere else, Jim. And not, *not,* NOT here! Not in this god-forsaken city. If you want us back, some big changes'll have to be made...."

Even Mimbo was now howling. I tried to soothe all three at once. Then I protested. Then shouted and raged about. But Inger seemed to have moved beyond reach.

Storming out the door with suitcases half closed, she and Grete flung themselves down the ravished hallways and past the ravaged bushes and into a taxi—my bewildered two-year-old son wailing in Inger's free arm. The cab door slammed shut with an explosive *BANG!* And there on the wet, slippery sidewalk they left me...still pleading and shouting, sweating and crying, hot tears mingling on my cheeks with the cold, persistent, oppressive rain—no less bewildered than Mimbo.

Chapter III

"A zillion eager American girls runnin' 'round out there...and you, knothead, have to go and marry a lousy foreigner!"

It was my father talking. We were sitting in the dark livingroom of his Detroit home, where I had gone to discuss the possibility of moving in after Inger's flight. I should have known better, for it was obviously I should not. In fact, I was getting madder by the moment—even while I realized it was useless to take my anger out on Dad.

"Okay, so she's a foreigner. But *lousy*? Sure, you might say she became buggy or even roachy...thanks to America. But lousy? No, Dad...not yet, anyway!"

"Now, now, I wouldn't be too sure Satan won't punish her with that, too."

This was Dad's second wife, Ellen, chiming in—the only person I ever met who knew all that's going on in both heaven and hell. She then spit out: "Be glad she's gone. It's good riddance, that's what."

Now really mad, I rose to leave, but was met with some gratuitous advice from Dad, who really liked Inger but was reluctant to show it in front of Ellen:

"Forget that two-legged smorgasbord, Jim! Get a divorce and find yourself a nice American girl—one without all those highfallutin' foreign ideas."

"Look, Dad, I...I haven't decided what to do. Or where to go. To hell, maybe...."

I spun on my heels and practically ran out of the house—my spirits close to the breaking point. *God, how I missed Inger!* Weeks had passed since we parted and I was still wracked by indecision over the future. What *should* a man do when his wife suddenly leaves, however justified her reasons? Could our relationship be salvaged? Was it *worth* salvaging? Or was the situation really as hopeless as Dad made it out to be?

Sister Betty was more discreet, but hardly more helpful. She maintained that every marriage, every sexual relationship is unique...and so filled with such a complex interplay of feelings, needs and demands that no outsider, however well intentioned, can come close to determining whether a particular combination is good or bad. Or what can be done to repair a rupture. So she tossed the ball right back onto my side of the court.

But, I asked myself, *was* there a rupture? Didn't Inger leave mainly for Mimbo's sake? And hadn't she virtually promised to return once I had gotten them out of this mess?

I thus wavered all the way from defending my wife with such questions and condemning her for abandoning me and our home. I banged around our empty apartment, longed for her and was tormented at night by her image, curiously mixed with creaking night sounds, until I no longer knew where thoughts ended and nightmares began. I took to drinking...but found that of little comfort. (As did my boss at the office.) I met other women—there were plenty around the office. But being used to Inger's minimum-makeup natural look and total lack of pretense, I felt repelled by what I ran into—too much paint, too much jewelry, too much witchery—too much of too much. Even the prettiest somehow looked like baboons alongside my Valkyrie.

On another occasion Inger would have scolded me for being too hard on her sex. Not every girl, she would have said, can look like a beauty queen. So she has to do the best with whatever nature gave her...and, if she can't look especially attractive, she's got to look at least *exciting*. And if a girl can thereby excite a man enough....who knows?...he, in turn, might even excite *her*.

To cut expenses, I sublet our apartment to a young couple from Wayne with a new baby, while retaining the small rear bedroom. I then decided on a singular way to stay out of trouble... and landed a job with Radio Cab driving from 6:p.m. to midnight. After a strenuous day at McGraw-Hill, driving and fighting traffic in the worst parts of the city for six hours was tough—and, I was warned, dangerous. However, most customers turned out to be harmless harried travelers, big-mouthed Big Spenders, beaten-down prostitutes and wayward drunks. Like the souse who pressed a hundred dollars onto me as a "tip"; his wife was plenty glad to get it when I managed to pour him into their house in Hamtramck. In any event, the extra job worked...for I had no energy left for much of anything after that.

When Bill Kearns, *Business Week's* likable young advertising rep in Detroit, found out about my double work schedule, he chided me: "Hey, Jim, you're trained to write, right? So how come you're wasting six hours a day driving a taxi when you could be free-lancing? The auto industry is filled with solid stories. Marketable, too. And you'd be making a lot more money."

Well, he was right...and I vowed to put that observation to use one day. But right now, I needed to be *doing* something, not sitting there thinking like Rodin's statue...and pining away.

A long, somewhat strange letter from Inger, postmarked Oslo, finally moved me off dead center. She rambled on about Mimmy, now almost three and jabbering in kiddy English...while his new-found friends in the local *barnehave* (outdoor kindergarten) jabbered back just as brokenly in Norwegian—with the two understanding each other perfectly. She went on about how odd her hometown, family and friends seemed after a long absence. Was she becoming "Americanized"? Etc, etc, she wrote...about everything except *us!* Nothing about her feelings for me, our situation, our future. Not a word. As though nothing wrong had ever happened!

The letter left me hanging in midair about the really important issues facing us. [How would *you* handle such a quandary?] Saddled with the stupidity of hurt pride, I couldn't bring myself to telephone. Rather, I decided to take action.

My first move was to talk with Bureau Chief Stan Brams to see if a transfer could be arranged to McGraw-Hill's Washington, DC bureau. I remembered well what a great impression our Nation's Capital had made on me when visiting Sis there during the war (she was then working at the Pentagon). Yes, the normally reticent Stan responded, he was aware I was having marital problems...but went on to say, "You think that's news? Just ask anyone. *Anyone!*"

And, sure, he would be glad to help out. But a transfer wouldn't be so easy. Each bureau within McGraw-Hill was run by its chief like a small fiefdom, and a transfer would be up to the Washington manager. A call to that distinguished Virginian got me nowhere: There were no openings, and none in sight. Besides, they preferred people with Washington experience. [Well, who didn't know that! And how do you get experience if no one will hire you without it?]

Stan then suggested New York headquarters...and arranged for me to meet *BW*'s managing editor in that financial center of the world. An overnight train ride later, I found the meeting going well...but a look around my Manhattan hotel did not go at all. Here were all the old familiar signs of urban decay and personal disintegration. New York throbs with soul, excitement and challenge, I concluded. But the innercity looked too much like Detroit. And I felt that another rehash of that would be disastrous for Inger. So I took the train not back to Motor City but to the *reporting* center of the world — to the place I really wanted to settle in—*Washington*! I planned to knock on doors all over the National Press Building and elsewhere around town and simply see what I could turn up.

I wasn't totally on my own, however. Joe Gambatese, McGraw-Hill's ace labor reporter and our *Detroit Labor Trends'* contact in the Capital, made a few calls on my behalf...and found that the Association of American Railroads was looking for a press representative. This led to interviews in the Transportation Building at 17 & H with AAR's public relations executives. Then, two days after my return to Detroit, Assistant Vice President for PR Albert R. Beatty, a short, balding, genial non-stop talker, telephoned...and posed this startling question:

"Mr. Sites, would you be interested in joining the AAR at $7200 a year?"

Would Mr. Sites ever! The offer amounted to *double* present pay. I tried to sound casual even while I struggled to get my voice back: "Oh? Wel-l-l...[properly dragged out] yeah, yes, yessir! That sounds fair. And please call me Jim."

Inger would have cracked that two times zero (present pay) still equals zero. Also, Washington price levels would soon come to bowl us over. Nevertheless, I felt Inger would consider this a hopeful harbinger for our future...together! Besides being a regular *Valhalla* for reporters, this sleepy southern town of 1.3 million people treated foreigners like anyone else...and maybe even better since, here, foreigners carried an aura of the exotic-seeming diplomatic world about them.

As for railroading, my only knowledge of that vast industry lay in memories of hearing that most mournful of sounds—a train's steam whistle—echoing down the Ohio River valley at night; skipping along the tracks as a barefoot boy and wondering why the crossties were always so awkwardly spaced for walking, and singing to our neighbor's guitar on Summer evenings on the front steps, "I've Been Workin' on the Railroad." In short, railroading struck a responsive chord in my heart. It was a blending of childhood, America's past, its strivings for the future, adventure and promise.

NOW, I decided, it was time to phone Inger.

I placed the call on a sweltering Washington June afternoon and waited an endless hour while the overseas operator tried to get a connection to Oslo. Then, at last, there was Inger on the line. Taken by surprise in late evening, she gurgled something in Norwegian, abruptly woke up to the fact that it was her husband calling...and burst out crying!

"Oh, Jimmy, Paasan and I miss you so," she blubbered.

"Me, too, Inkie...so how come you're there and I'm here?"

"Because you haven't asked me to come ho...er, back!"

"Well, how 'bout right now?"

"*Ja, ja!* We'll catch the first boat."

"SHIP! Ink. Boats don't cross the ocean. They sit *on* ships...like lifeboats."

"*Du da...jeg gir blaffen hvor de sitter!* [I don't care where they sit!]," she shot back, her old fighting spirit reasserting itself. "In fact, I don't even know where *you*'re sitting...."

"I'm calling from Washington."

"Oh...the state?"

"No...the District of Columbia. Peoria on the Potomac. The capital of the USA. The capital of the world!"

Inger got so excited she reverted to an earliest problem with English: "Vashington!. That's vonderful! It's vild! Ve'll leave on the first bo...er, sheep!"

Overjoyed, I told Inger about the new job and about a garden-type apartment I had rented for the three of us in Bethesda. We finally kissed via long distance and hung up...and for the first time in ages, I found myself whistling, "Let me Call You Sweetheart."

Seeing Inger again at Pier 14 on the Hudson was like rolling the clock all the way back to her arrival in Baltimore. There she stood at the railing of the Norwegian America Line's smoke-breathing *Stavangerfjord*...holding Mimmy's hand and throwing kisses and flashing that big, radiant, dimpled smile. I felt as though someone had hit the jackpot on a slot machine. Rotors whirled, bells rang, coins jangled...and the whole pier jumped. Inger normally shrank from public display of private feelings, but this time was different. Mimmy even got a few High C's in on our happy reunion chorus. And not even the trainside view of the dingy backyards of Newark, Trenton, Philadelphia and Baltimore could dampen our spirits as we sped homeward.

Things now *were* better, just as I had hoped. Inger felt an unaccustomed sense of security...and coziness...in the parklike apartment complex off Piney Branch Road in the Maryland suburb, Silver Spring . Our brand-new first-floor two-bedroom unit had parquet floors and was sparkling clean. We gradually picked out reasonably priced furniture and furnishings—all bought on credit. Best of all, right outside was a big sandbox where Mimmy could play with our neighbors' children—including those of the incomparably personable southerner, Mary Anne Hodge (and PR consultant Herb) and of reserved Canadian Nancy Hudson (and English physicist Ralph). The place was filled with people of similar age, education level and career status—people who showed promise of improving on that status—and we made many close, lasting friendships.

For the first time in America, the tensions melted away...and Inger became playful, buoyant. We wrestled with Mimmy on the lawn, shopped in Georgetown, went for long walks along the C&O Canal, drove to the Skyline Drive and hiked over the Appalachian Trail, toured the Capital's incomparable memorials and public buildings—especially the Smithsonian's—picnicked at Mount Vernon, went swimming in Chesapeake Bay, and visited the National Zoo so often that Mimmy came to know the names of every beast in every cage. To Inger, it was all a new and wonderful world—one in which we could live and work without the old overhanging threats of disruption and doom.

Not forgotten, however, was the original reason that brought Inger to America. She soon signed up for the Master's Degree program in Library Science at Catholic University. Here she was the one Lutheran in a whole college filled with nuns and fathers...and they didn't even try to convert her! She also got a part-time job, at the lowest imaginable salary, at the Georgetown University library. I thought she deserved a medal just for handling the fearsome logistics that all this travel entailed. There were innumerable trip transfers and long waits for busses that never showed up. But she worked it out, though with much grumbling that public transportation was much better in Europe. But isn't America the realm of the private car, not public transport?

Wonder of wonders, Inger even found an old friend working on the political desk of the Embassy of Norway on Massachusetts Avenue. Through her, we began reading regularly Oslo's outstanding newspaper, *Aftenposten* (anyway, I *tried!*). We were also dragged off to assorted receptions where hardly anyone spoke English: *I* was the foreigner. Strange affairs, they were. No one showed the slightest interest in anyone else except for ambassadors and other top dogs (plus the occasional ravishing Mata Hari) and one and all concentrated on swilling down vast quantities of the finest beverages...and swarming like a plague of locusts over tables groaning with gourmet foods. Yes, I was assured, *this* is the fabled diplomatic whirl which many outsiders think is right next to heaven....

A surprising new side of Inger emerged at such events. If an especially pretty woman came by and was extra friendly toward me, Inger would *bristle* underneath her normally pleasant exterior. And if the newcomer batted her eyes, licked her lips or flaunted her sex in any way, Inger's own eyes would blaze with danger and she would prepare for a frontal assault. Worst, if I myself reacted too warmly to such a temptress or even showed ordinary friendliness, I would be raked over the coals afterward. Thus I learned how fiercely possessive my wife was of her man—*and* protective of our home! She wasn't about to put up with the tricks some women play on men. I also learned to keep a *very* straight face when confronted with such provocations.

Echoes of this attitude sounded at an embassy reception sometime later when a friend of a friend of Inger's—a Washington party type— sidled up to Ink and asked in a low voice if she and I would like to join a "swingers" group she was putting together.

"Swingers?" asked my baffled wife. "Like monkeys? From trees?"

"No, no! Ha, ha, ha!" boomed the response. "No, we're humans. You know, couples. Like Arnie and me. Three or four of us get together every weekend...and, you know, have a party. And then switch partners. You know, for the evening...or maybe the whole night."

Inger was shellshocked. "You mean you—a *married* woman— would make love to another man? NOT your husband? And let another woman mess around with *your* man?"

"Sure. It's the modern thing to do. It's fun—monstrous fun! Why, our marriage hasn't been the same since...."

"No, you idiot, and it won't be much longer!" burst out Inger, to the delight of everyone within earshot. Then, lower, through clenched teeth: "*Du stakkars duming!* You and your marriage are both headed for disaster and you don't have sense enough to know it."

"Well, you don't have to get so huffy about it."

Inger's eyes narrowed to hard slits. She set down her drink and gripped the swinger by the wrist. Her voice became a menacing whisper: "Look, you ever come sneaking around me and my husband proposing something like that again...and you're dead!"

That message got through. We never saw the swinger again. But she left us chewing over a mystery: How could anyone be so 100% offbase in her targeting? For she had unknowingly, stupidly singled out the one person in that whole room who considered her children, home, husband, marriage absolutely sacred...over and above everything else on earth.

As for the job at AAR, the centralizing organization of the major rail lines of North America, both Inger and I were surprised to find that my work in this intriguing, ephemeral field of public relations wasn't all that different from my tours with *Chrysler Motors Magazine* and *Business Week*. PR people originated information; news people disseminated information. We at AAR were selective with the facts we gave the press, always (like legal advocates) putting our case in the most favorable light; reporters were selective in what they picked up and passed on to the public, always emphasizing the unusual and dramatic (and often most negative). Sad to say, out of these two filtering processes—even assuming both sides' dedication to factual accuracy—the public gets only the flimsiest end-of-the-line fragments.

Inger threw up her hands at this analysis: "But how can people get any valid perception of real-life situations from the news? And isn't that crucial to making democracy work?"

Trying to explain such inexplicables, I told her about the poem from *McGuffey's Fifth Reader* which I memorized as a boy. Seems there were six men of Indostan, who, "to learning much inclined," went to see an elephant, "though all of them were blind." Depending on which part of the beast they touched, each came away with directly contrary ideas of an elephant...as a spear, fan, tree, wall, rope, snake. Concludes the poem:

And so these men of Indostan disputed loud and long—though each was partly in the right and all were in the wrong.

Inger shook her head: "So you mean that a reporter's fidelity in covering one part of a story can backfire in distortion of the over-all picture?"

"And how! Can and does, every day," I responded. "But don't give up hope! The real genius of a free press is, if you have enough people communicating enough points of view, the public just might get a pretty good idea of what's going on. They might even see the elephant!"

Inger was also puzzled about how the many private US railroads could possibly work together so that rolling stock can move throughout the continent. In Norway, that's easy to grasp, she said: The rail system is state-owned and run like one big, happy (?), bureaucratic family. The US answer, of course, is the AAR itself—which we soon discovered wasn't just a lobbying and PR entity. Its Operations and Maintenance Department coordinated technical developments throughout the industry, and its Car Service Division routed freight cars to meet transport needs across the nation. Right now, for instance, rolling stock was being channeled to points serving West Coast ports to meet military transport needs for Korea, where the Communist North had blasted its way across the 38th Parallel and was now being pushed back at terrible cost to US and other forces fighting under a UN mandate.

The AAR was also blessed with many loyal, dedicated people, especially within the law and economics areas, who provided sound research and argument for every controversy. Nor was there any lack of these. For here was a field regulated from locomotive to caboose by the Interstate Commerce Commission. Railroading was still considered by much of the public, including many people on the inside, as more of an institution than a business. Unfortunately, this almost sidelined the industry until regulation was relaxed and tough new leaders took over and made railroading more competitive with expanding road and air carriers. But the industry also lost mightily in the process.

I soon met the president of the AAR: The able, articulate lawyer, William T. Faricy. Whether testifying before Congress, making a major speech or running the organization, he always stressed the nation's interests ahead of the railroads'...and thus struck Inger and me as that rarest of people, a business statesman. [How many like that can you find today?] His executive assistant was a real character, however. Despite being well paid, this able-though-modest man wore a frayed topcoat, lived in a barren room above a funeral parlor and often stopped by my office to borrow newspapers instead of buying them. Yet, when he died, his desk was found to be filled with uncashed checks, shoved far back in the top drawer. *Then,* as often happens, scores of relatives who never spoke to him turned up to cash in on his estate.

AAR PR leaders like Albert Beatty taught me (and Inger) how to prepare solid news releases and background memos, how to cover meetings and hold press conferences (also in New York and that key US rail center, Chicago) and how to deal with news people (carefully!). AAR also paid the bill for me to become a member of the Public Relations Society of America, thus providing a chance to meet others in the field (including arch competitors) and to begin the long journey toward PRSA professional accreditation.

Our best teacher of all, though, was the vice president for PR, Robert S. Henry, a scholarly, eminently civilized Tennessean with a kindly countenance rivaling that of Santa Claus. The Colonel, as everyone called him because of his WWI military service, did much to offset the industry's Robber Baron image. His classic book, *This Fascinating*

Railroad Business, was virtually memorized by Inger and me. He also wrote several authoritative books on the "War between the States"— never referring to that terrible national tragedy as the Civil War.

At AAR Colonel Henry had built up one of the nation's truly outstanding public information programs. This embraced School and College, Advertising and History services, Special Studies and the News Service under Harry Hammer—with whom I shared an office for two years (and who never got upset despite my making some colossal beginner's blunders). Harry, capable and the soul of friendliness, turned out to be a journalism graduate of the University of Missouri, where he had excelled in broadcast reporting. He wrote as effortlessly as one talks...and showed me and Inger how to craft one-minute commercial messages for the AAR's weekly hit program, "The Railroad Hour" (with Gordon McRae). These signed off with this simple line, which we still hear many people playing back to us:

This program has been brought to you by the Association of American Railroads—the same railroads that bring you the food you eat, the clothes you wear and all the other things you use in daily life.

One memorable, sleepless night, Harry and I rocked and rolled over the tracks on a totally misnamed B&O "express train" from Chicago to Washington...writing the script for a lively 20-minute motion picture the AAR planned to do on modern railroading. Earlier, Inger got us unstuck on what approach to take...by asking the simple question, what would a reporter discover if his editor assigned him to dig into the subject? So the film began and unwound just like that, at the reporter's desk. The morning following our rough ride found us plenty groggy. But that didn't seem to hurt the film: It was shown throughout the nation for many years.

Inger quickly discovered the glories of free train travel. FREE! Mimmy in hand, she was soon traveling as a "deadhead" on as many trips as she could sandwich in between studies and work. She loved it...and that's the way she really discovered the sweeping panorama of America—through the ever-shifting scenery of a train window. Chicago became a recurring destination of these trips, mainly because it was home to distant relatives—descendants of Norwegians who had immigrated around 1900—like the lovely Sigrid Krogh (a model married to a strict Iowan doctor) and Egil Krogh, vice president of that great department store, Marshall Field. Egil and wife Josephine lived in Winnetka with their three children, in a spacious house filled with the finest finery of the American home. Inger was impressed, for here in living color and everyday use was the striking abundance that foreigners normally see only in ads and movies.

Harry and his wife Midge virtually adopted Inger, and we had much fun together...often at the National Press Club, where I became a member early-on, again courtesy of the AAR. This led, among many other wonders, to a hilarious train trip for the press to Harper's Ferry. At our instigation, the B&O outfitted a baggage car with a bar with free beer, with Inger serving as a volunteer barmaid. This led, in turn, to some pretty raucous singing. Grand opera, it wasn't!

NPC also enriched life with its famous headliner luncheons, featuring the world's great and wannabe great, Thursday evening roast beef buffets, the annual summertime Family Frolic, where Inger (Ol' Lucky!) won door-prizes three years in a row, and Magic Shows for Mimbo (having shed the name of Mimmy because of his advancing age—five).

Inger and Midge took part in another special labor of love—helping host the AAR's popular annual Christmas party for reporters at the Carlton Hotel, where we sang songs (again, unimaginably off-key!) far into the night. Ink showed up at the first of these events in a sleek, unadorned black sheath, and became *very* popular. Here we traded notes with stars from the transportation press and local newspapers—the *Post, Star, Daily News* and *Times-Herald*—and became friends with such grand people as Bob Young of *The Chicago Tribune*, Kermit McFarland of Scripps-Howard, Jack Adams of the AP, Doug Larson of NEA, Paul MCrea of *Nation's Business,* Andy Brown of *National Geographic,* Ted Koop of CBS, Lu Warren of the *Buffalo Courier-Express,* Frank Holeman of *The New York Daily News,* Ben Grant of *US News & World Report* and Jack Horner of *The Washington Star.* (The last five eventually moved on to the exalted status of NPC president.)

Inger loved them all — platonically speaking! — and her regard was reciprocated...in spades. She found Washington reporters to be perceptive and sensitive (sometimes too much so), knowledgeable, deeply skeptical about people in power, serious about their calling but with a great sense of humor about life in general, and as open and direct as she herself was.

It's no accident that, like Abou Ben Adhem, Bob Young's name leads all the rest in the foregoing list. For after dinner at home one evening with wife Millie, he provided the ultimate description of Inger: "She's one of the few I've met in this crazy town who has her head screwed on straight."

This in a place where heads are screwed on every which way, and some not at all!

We both agreed that only a wizard like Lewis Carroll could do justice to the story of Inger's adventures in Washington. And he would surely call his work *Inger in Blunderland.*

For instance, who can forget Senator Joe McCarthy? In 1950 he claimed he had a list of 205 communists in the State Department — never named, of course — and thereby unleashed a notorious communist witchhunt upon the nation. This ordeal lasted four long years until the US Senate finally screwed up its courage and voted condemnation. Happily offsetting this madness, however, was the shoo-in election in 1952 of General "Ike" Eisenhower, who provided eight years of needed stability in a very insecure world rattled anew by the portentous explosion of the first hydrogen bomb in the Pacific. Unfortunately, Ike's victory was accompanied by the defeat of Inger's favorite (*only* favorite) politician—the thoughtful, inspiring Adlai Stevenson.

Inger found other happy offsets of the times, however. There was Walter Cronkite and Edward R. Morrow briefing the multitudes on TV; Imogene Coca and Sid Caesar making us laugh uproariously...and "I Love Lucy;" Patti Page singing the beautiful "Tennessee Waltz;" *Life Magazine's* daring publication of the whole of Ernest Hemingway's "The Old Man and the Sea"...and, right down my wife's line, Gian Carlo Manotti's Christmas broadcast creation, *Amahl and the Night Visitors.*

One day Joe Gambatese confided to us his secret for success in this mad, interacting milieu of politicians, lobbyists and the press: Emulate the Boy Scouts and do a "good turn daily" for someone — anyone! Look for chances, he said, to help people develop information, win promotions and get raises, make important contacts, join desirable clubs and professional groups, etc, etc. After a couple years of this...lo!...you'll develop an unbeatable network of essential contacts and supporters...and become an "old Washington hand."

Above all, he added, while making friends, be careful to make no, NO enemies! Avoid antagonizing anyone, even your fiercest professional opponents. Why? Because in Washington alliances shift every day, depending on the issue you're dealing with. And the guy you violently oppose today may well be needed as a supporter tomorrow. So keep all your bridges open, both for forward charges and hasty retreats.

Inger herself came up with another essential, what she called "the Washington survival drink." When invited to drink-fests and feeding frenzies, you eat only the safest, blandest foods—avoiding like poison exotic dishes, meat sauces and salad dressings. Then, when you drink, take, say, a scotch and soda; drink half of it; fill up the glass with soda; drink half of that; fill up with soda again, etc, etc. Thus, while everyone else is flying higher and higher and heading for a calamitous crash, you remain in control—THE survivor!

All good things seem to come to an end all too soon. And so it was that one day Harry announced that he and Midge would be leaving town: He to become PR director of the Reading Railroad in Philadelphia. So what limb did that leave me dangling on at AAR? I didn't know...but Colonel Henry, Al Beatty and President Faricy did! First, they had to come to grips with a huge stumbling block—my age. I was 29...and, in railroading, people apparently had to wait much longer before moving upward. They must have swallowed plenty hard. For despite my age and all my blunders, I suddenly found myself the new News Service manager.

The new post wasn't all drudgery. For instance, there was my celebration of his birthday with Ben Miller, an experienced broadcaster I had hired to fill my old vacant seat. Aiming to do this in style, I invited him to that most convivial of Washington watering holes, the noted (notorious?) Press Club bar, where we decided to have a martini— one. However, before that could be consumed along with the free bread (his "birthday cake"), an old buddy came by and decided we all had to have another martini...on him. That put away, there suddenly appeared another buddy who, against all protests, ordered still *another* martini.

After this three-martini nirvana, Ben and I swayed our way back over the six blocks to the Transportation Building, an hour late for a scheduled meeting with Albert Beatty...and absolutely certain this would be the end. So what happened? Albert, a former child evangelist orator, had just converted to Catholicism...and spent the rest of the day haranguing us about the glories of his new religion! While we saw him dimly...*very* dimly...through a thick fog, heard him from far afar...and fought desperately to keep focused and look attentive.

Two important events now occurred for Inger. Obviously, her explorations on how to live in America did not keep her from either living or loving...and the day came when a new son was born. Erik Krogh, he was christened—thus including Inger's family name in the middle. Actually, the event happened on a cold night—the 12th of January— one of those rare occasions when Washington was virtually shut down by a snow-sleet-rain-ice storm (in precisely that sequence). I helped Inger into the Blue Streak in between attacks of pain and slid over the five miles to Georgetown Hospital in second gear, squeezing the steering wheel into a pulp all the way. Things went well, and our doctor shortly came out of the operating room bearing another big blond baby boy in his arms: "And look, Mr. Sites, he's been born with skis on!"

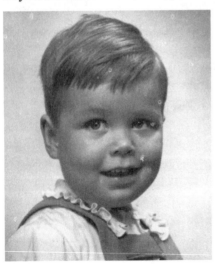 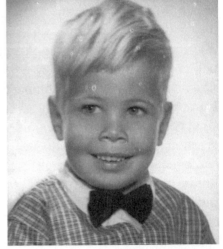

Inger's pride and joy! Mine, too. Here are sons James Philip Sites (left), born September 17, 1948, in Detroit, Michigan, and Erik Krogh Sites, born January 12, 1954, in Washington, DC.

[That remark did not come from outer space, for, much to Inger's delight, Norway had rampaged through the 1952 Winter Olympics in Oslo, with that small country winning eight gold medals—*double* the number for contender No. 2, the USA.]

How did Inger feel about sex? I myself had long since found that this was a subject she *felt*, period. No talk, please! Talk for her made such intimate things common, mundane. She also couldn't stand bathroom, bedroom, off-color or "plumbing" jokes—they befouled, besmirched and contaminated. She viewed sex as a fragile, ephemeral wonder, easily injured or destroyed by over-indulgence or perversion. Push sex too far or try to get too much out of it, she felt, and you wind up with emptiness. Or, like eating only the icing on a cake, you become surfeited and sick of it—*and* with your partner.

Inger could not understand why so many men and women rely on sex as the mainstay of their relationship, instead of simultaneously building a uniting web of common interests and activities. She knew instinctively that sex alone cannot support such a load, and certainly not on an enduring basis. Too many also seemed to her to treat sex as some form of calisthenics. Witness, she said, all the talk and titillating publications on mating positions and erotic techniques. What room does all this leave for beauty and spiritual value?

Most disturbing of all sexual negatives for Inger was the American culture's concentrated drumbeating on the subject on sex and its close relative—personal appearance. As though the wrapping on a package is more important than its contents. Contents like character and what Inger saw as the four dimensions of the truly developed human being: Knowledge, cultural awareness, spiritual depth and considerateness toward others. Then comes the final irony: Even when these factors are mentioned at all, they're often sold as "improving your sex life."

The Four-Dimensional Human!

"What if..." Inger asked, her blue eyes darkening [they actually did when she got serious], "what if...instead of succumbing to the siren lures of commercial interests—all those selling sex, luxury and pleasure in all its forms—what if every person had this primary goal in life: To become a 4-D human? To become an informed, cultured, spiritual, considerate person? Think of how different people would be! Think of what a different world we would have!"

"Ah, now, Ms. Socrates, you're moving onto very dangerous ground," I said. "You're questioning our society's entire *raison d'être*! Witches used to be burned at the stake for less. But you'll probably get special handling—you'll get a chance to drink hemlock."

"But isn't that what every liberal thinker in history hoped...that man, given freedom, would become? Four-D humans! Just look at the founders of this country: Isn't that what they themselves were?"

"Yes, but we're talking about today...and, today, you're the only 4-D person I know."

"Be serious!"

"Okay, Honey, here's the situation: You can tinker around the edges of change...but forget changing a whole system. It can't be done. Too many powerful interests have a stake in continuing the present travesty, promoting sex, goods and goodies, drinking, gambling...the sweet life. They would either silent you by ignoring you...or conspire to crucify you."

"You mean things are hopeless? That people can't do anything about this mess?"

"Sure, they can. Just like you: *Turn it off!* Don't buy the ad media's trash—the PR garbage—the entertainment industry's sewage. If enough people do that, you'll see less of it."

The commercial world's awesome sex barrage that Inger was so distressed about hits people from all sides through advertising, films and TV, magazines and books, the news media [and now the Internet]— the whole of what we came to call the Media/Entertainment Complex. And, oh! how the same phenomenon was sweeping Norway, too! Why, she pressed on, had our societies become so sex-saturated?

"Because 'the mass of men lead lives of quiet desperation.' You might even know that quote, Inkie—it's from Thoreau's *Walden*. I'm afraid most people are bored to tears with the lives they lead. They're living in unconscious despair. They're dying for excitement. And the Media/Entertainment Complex is only too glad to give that to them. For an awesome price, of course—not only in money but, more important, in their lives."

Yet, there was an even more simple answer I tried out on her—that

SEX SELLS. Like the story of the guy who ran an ad announcing he had a car to sell...and bordered the ad with an endless chain of the word, *sex*. Well, the ad had nothing whatever to do with sex BUT...my, how it got attention! In short, in an economy based on *laissez faire* (more or less), commercial interests—all those producing and selling things with the hope for profit—rule the roost. Backing them up are their marketing hirelings—led by clever, aggressive advertising agencies—who exploit sex in all its forms, open and subtle and all points between. With pretty faces, enticing breasts and tantalizing bodies. Then the rest of the Media/Entertainment Complex joins in, with everyone trying to outdo each other in order to get attention...and collectively going hog-wild on the subject. So now, everywhere you look, you see the grisly debris: Drugs and alcoholism, especially among the young, prostitution, violent crime and rape—including sexual abuse of the most defenseless of all in society, our children.

Well, Inger didn't like either the situation or my portrayal of it...just as many blame the messenger for the message. If, as she believed, truly rewarding love is as much a union of the spirit as well as the body, and if it is to give real returns in both respects, then, she felt, people today are in for trouble, indeed. She predicted, sadly, that the Media/Entertainment Complex's avid promotion of the shrill new world of permissiveness, pornography, perversion and promiscuity will yield only heartbreak for people...and disorder and decline for Western society.

Important Event Number Two exploded on the scene when Inger announced that she intended to become an American citizen. I couldn't quite believe what I was hearing. But, yes, she assured me, she had come to love America, and especially the American people, despite her rough experiences. Moreover, she never considered Norway's culture, or its foreign policies, inimicable to the USA's...so she never had to make the agonizing choices that switching countries imposes on many immigrants. Hadn't she said that her homeland and the USA were becoming so similar that Norway now seemed more like our 49th state?

On a more personal level, she didn't feel particularly "ethnic" and didn't consider herself very different from most Americans. (I didn't, either.) Yet, what really moved her was her perception of the boys' future here vs. there. The US was big, diverse, dynamically changing, singularly involved with the world and the immense diversity of human strivings. It was a giant stage on which people could play out whatever role they might choose and become whatever their vision, intellect and will permitted. And that should and would include our sons, too....

So we went over the INS examination questions together, with my finally concluding that...oh, boy!...it's not often we get a new citizen like *that!* It was then on to the courthouse at Rockville, Maryland, where the swearing-in took place. I had earlier found out that the *Times-Herald* reporter there was the astute Neil Regeimbal. He arranged a photo of the new citizen, and there Inger appeared on the front page of the paper's local news section waving an American flag. Our friends were elated. My own reaction: Will wonders never cease!

Now that we were four, Inger and I decided the Goodacres apartment was getting much too cramped. So we scrimped and denied and saved and finally came up with enough money for a down payment on a modest two-story house behind BCC Highschool in Bethesda. Even though this would force Valkyrie to run up and down the stairs all day to take care of Erik. The best of it, though, was that, as luck seemed to have it wherever we lived, we got some fantastic neighbors. Dottie Breedlove (husband Joe was in real estate management) and Edna Sprague (Dean was a Ph.D., government budget officer and author of the book, *Freedom Under Lincoln)* were both educators, and Inger hit it off with them from Day One. This led to long discussions with Dottie and Edna about literature and to equally spirited talks with Dean on public policies. Dean proved to be that rarest of Washingtonians—a *conservative* bureaucrat. As he explained, though, "no one knows better than us insiders how really screwed up things get when government tries to implement some screwball politician's grandiose schemes."

The big fly in this new concoction turned out to be me. I enjoyed the AAR and PR work, perhaps because I never stopped being a reporter. Indeed, I had crossed over to the other side of the communications street and had become a news source, but I never stopped wanting to continue to report on those sources. Most of all, I never stopped wanting to get into *Washington* reporting. I was dying to get involved in the big issues of our time and in the government/ political machinery that dealt with them. So when the chance came, I went!

Photo from Washington Times-Herald

Inger becomes a US Citizen! This Washington Times-Herald *photo shows Inger (right) as she and a native of Austria "take the oath" along with 40 others on January 27, 1953, at the Montgomery County Circuit Court in Rockville, Maryland.*

John Rudy, a pal at the capital's oldest newsletters, *The Whaley-Eaton News Service,* alerted me to an opening there. It was appealing because the service covered the waterfront: Its *American Letter* covered the US, its *Foreign Letter* covered the world, and its *Atoms for Peace* reports (Rudy's baby) covered the expanding field of nuclear technology. BUT the job paid less than present earnings—a disgusting 15% less. So back to Inger I went with the bad news.

"Fannen tar det! [The devil with it!]," she said in affected pain. "I should have married a rich publisher, not a penniless reporter."

"Well, maybe you did, sweetheart. Unfortunately, you might have to wait a while...."

The AAR gang put on a small farewell ceremony for us in our Conference Room, where Albert Beatty spoke with many oratorical flourishes about my four years on the rails. As I listened, I kept thinking of how I would miss his warm involvement in everything: His urgings at press parties to "mix it up!" His solution of difficult railroad policy positions: "Blur it up!" The caution he voiced in difficult situations: "Don't stir up the animals!" Above all, the way he would always charge down hallways with a piece of paper in his hand—*any* kind of paper; this showed conclusively that here was a very important person on a very important mission!

Inger, I knew, would also miss Beatty and his affable, gregarious nature. Like the time Mamma came to America, and I introduced the two at an AAR meeting at the Waldorf-Astoria in New York City. "Yes, of course!" he said without one moment's hesitation, "I knew that anyone like Inger would have a beautiful mother!" Well, *both* thought he was the greatest!

Then, of all people, President Faricy showed up...and made this prescient statement along with his so-long-and-good-luck comment: "Jim, I have a feeling we'll meet again...."

That was nice to hear, all right, but I didn't put much stock in his remark. Doesn't everyone involved in Washington meet everyone else who's involved here sooner or later?

Chapter IV

My Washington reporting career began not with the bang I had anticipated but with a whole series of misfires and backfires. Not that any of
this bothered Inger. Far from resenting the big pay-cut the change entailed, and the trouble this led to, she excitedly positioned herself to
plunge into this new news business just as she plunged into everything
else I had undertaken. For here, indeed, was another chance to un-
cover more of what America was all about. She struck me much like
an eager archaeologist digging layer by layer into the mysteries of an
evolving civilization.

Stan Shaw, a balding, soft-spoken former investment analyst who
was now Whaley-Eaton's editor, assigned me to work on the *American Letter*, which covered virtually everything happening in Washington of consequence to business and the economy. (Subscribers were
mainly business executives and public officials and, not so strangely,
perhaps, news people.) This was like throwing me straight out into
deep water—like saying s*ink or swim, you rascal!* The result: I almost
sank. Despite my previous writing experience and all my studies, readings and personal inclination, I found out quickly that I really didn't
know Washington or the ever-changing issues and their nuances that
reporters here wrestle with daily. Trying to find out sent me home in a
daily daze. And when Inger asked how it had gone that day, the only
thing I could do was roll my eyes toward the ceiling...and collapse.

Fact is, I was monstrously confused the first days and weeks on the
new job. Confused as to whom to turn to and how to get reliable information out of the White House and its solar system of Executive offices, out of the vast and seemingly impenetrable Federal departments,
out of the alphabet soup of regulatory agencies, out of Congressmen's

offices and the myriad Capitol Hill committees and subcommittees. Confused as to who's-who and where's-what among the lobbyists and special-interest groups, the political parties and "think tanks"—not to mention all the government reporting services and private analysts. I felt lost in a labyrinth.

"How in tarnation," I asked Inger in bewilderment, "do the other reporters do it and still look so relaxed at the Press Club bar!"

"Ah, but most specialize—they cover one beat. You're trying to cover the waterfront. And I bet most have developed a system. Can't you, too?"

Yes, so they had. And so, I vowed, would we....

With Inger helping out on research and learning a-pace, I burrowed for months into the ocean of information overload that inundates Washington...and began to sort out the dozen or so major issues that occupy people here. That's right, there aren't that many—BUT, like trees, each can have many branches. We identified each issue's nature and graded its importance, singled out who's involved in it and the constituent pressures and lobby conflicts pulling and pushing behind the scenes, where the balance of political pressure lies...and, most crucial, where the issue's resolution is going. In this long, arduous process, we came to see with new clarity that most reporting sadly deals only with the surface ripples in this outsized stream of information, not the underlying currents. But that's why people bought our newsletters!

We spent still more time hashing over all this with other staffers—John Rudy and Sid Levy, in particular. They and Stan Shaw already knew! Sid was a truly knowledgeable, focused, serious reporter. John, on the other hand, bubbled over with new ideas (some even workable!) and fresh viewpoints on Capital maneuverings. The soul of tact, he never disagreed with my ramblings—only muttered under his breath, "You'll see! You'll see!" Then one day Harry Vandernoot joined the staff. A refugee from UPI, he turned out to be completely allergic to work...but irresistibly good-humored. He would often slip into my office, clap me on the shoulder and sing out, "Jim, you're doing a g-r-a-n-d job!" Even when he knew I wasn't.

No one seemed to me to know Washington better than the Letters' owner and publisher, the wizened, brilliant Percival H. Whaley. Now over 80, he had founded the service 40 years before, in 1916, as the original Washington newsletter. Our major competitor was *Kiplinger*. Once when with AAR, I was invited by Kip staffer George Kennedy for a private lunch at that service's headquarters...and who should join us but Willard Kiplinger himself! So I knew what kind of tough rival we were up against. Mr. Whaley was much more reserved. He came into the office seldom but kept a close rein on the company pursestrings. Unfortunately, as I shortly found out, this came to pose a host of problems in terms of selling the service to new subscribers...and surviving.

My nearterm reporting goal was to pin down a half-dozen or so truly reliable sources on each major issue...and thus build an invaluable network of personal contacts. For it's the size and quality of these that often determine one's skill in cutting through Washington's ever-present overlayers of muck, red herrings, smokescreens, mirrors and political posturing...and getting to the facts. "Calling around the circuit" on a given new development, we found, often did wonders in putting a story into perspective with reality, or in revealing an entirely fresh and more meaningful angle. Such contacts effectively spanned the range of thinking on a subject, from reactionary to radical, from the Chamber of Commerce to the AFL-CIO, from GOP leaders to the Dems, from liberal Brookings to conservative American Enterprise Institute.

My own perspective could use an overhaul, as well, I heard directly one day from the editor. Sorrowfully wagging his head, Shaw said my reporting was too arms-length, too analytical, too focused on policies and problems...and not, NOT enough on personalities and politicking. *This* is what makes the Washington merry-go-round go 'round, he said. *This* is what people want to read. *This* is what sells: Who's in, who's out; who's going up, who's going down; who's winning, who's losing; who's amassing power, who's losing it.

For instance, there was that special four-page "Transportation Report" I wrote for our promotion service. Okay, it did a fine job of showing how totally out of balance government policies were in this area, especially in their treatment of highway, air and water carriers vs. the railroads. But where were the fireworks? he asked. Where was the coverage of the clashing lobbies, Congressmen, bureaucrats and industry personalities? Where was the revelation that the highway lobby, led by truckers, road builders, vehicle manufacturers and Big Oil, is perhaps the strongest in Washington...and can demand and get almost any amount of Federal money for better roads—with auto owners paying a disproportionate share of the bill compared with the road-busters (heavy trucks) because they are largely unorganized. (And why aren't the big automobile insurance companies helping auto owners make their case on The Hill? Shouldn't they be fighting your battles for a fairer deal? *Sorry,* motorists! The insurance companies are too busy making a fortune selling insurance, period.)

Or how about the "pork barreling" by everyone and his brother through the notorious Rivers and Harbors Bill and its annual raid on taxpayers...to the benefit of waterside industry and the commercial carriers plying our inland and coastal waterways? Sure, but don't these construction projects benefit every community near whatever creek can be made into a navigable stream? And in every port city? Since every associated Congressman loves to bring home this kind of bacon, here in this profligate plunder you have the most "natural" of all lobbies. As Congressional action proves year after year, it's unstoppable!

Sid Levy, I noted, wrote fluidly along this line, and I began to copy him and work the political ramifications into virtually everything I wrote about—much to Inger's chagrin. On a dull-appearing Labor Department release of rising unemployment statistics, as an example, I wove in the concerns of the "ins"—Eisenhower Republicans, in this case—regarding the effects that greater joblessness would have in turning off voters at the next election. This was then contrasted with the barely concealed jubilation among the "outs"—Democrats—who saw in the figures not indications of rising human suffering but, rather, rising prospects of a big political pay-off at the polls. For doesn't everyone vote according to his pocketbook? Likewise predictable were the President's sympathetic-*sounding* follow-up action recommendations, as well as the opposition's denunciation of these as "much too little, much too late."

Inger's chagrin was well based, I had to admit. For in this changeover in approach and style, my reporting somehow lost depth and began to sound more superficial. Like Washington itself. In any event, the objective was to better reflect the real, everyday Capital whirl. While readers might thereby come to understand less about public policies, they would grasp more about the political reality underpinning these. Indeed, that's what the Washington game is all about...and I came to feel it's vital that people understand *that*.

Other tricks of the trade were picked up in time, as well. Under Inger's oh-so-bland questioning, a top columnist revealed that his forecasts, like so many others' around town, were purposely cast as worst-case scenarios.

"But why on earth would you purposely add to public uneasiness and fear? To the negative tone of society?" she asked innocently. [Foreshadowing Vice President Spiro Agnew's unforgettable branding of Washington reporters as "nattering nabobs of negativism." This also echoed Inger's own description of the advertising business as "muttering merchants of malcontent" and, perhaps more to the point, "expectorating exponents of extravagant expectations."]

"Well," came the replay, "since no one can know what the future holds, it's just as well to be prepared for the worst. Then, if you're right, people praise you as some sort of modern-day prophet. And if you're wrong, they're so relieved they gladly forget what you said!"

Significantly, Mr. Whaley would not tolerate anyone predicting anything. We could talk possibilities, even probabilities, and underscore directions and trends. But no predictions, please! He felt our readers were too smart to fall for that kind of baseless bait. For who can predict the future? So we worked doubly hard to make our reporting *responsible*. We smugly contended that the competition—namely, *Kiplinger*—wrote more to excite and sell, while *Whaley-Eaton* wrote to inform. That was plenty dumb, for in terms of market response, while Kip's services prospered and waxed, ours waned.

Another principle Mr. Whaley stressed was that we should never hesitate to report the obvious...or to take the directly opposite tack from the prevailing consensus. (As Inger invariably did!) Note, he said, that most reporters scurry around town, trying to unearth the most dramatic or unusual angle on a story (hopefully, maybe even an embarrassing scandal)...leaving it up to a bare handful (namely, us) to "tell it like it is." We few—we unhappy, readerless, poverty-stricken few—are then hailed for our singular intelligence and insight!

Another important point he stressed was that most of the world has its eyes on the wrong target area in trying to chart the direction of political trends. People, military factors, government decisions, propaganda noise...aren't that decisive, he said. What is? The *economics* of a situation. Follow the money trail! Figure out where economic pressures are heading, and you'll have the best chance of determining where the political outcome is heading.

This led us to the most important—and simplest—discovery of all: That a given report is no more solid than the reporter behind it. In scanning continually a wide range of newspapers and magazines and tuning in to many commentators, we had a chance to compare all kinds of approaches against a given set of facts that we had personally checked out. This laid bare a disheartening display of prejudice, partisanship, shallowness, distortion and outright meanness. But it also pinpointed some of the world's best reporting. Yes, it's rare...but it *does* exist!

Inger proved adept at this game. To her, accustomed as most foreigners are to party-owned, union-owned, church-owned and other unabashedly partisan news outlets, there was nothing anywhere quite like *The New York Times*. She came to consider its writers on books, music and the arts—her own spheres of knowledge—as *the* authorities. And she assumed the paper's writers in other fields were the same...as she noted, with considerable disgust, my diligent clipping of its Washington and foreign economic news sections. She despaired of reading the paper after that; it looked as though it had been used to make paperdoll cut-outs.

Were others doing this kind of "underhanded plagiarizing"? Inger wanted to know.

Absolutely! I answered. Almost everyone in town was using the *Times'* coverage of a developing story as a reference point for checking out his own version. This is why it's said that you can hardly ever correct a *Times* error; it had likely already spread everywhere on the wings of emulation and become historical "fact".

Despite its obvious faults, however, America's free press had one overriding virtue to us that far offset its faults: The threat of exposure. "How will it look on the front pages?" must surely be the most effective force ever conceived for compelling people in the public arena to avoid wrongdoing, chicanery, corruption and dishonesty. Obviously, many do so anyway, as the press reports regularly. But what kind of society would we have if that subtle protection wasn't there at all?

Inger's response: "You really want to know? Ask the people in Communist Russia—or any other dictatorship. A free press is the first thing to go."

Six months into the new job, I screwed up enough courage to try my hand at also writing for our *Foreign Letter*. It proved hardly that awesome. We had stringers ("moonlighters" with other services) in London and Tokyo and at the US State Department (broadcasting reporter John Scali eventually became US Ambassador to the United Nations). These aides supplemented other stringers around Washington, like the capable Bill Theis, head of the UPI Senate staff, in feeding us a steady flow of alerts on new developments...and in providing solid soundingboards for story directions. We also followed closely IMF (the Fund) and the World Bank and many foreign publications, of which there was nothing like *The Economist*, of London.

As fate would have it, the minute I touched the typewriter in this field, all hell broke loose. On two fronts! Egypt took over the Suez Canal, precipitating separate attacks by Israel and British-French forces. I had passed through this waterway in 1944 during a hellishly hot voyage to the Persian Gulf and knew firsthand its strategic importance. Even so, few were prepared for the alarm that swept governments and global businesses over the sudden disruption to world commerce. Overnight, Whaley-Eaton put all its resources into coming out with a Special Report for our readers, then used it as the basis for a promotion mailing. Returns in terms of new subscriptions were unbelievable! So Stan Shaw went to Mr. Whaley and proposed that more money be plowed into even heavier promotion. He didn't get a cent.

Explosion No. 2 came as the Hungarian people rose in revolt against their communist jailers. The hour for freedom had struck! Here was a heroic people making a bold attempt to break their bonds and rejoin the Free World. Inger and I stayed up night after night listening to the radio for scraps of news, biting fingernails, wringing hands, remembering Poland, praying. The gauntlet had been flung and the times called for decisive action. But the fear of setting off a MAD (Mutual Assured Destruction) atomic holocaust prevailed. America and the rest of the world did nothing. Russian troops marched into Hungary, leveling murderous fire against crowds armed with rocks, crushing the revolt and triggering a massive flight of refugees to the West. So we watched helplessly as Hungary slipped back again behind the Iron Curtain. And we raged over our impotence and the abandonment of people fighting mankind's ancient battle against tyranny. It was a terrible time for personal agonizing over the limits of America's power—a time when we lost political innocence forever.

Inger was the first to note that my intensive learning in the Washington school of hard knocks was taking its toll on health. Playing catch-up for the lost war years and trying to do in six months what should have taken six years brought on strange attacks of dizziness. While phoning, typing, running to press conferences and hearings, I smoked heavily—far too much.

And that first cigarette in the morning almost put me back into bed. So both of us stopped smoking...completely, permanently. Inger's "science of alternatives" helped: Every time I reached for a cigarette, I got a lifesaver or chewing gum, instead.

Anyway, what's the gawdawful rush? Inger wanted to know.

I replied, lamely, that it was necessary...quickly...to develop professional standing. In fact, you couldn't get anywhere in Washington without that. But the real reason—one I could not divulge—was Inger herself. I felt driven by an overwhelming compulsion to make things better for her in the USA, to make up for her abandoning family and homeland for me, to make her like America and living here better—to make her happier.

Inger got me to go to a doctor, who diagnosed the dizzy spells as sinus pressure. Not really that serious, he said: But, mister, he said, you've *got* to let up on the work pressure. Spend more time with your family. Get away for a while. Have some fun!

What a grand doctor! He could go right to work in Norway, Inger said, for there everyone always seemed to be either on vacation, planning one, or coming home from one.

Leaving Editor Shaw muttering over the "medicine," Inger and the two boys and I piled into the car and headed east 130 miles for a week at the Atlantic Ocean at Rehoboth Beach, Delaware, hailed as "the nation's Summer Capital." It was the perfect remedy for all of us. We stayed in a beat-up "apartment" above a garage on Hickman Street two blocks from the beach and lugged our gear back and forth under a scorching sun. But who cared! One look at the roaring, rumbling surf and we felt again the old pull of the sea—the pervading presence of the endless, the eternal, the uncompromising, the all-powerful. On the far horizon, I saw again vague shadows of gray ships plodding along in convoy and heard again the roar of dive-bombers and the blast of depth-charges. But, no, that was yesterday (thank God!). Today was different. Here beside me was Inger—and Mimbo and Erik. We held hands, and our spirits soared with the seagulls...as they glided, wheeled, dove and pirouetted along the shimmering sands.

"Three hours' drive from Washington...and a million miles from hell!" was the way Inger described Rehoboth.

And then and there we made a pact that, regardless of what the world did to us, we would return to this spot to renew our spirits (and our Promises). And what better way to do that than to walk down to the lonely shore at night...and, standing there nakedly alone before heaven and God, face the enormous ocean and ancient source of our birth and, overhead, the measureless, star-filled canopy of the sky? And despite how small and insignificant all that wonder made us poor humans, thrill to the greatness of creation and the sheer glory of being alive and being able to feel and experience it all....

Descartes, Inger added one spectacularly starry night, missed the point: Instead of "I think; therefore, I am," he should have gone on to say "I *feel*; therefore, I *live*!"

Returning to the job with new energy, I complained to Inger that the trouble with reporting in Washington is that you never feel you've finished your work: "There's always an endless range of good stories that you should and could be covering."

"Okay," she replied. "If you're going to knock yourself out, we may as well do it together. So you do the writing, and I'll do the research and typing."

We thus began to look around for free-lancing possibilities. Actually, reporting for Whaley-Eaton gave us a head start. In condensing a long story into a couple paragraphs for one of the letters, we had to compile enough information for a column and, sometimes, even for a full-length feature article. And wasn't just about every reporter in town reworking information into several different forms and "moonlighting" in this fashion to some extent?

John Rudy's field—peaceful uses of atomic energy—struck us as a goldmine of new, salable ideas. So, with John's generous help, we summed up a couple story ideas in brief query form...and, a bit apprehensive, sent off letters to a half-dozen likely publications: Would you be interested in an article on prospects of atomic power generation, research into radiation of food, use of isotopes for better health, etc?

And waited for a positive response. And waited.

Inger wouldn't give up, though. Each time an editor turned down an idea, we shot off a second letter proposing still another. She felt life situations should be treated the same way: Whenever you get hit by a setback, start something new and different right away...that gives you an offsetting hope of a positive outcome. Sometimes this even works!

At last, a breakthrough came in a phone call from the editor of *The American Legion Magazine*—and I blew it! The distinguished Joseph C. Keeley himself came on line, announcing he had received my letter and, instead of the article I proposed, would like an 1,800-word piece comparing the political parties' positions on national security issues—all this looking ahead to that Fall's election. AND would pay $250. for my efforts. I paused, did some fast calculating and replied that I thought such a lot of work was worth more money—say, $350.

Well, what followed was an ear-splitting explosion...as the editor hung up the phone! Or did he throw it against the wall? So there I sat, aghast at my stupidity. How could I possibly explain my moronic, abject failure to Inger?

Fortunately, I didn't have to, for heaven must have assigned a whole flight of angels to help morons. Next morning, against all odds, the phone rang again and there was Editor Keeley...saying (astoundingly!) he agreed with me. *Agreed!* He said he felt the magazine's rates were too low, and he would gladly pay the higher figure. "And, oh, yes, please call me Joe."

What a guy! This kicked off a lifelong friendship as well as a close working relationship. Inger and I thereafter put together two long feature articles for the magazine. We also worked out with Joe a monthly feature that continues to this day in *The Legion* magazine: It's called "Washington, Pro and Con" and includes two Congressmen on one page, taking opposite sides on a major public policy issue.

Then came *Nation's Business* with a request that I do a Q&A interview with Senator Clinton P. Anderson, chairman of Congress' Joint Atomic Energy Committee...on the future of the atom and related Washington policy approaches. Another Q&A followed, this time with Arthur Gass, the dynamic chairman of the AAR's Car Service Division, on what the railroads were doing to head off boxcar shortages during the massive upcoming western grain harvesting season. In both these cases, I found to my surprise that I could remember almost every word said during the interview—as long as I wrote it all down within a couple following hours. Later, I got wiser and used a tape recorder; it's always best to have a subject's views *on record* just in case questions come up as to what he *really* said.

An assignment with downright weird results next came from *Steelways* magazine: Could I possibly get an interview with the controversial Admiral Hyman G. Rickover, father of the first nuclear submarine, the *Nautilus*? Yes, I could, I thought...and did. It wasn't easy...but, man, was it ever instructive! I found Rickover sitting with rolled-up sleeves in an unadorned workroom—small, lean and keen and looking much like an eagle preparing to pounce on his prey. Aware of his reputation as one difficult leader, I began the interview with some soft, warm-up questions.

"Young man," the admiral cut in impatiently [I was then 34], "you sit and take notes. *I* will ask the questions and *I* will provide the answers."

There followed a fantastic account of how he was fighting day and night to get his fellow military officers, politicians and an American industry rooted in a business-as-usual past to adjust their thinking to the entirely new level of technology required by atomic power development—in metallurgy, machine clearances, plumbing, fittings and gaskets, operating skills, etc. No wonder people thought he was difficult! The lesson he taught, though, was that you don't get anywhere in implementing a revolutionary technology by being a nice guy. The Brooklyn Dodgers' Leo Durocher put this well: "Nice guys finish last." And Admiral Rickover, who was born in Russia, wasn't about to let the USA lose out to the USSR in this increasingly crucial arena.

One surprising lesson Inger and I learned in our free-lancing was that editors aren't all that concerned about a free-lance contributor's *writing* ability. They assume you can write reasonably well—otherwise, you wouldn't be in the writing business. What *really* concerns them is an outsider's reliability regarding facts, article content and interview quotes (think *libel*!). AND your ability to meet deadlines. An unforgivable, permanent blacklist awaits those who leave an editor facing a blank page at press-run time.

My first visit to Norway also resulted from our expanding freelancing work. I knew that, as usual, Inger was dying to get back to her home stomping grounds, so I arranged some reporting assignments to pay for the four roundtrip tickets we would need to travel on the Norwegian-American Line. And found myself falling in love with a country with an inimitable nature—with glorious fjords and fjells and forests and waterfalls. So I came to admit that Inger was right when she said, "If you like nature, you'll love Norway!"

We also visited Denmark and Sweden, where we talked with assorted experts on what makes Scandinavia tick. And duly reported these developments in news columns stressing the three countries' economic outlook...for *The Christian Science Monitor*.

One more assignment must be mentioned, for, as I found out later, it actually amounted to a "put-up job." *Wheels* magazine called and asked me to do a joint interview with the AAR's retiring William T. Faricy and its incoming president, Daniel P. Loomis. Some big developments were in the wind concerning the railroads' long-standing problems with their labor unions over "featherbedding" work rules, and the interview was aimed at exploring these. Little did I know that the real purpose was that both of these executives wanted to look me over, close up—Faricy anew and Loomis afresh. So shortly after the resulting article was published, my old boss, Al Beatty, phoned and asked, "Say, Jim, would you be interested in rejoining the AAR?" More on this shortly....

"A news entrepreneur—that's what you're becoming," Inger said proudly as she tore open an envelope with the latest check from one of our publishers.

"Where did you get that funny label?" I wondered.

"From your friend, John Rudy. Where else?"

"Well, he's only half-right—maybe even less. We still have a long row to hoe before reaching such an exalted status."

Ink was referring to my regular reporting job plus outside writing. Looking around at more experienced Washington reporters, however, I noted that the best were also giving speeches around the country, getting books published, appearing on TV interview programs, lecturing at universities, etc. They *were* entrepreneurs. They were turning their journalism craft into a full-fledged one-man business...and making a small fortune doing it.

In the meantime, we weren't doing so badly ourselves. Now, after two years of double-duty at both Whaley-Eaton and "our" magazines, checks for $200. for "Pro & Con" and $450. to $750. for articles/Q&A's were appearing regularly in the mailbox. In fact, working most evenings and weekends, we were earning as much from free-lancing as from my regular job. Not that it made any difference in our living standards. Oh no! Inger sent every "outside" cent straight to the bank. (She must have read the book, *Mama's Bank Account*, forerunner of the noted movie, "I Remember Mama.") All this was in line with her views that you should dwell *above* your means, dress *at* your means and eat *below* your means. Of course, few Americans went along with such a tough prescription: For them, *everything* was above. (And so were their debts!)

So what was all this saving for? For one thing, Inger announced that we had to move from Chase Avenue. There were too many speeding cars on the street and too much danger for the boys. After much looking around, we found a dead-end street full of new houses being built...on Ogden Court in the Springfield section of Bethesda. And by selling our current house and raiding the bank account, we came up with enough for the down payment. After a half-year of wrestling with the builder over every conceivable construction problem, including several postponed occupancy deadlines, we finally moved into a modern split-level—four levels a half-floor apart, which we found added up to a perfect living arrangement.

Then came another important thing involving money: Inger wanted to do something special for her parents—which boiled down to a free (for them!) trip to our new home and America. Mamma and Pappa thus became our honored guests all over Washington. They loved it! And so did we. Mamma turned out to be a shrewd but fun-loving gal, and we became close pals. The secret? On her advice, every morning as I shaved I looked into the mirror and said three times: "I love my mother-in-law. I *really* love my mother-in-law." And it worked!

A grand family celebration came next. After spending eons commuting to the Library of Congress, Inger completed her Master's Thesis—on Norwegian literature available in English translation—and finally received from Catholic University her Master's Degree in Library Science. Mamma thought she should have received a degree in perseverance. To paraphrase Churchill, this awesome challenge had progressed by stages from adventure to mistress to master to tyrant to monster. But Inger had finally justified, at least to herself—and *that* was important—America's award to her of that long-ago scholarship to Kalamazoo College. I spotted a news photographer on campus and talked him into taking a picture of the new graduate and us three admirers. This appeared in *The Washington Post* over a caption that began, appropriately:

A new country, three schools, several jobs, two children and eleven years later, Inger Krogh Sites finally made the grade!

Were things going too well in my wife's long struggle to find a foothold in her American adventure? Perhaps fate thought so. After all, one of Inger's frequent quotes was the sobering Norsk warning: "For each moment of happiness in life, you will pay with a moment of sorrow."

One day Inger happily announced that we could expect another heir in six months...but her buoyant mood changed to tears when a miscarriage threatened. We went to see her doctor—a smart young character who had delivered Erik and who assumed the position of knowing all the latest about medicines and techniques. He urged the drug, *stilbesterol*, for Inger. This kicked off a lengthy debate, in which

Decked out in graduation gown, Inger receives her Master's Degree in Library Science from Catholic University in Washington, DC, fulfilling the mission that brought her to America as a first postwar exchange student—11 years, 3 schools, and 2 sons later. Here she's shown with the rest of the "Gang of Four", courtesy of The Washington Evening Star, June 10, 1957.

both of us took the position that nature was trying to tell us something...and that it was perhaps best to allow the miscarriage to run its course.

"Oh, no—nothing to worry about at all," was his answer. "Stilbesterol will do the trick. Everything will work out fine."

So Inger and I yielded in hopes that our misgivings were unfounded. The medicine (or should I say *poison?*) did do the trick, the miscarriage was stopped, and in half a year Inger gave birth to another baby.

I was at the hospital when the doctor came out of the delivery room.

"Congratulations!" he said with the barest hint of hesitation. "You've got a fine big boy—a mongoloid."

"What in holy hell are you saying?" I shouted, not knowing whether to weep or smash in his face on the spot. While alarm bells rang: How will Inger take this?

Well, the news hit her hard at first, then more softly as she came to grips with the new reality. She was told that mongoloids were usually sweet and lovable, though they were poorly developed mentally and physically and would remain essentially babies their whole life.

Yet, the more I saw her trying to rationalize this raw deal, the angrier I became. I played for a while with committing mayhem on the doctor—but, instead, talked to a lawyer friend about a possible suit for malpractice. He shook his head. No, he said, drug experts and other doctors would have to be brought into the case as expert witnesses— and he saw no real hope of getting them to do so:

"They're all members of 'the medical club.' It's shut tight against outsiders. And you're the outsider. Members will simply close ranks against you...and you won't be able to prove a thing."

Dissatisfied with that opinion, I consulted another lawyer who specialized in liability cases. Same result. The lawyers seemed to me to care as little about the human impact of this blatant case as the doctors. To me, stilbesterol was a disaster and should be banned immediately before it wreaked further damage among hopeful young women and their families. But who was going to stick his neck out and force the profession to do so? ONE would have, and that was a Ralph Nader-type doctor/lawyer team. But I never managed to find that out until much later—to my everlasting regret and sorrow.

Lars, our new baby, *looked* so fine and normal—almost like Mimbo. But he had slightly slanted eyes and an oddly repetitive, heart-rending blinking in the inner eye. His digestive tract was also apparently so undeveloped that he couldn't swallow or digest food. So home care went from bad to worse. And after a long row of sleepless nights, Inger began to come unglued in both nerves and emotions. A pediatrician helped; he recommended a private home for deformed babies. Here, he maintained, the baby might get enough expert care to get a real start on life.

The home, located in a rundown house in Silver Spring and run by "a good Christian nurse," as the doctor put it, struck Inger as a scene right out of a nightmare. Occupied cribs were lined up side by side in the livingroom/diningroom and bedrooms, and weird noises and awful odors filled the air. A dozen mongoloids peered and jabbered at us visitors. They seemed the most normal of the patients. Other babies had outsized heads and grotesquely twisted bodies, and some writhed about as though in wrenching pain. Inger was appalled. For here were strewn the bitter ashes of once-radiant dreams—cast-offs of a nature that somehow had gone terribly wrong. I wondered how many were the grim results of some doctor's ignorant, indiscriminate use of stilbesterol....

In stark, almost scary contrast, the aged caretaker who came to meet us at the home bore an angelic expression and seemed unperturbed by her surroundings—to the point of being almost cheerful. Yes, she told my anguished, ashen-faced wife, she would gladly take care of "God's little one." So we hurriedly made the necessary financial arrangements, kissed Lars goodbye and left, torn and heartsick over the unspeakable tragedy that had befallen these poor souls—and now one of our own.

At home, Erik started giving Inger a bad time. Now four and more sensitive and excitable than the four-years-older Mimbo, he was beside himself over Lars' absence.

"Where's the baby brother you promised me?" he asked plaintively day after day.

"At the hospital. You know he's sick. But getting well!" A harried Inger said this with the lightest mood she could muster...which didn't fool our son a bit.

In between mollifying Erik and reassuring Mimbo, Inger subjected herself to the torture of repeated visits to what I came to call the House of Horrors. This did neither Lars nor her the slightest good...and after six more weeks of drawn-out agony, the baby died.

I guess both of us were too spent, too drained to feel either sorrow or relief. We stumbled through the final arrangements and then the four of us took off for Rehoboth and the thundering, wave-whipped seashore—the wild wonders-working world "where the wind's like a whetted knife." It could cut right into your innermost recesses and restore the stricken spirit. I felt furious over this setback to all I had done to make Inger happy in America. But as she said, it was time to pull ourselves together and move on.

It was also time for the second shoe to drop. Inger's close friends maintained that the only way for her to get over the shock of such a loss was to have another baby right away.

"You don't mind that kind of advice, do you," she asked, renewed hope in her voice. She also revealed for the first time that she wanted us to have six children. Six!

"Hey, wait a minute, who's going to support all these big eaters?"

"*Uf da!* YOU! With my help, of course...."

She got serious: "Look. Jimmy. My family's far away...and your family's read itself out of the picture. So who will our kids turn to when we're gone? To each other! I mean, if we're going to start a brand-new family here in America, we need all the children we can get. And you, their father...how could you be so lucky!"

So Inger did become pregnant again and, as forecast, her mood did become lighter...for a while. Eight months along, however, alarm bells started ringing once more. Our new gynecologist, who avoided use of drugs whenever possible, said Inger was retaining too much fluid in the abdomen. Something was wrong again....

Wrong, indeed. This time our baby was born with simple stubs in place of hands, a deformed foot and grave respiratory problems. Inger herself barely survived the delivery, and everyone joined me in trying to withhold the truth about the baby from her to give her time to re-cover. Nor did anyone want, above all, to tell her she could never again bear children.

But who can fool a mother in such circumstances? When the nurses made excuses about bringing in her baby, Inger dragged herself to the intensive-care unit and saw what had happened with her own eyes. She collapsed.

For days, I sat by her bedside and watched as she slowly came out of a semi-coma. Then came long, tearing sobbing spells. Our Lutheran minister came to visit, but Inger sent him packing. Likewise a psychiatrist I tried to have her talk with.

Some knowing soul sent not flowers (her room was filled with them) but a bottle of Chivas Regal. And when Inger couldn't get the bottle open the following night, she broke the neck off over the washbowl...and drank a whole glassful. After that I stayed with her around the clock, for the nights were especially bad. There were harrowing hallucinations: Once she found herself back on her first ship, the *Byron Darnton*, and the ship was sinking in a frightful storm. Mountainous waves crashed over the bed. Whirling pools of ice-filled water dragged her down. She screamed and threw pillows and bedclothes and fought desperately to stay afloat.

Breaking all the hospital's rules, I stripped down to my underwear, lay down beside and held her as tightly as I could, hoping to drive some of my own strength into her body and some security into her soul. She, in turn, locked her arms around my neck so hard that I almost choked...as she struggled, literally, to hang on to dear life.

I talked with the doctors about what had gone so wrong. Their conclusion was that carryover effects of the stilbesterol from Lars' birth, together with some sedative she had been given, combined to produce a defective embryo. The baby wasn't breathing well, and was being kept alive in a respirator.

"I want that damn thing turned off!" I told our family doctor. "If the little guy can make it on his own, that's fine. But, please, NO artificial measures."

"You'll never get the hospital to do that," he replied. "Doctors are here to preserve life, not end it."

Say no more, please! At that moment, I was hardly in a mood to hear anything positive about doctors or their pharmaceutical friends. Modern medicine had taken a strong, healthy, vital woman and ruined her reproductive system and killed off two of our offsprings—the last she would ever have. I felt frustrated, helpless and furious at the whole pack.

Sick about whether Inger herself was going to make it, I watched with mixed feelings as our crippled boy dwindled away day by day—while the medical staff worked feverishly to keep him alive. Then, finally, he, too, gave up the ghost of life and died.

Inger, wrung out in body and soul, took the news with fatalistic calm. Too calmly, I feared. Yet, it was our two existing sons who made the final difference in her recovery:

"We'll never have those six children you wanted," I said, "but, sweetheart, we *do* have two...and they're fantastic. And, I might add, they need you desperately...right now!"

Drawing on some fathomless inner sources of strength, she gradually got back on her feet and returned home...to Mimbo and Erik's wild jubilation. Her condition continued to worry all of us, though. She acted listless and withdrawn. And seemed to be going on sheer courage and willpower.

Trying to push her thoughts into other channels, Inger landed a half-time job at the local library. Or, more accurately, it landed her. No ivory tower of hushed learning, the suburban library branch proved to be an open house overrun by noisy children. Plus their desperate parents. Inger also found out that anyone bold enough, like her, to try to impose order was simply swept aside under the melee. Yet, the changeover to battling instead of thinking...and sorrowing...helped enormously.

Inger even got to the point of urging me to respond to Al Beatty's invitation to explore the new position he mentioned at the AAR. "You need a change, too," she said.

And what a change it turned out to be! The nation's railroads had decided to slug it out publicly with their unions—the "brotherhoods"—over long-standing featherbedding work rules that added huge costs to operations—costs paid by travelers, shippers, investors, even the work force itself in reduced, more insecure jobs. Basically, featherbedding boiled down to pay for work not done or not needed. And the solution the railroads proposed, in a nutshell: *A fair day's work for a fair day's pay.*

The carriers had given up on trying to correct this problem through direct negotiations with the unions. For instance, it was obvious that the Fireman's union would never agree to eliminating the fireman position on diesel-electric locomotives, even though the fireman had nothing to do; this would mean the end of the union itself. So the carriers' strategy was to launch a major public information program that would tar featherbedding with such a black brush that when a national shutdown crisis arose and the federal government got involved—as was bound to happen—the unions would be forced to accept reasonable work rule changes.

AAR was to be the action center for this campaign, and major internal personnel changes were being implemented accordingly. Dan Loomis was being chosen to head the Association because of his long experience in rail labor negotiations and good working relations with union leaders. Col. Henry, the grand old man of railroad PR, was being retired (or, more accurately, shunted aside) and replaced as vice president by J. Handly Wright, a non-railroading PR pro who promised a greater ability to wage what was sure to be a rough nationwide PR war. My own role? At my first meeting with Wright (it went well!) he revealed that I was slated to be the workhorse writer of the mass of information materials that would undergird the campaign.

Like the Colonel, Handly Wright was another Tennesseean. He spoke with a warm drawl and exuded friendliness...but was tough as cowhide underneath. This didn't bother me since I had long since learned from the likes of Jack Meagher, Stan Brams, P. H. Whaley and Admiral Rickover that pussyfooting around gets you nowhere. And I felt that if the AAR was going to pay me well, I was going to produce well. And I knew Inger wouldn't have it any other way. Handly was also a born delegator of work (onto me!) yet proved personally supportive and eager to do things for his staff. For instance, who could complain about all those "strategy meetings" we came to hold at the exclusive *Sans Souci* restaurant, a favorite meeting-ground for Art Buchwald and other reporters and politicos a half-block from the White House/EOB?

Oh, yes, *pay*! Something unbelievable happened on the way to a final agreement. The AAR put forth a suggestion which I thought (for the second time!) was fair enough—in fact, it was more than my reporting salary and free-lance earnings, combined. But then came news that the Federation for Railway Progress was being disbanded. This had been set up as a competitor of the AAR but had now run out of financial support. And FRP's director, Bill Merriam, was to be taken in by the AAR as part of my staff, which also included the News Service (my new title was Assistant to the Vice President). This meant, naturally, that I had to be paid more than

Merriam. So, lo and behold, without working one day, I got a $3,000. annual raise! Meaning the AAR was more than doubling the salary I had when I left two years before.

All this led Inger to proclaim that the way to get ahead in a big organization isn't to slog your way slowly, bloodily up through impenetrable bureaucratic layers...but to leave, make yourself desirable, then come back later when you're really needed. With a huge raise. [Just don't ask us to recommend your doing this!]

We also quickly found that big pay generally means big work [unless you're a modern CEO?]. The railroads had documented in detail their case against burdensome work rules in three huge volumes. These I pored through with Inger over the next month, singling out the most pointed materials and putting these into myriad forms—a press kit, booklet, speaker's manual and a tightly condensed leaflet called "Featherbedding Hurts Everybody." This item was designed for mailing by the millions, as enclosures by railroads in their regular postings to stockholders, shippers, suppliers, etc.

Handly Wright then arranged a grand experience as far as Ink was concerned. Whitaker and Baxter, the famed couple that was using radical PR approaches to shake up California politics, was being hired as consultants on our anti-featherbedding campaign. And Inger and I were to join Handly and his wife, Mary, on one of the world's great train trips—the route of the Burlington Zephyrs—in order to meet and confer with the two in San Francisco. It was breath-taking! Two nights and days out of Chicago—rolling in spacious dome cars over wide prairies and cattle-strewn uplands, through deep canyons and the snow-covered Sierras and on into one of the loveliest cities anywhere.

Inger was absolutely enchanted with this, her first look at the whole of America, coast to coast. Mary Wright was enough of a gracious native of Florida to appreciate my wife's "difference" (isn't everyone in the South different?) and they spent hours discussing the latest books, music, etc—while the wheels hummed their wondrous song of travel and adventure. Inger was knitting a ski sweater for me—dark blue with big white snowflakes worked in around chest and shoulders—and, almost without her looking, her fingers danced along with the wool yarn, European style. Every woman on that train must have stopped by to behold both the technique and the developing result; it was obviously going to be beautiful (it was...and is!).

We met the Whitakers in their penthouse suite in the grand Fairmont Hotel on Nob Hill, where we stayed, as well. Clem, older and wheezing badly (he carried an oxygen tank in his silver Rolls Royce), looked much like the lean, intense, mythical Baptist minister he often quoted, while Leone provided the couple's touch of glamour...with intelligence. We got right down to business—our national PR strategy—and the first question resolved was whether to use the word "featherbedding" at all, since union leaders considered this one big red flag. Clem argued, however, that words alone are insufficient to get a vital message across to the broad public; you must be able to sum up such a campaign with a *visual* image. Society is more and more turning to picture forms to convey thought content (think TV, films, political ads, PC screens, etc). And aren't even dreams made of visual images? The result of all this debate is now history.

"Ten commandments" were also to be drawn up, as do-s and don't-s for all management people addressing this problem. Actually, these amounted to only eight (but, as someone put it, most people aren't very good at math)—with the most important stressing that rail workers themselves are NOT to be blamed for featherbedding. The fault lies, rather, in outdated work rules...that penalize workers no less than others. Without giving away bargaining points, management also pledged to work with the unions to cushion the impact on workers of work-rule changes (which turned out to mean cutting back on surplus jobs mainly via the painless method of "attrition"—retirements, transfers, resignations, etc).

The speech in which AAR President Loomis was to announce this drive was also discussed at length. This was to conclude with an appeal to President Eisenhower to appoint a special commission to study the issue and recommend solutions. By someone's ingenious twist, however, this turned out to be an appeal, instead, *to the brotherhoods* to join management in making the appeal to the President. Which put them squarely in the middle. Clem also contended that featherbedding work rules had become an albatross around the industry's neck (another visual image—thanks, *Mr. Coleridge*!). This, too, went into the speech.

(For one fleeting minute Clem lost me as his audience...as I slipped away into totally irrelevant thinking about that albatross. Coleridge wrote in his famous *Rime of the Ancient Mariner* that it was only after his Old Salt turned his eyes to heaven and prayed that the albatross slid from his neck and fell into the sea...and the curse that had so disastrously becalmed ship and crew was lifted. So I began to wonder how many railroad CEOs would be praying for deliverance from the scourge of featherbedding. Or were we all too busy drawing up battle-plans and loading our guns? And if the union leaders also turned to prayer, what would they be praying for? Reprieve?)

Clem also talked much about PR philosophy, which I swallowed in big morsels. For instance, he said you must equate what you want with what the public wants, then hammer continuously on the *public's* stake in the outcome—NOT your own. Also, like that Baptist minister he frequently alluded to, you must paint a picture of both heaven and hell. Show the wonders that can result by solving the problem (our way, of course) and the dire results that'll befall the nation by drifting along as at present. I got the honor (?) of doing a first draft of the speech, which included most of this approach—and which was worked over many, many times before completion and delivery.

Leone got into the act mainly in urging methods to involve "third parties" in the effort. That is, we should go to outside public groups who would benefit from strengthened railroads and get them to pass resolutions (for legislative and public consumption), use their own internal communications to support the cause, contact public officials, etc. This approach had been pursued effectively on specific issues within the state...and would now be exploited nationally. Inger got caught up in all this, too, with the result that Leone taught her (Ink) the ropes...so that she (Ink) could help out in this area, too.

Perhaps the most effective impressions the campaign made on public consciousness came in a series of ads, one of which went into every newspaper in the country. Incorporating high-impact photos, these compared losses from featherbedding with the worst natural disasters that had hit America: The Chicago fire, the San Francisco earthquake, the Texas City explosion, the devastating Ohio River flood of the 1930s (which I myself lived through as a 13-year-old boy on my grandfather's farm in southern Ohio).

Another wise step taken in the campaign was to go to the newspaper publishers national association beforehand and explain what the railroads were up to...and how this could set a precedent for the press itself (in ending wasteful make-work rules in the print shop). This was followed at the campaign's launch by personal letters, with supporting information, to publishers of the 500 largest newspapers. One telling result: Editorial writers and cartoonists everywhere had a field day with the subject, showing well-occupied featherbeds smothering struggling trains and every other aspect of railroading.

Another stand-out publicity achievement was assignment by *The Reader's Digest* of a contributing editor to cover this developing story. Al Steinberg, a pleasant news pro, talked with both union and AAR people at length, then worked around my office for two weeks—boiling down information and checking out facts and sources across the country. We next went out into the field, visiting yards and shops and actual scenes where featherbedding was chewing up $$$. Then came the fun part: Riding the luxurious 20th Century Limited from New York to Chicago, one of the most infamous of the wasteful "red apple" runs. Inger joined us on this trip, laughing all the way and thoroughly diverting Al's attention from his work. When his story finally appeared, it was reprinted and mailed by the thousands to news people, public officials and thought leaders in all the states.

The foregoing actions must surely sound much easier than the way they happened. Truth be told, the campaign was nothing if not arduous. Every PR action step was hashed over innumerable times with industry people long before implementation. And Handly Wright was the guy in the middle of it all...demanding results from our consultants and ad agency, clearing everything with the lines' CEOs through the AAR Board of Directors, tying in the carriers' PR directors and Washington lobbyists, and checking every move with the industry's labor relations executives. Luckily, we found an amazingly informed, articulate and precise public spokesman in "Doc" Wolfe, labor negotiator of the western carriers—a PR man's dream. Handly also held hands continually with the executives and others who pay bills, and kept our budget intact. His was one tough, unenviable job, but he succeeded in writing a textbook case in the application of modern public relations to public problems. Perhaps *he* was the real PR dream!

The result of all this? A nationwide explosion of publicity followed the Loomis speech. This continued for months, and I don't think that those protecting the old work rules ever quite knew what hit them...or ever managed to recover. When the issue of the unneeded locomotive fireman finally came up in Congress in form of a bill requiring arbitration of the problem, only a handful of votes were cast against it. Obviously, few Congressmen dared to stand up against solving what had been proven conclusively to be an onerous, anti-public problem.

[Many may wonder how this insider's report on a major PR/political campaign from many years ago can be relevant to today's fast-changing world of clashing interests and multi-media complexities. The answer: While tactics change, the principles remain the same. And people badly need to know how to separate fact from fiction, appearance from reality, in today's communications deluge. The devil often comes cleverly disguised as an angel. The railroads won their noisy national battle against featherbedding because the ends they sought accorded with what overwhelming sectors of the public thought was *right*. How many current PR/political campaigns can meet this test?]

Inger moved in and out of the railroad strategy meetings over the months with wide-eyed wonder at this example of modern America in action. It was like a gigantic prizefight, of power pitted against countervailing power. She offered countless ideas, mainly in trying to "humanize" our efforts. The best were duly worked over by the campaign's daunting clearance processes and, like my own, emerged virtually unrecognizable. The campaign also provided chances for additional inspiring train trips—for instance, down the Atlantic Coast Line to a meeting at the beautiful Spanish-style Boca Raton Hotel and Racquet Club in Florida...with sun and surf, cocktails, delicious dinners, putting contests and long walks along the sea..

Despite all this involvement, however, Inger would occasionally give 'way to worrisome bouts of depression. I frequently found her staring off into space...or right into a blank wall. She simply wasn't getting over her lost children. Once she greeted me with these melancholy lines:

Ah, that Spring should vanish with the Rose!
That Youth's sweet-scented manuscript should close!
The Nightingale that in the branches sang—
Ah, whence, and whither flown again, who knows!

I knew this as her favorite quatrain from Omar Khayyam's hymn to that transitory, thin wisp of a dream called life, *The Rubaiyat.* But she looked so forlorn in quoting it that it startled me. Even more so when she added with a deep sigh, yes, Jimmy, *the Moving Finger writes; and having writ, moves on....*

But, Inger, I said with what conviction I could muster, you and I *can* grasp this sorry scheme of things...and rebuild it *nearer to the Heart's Desire.* She didn't look at all convinced—just more forlorn.

I went to see our sympathetic family physician, who suggested that Inger probably needed a psychological transfusion—a re-affirmation of life. He asked if there was anything that she really wanted to do— something I could provide that was truly near and dear to her heart.

Well, one didn't have to look far for an answer to that one: It was *Norway!* So I began thinking seriously of ways to get her there...for much longer than just a halting visit. And the Eisenhower Exchange Fellowships popped up in my thoughts like the rising sun sweeping aside the canopy of night.

Why EEF? While reporting at Whaley-Eaton, I had heard about this distinguished group from a fellow member of the Press Club. Designed to promote international understanding, it had been set up in 1953 by wealthy friends of Ike as a birthday present, and was said to be the "Cadillac of Fellowships." It provided up to a year of expenses-paid travel abroad for mid-career recipients and their spouses. Which sounded too good to be true. While it was targeted now mainly at bringing a score of foreigners to the USA each year, one American was usually selected to go abroad. Top Washington reporter Clark Mollenhoff of the *Des Moines Register and Tribune* had recently been honored with a six-month tour of Africa. As he told me, the trick was to find a subject area that was uniquely important and really appealed to EEF contributors.

Well, Inger didn't consider that so hard. A year before, while digging up material for the *Foreign Letter*, we had both become fascinated by the mounting trade moving across the Iron Curtain between East Europe and the West, and began wondering: Is the Curtain really *iron* any more, or does it just stay stuck that way in our thinking? (Remember Churchill's speech on that long-ago ship?) So I got in touch with the EEF president in Philadelphia—the genial, sophisticated J. Hampton Barnes—and proposed having Inger and me follow the Iron Curtain from the Baltic to the Med...then sum up the reality of what's happening along the way in a special report to the public. Inger would be essential because of her command of German and French. Barnes proved as fascinated as we were...BUT, sad to say, my return to the AAR ended those talks.

Now, I decided, a way had to be found to switch the EEF train back on track. Literally!

I had an idea of how to do that, too. For decades there had been a lot of loose talk in America about nationalization of the railroads. Growing government-aided competition from road, water and air carriers was diverting their lifeblood traffic; yet, they were still expected to serve every nook and cranny in the nation, profitable or not. So as their losses grew, so, too, did talk that government (all of us taxpayers) should shoulder this burden, as well—that takeover was THE way to keep essential rail services going, needed or not. As an example, the *New York Times'* Arthur Krock, dean of Washington correspondents, told me in a personal interview: "Nationalization of the railroads is coming. In fact, it's inevitable."

Strangely enough, despite the looming importance of this issue within the USA, no one had ever done any in-depth research into nationalization of railroads overseas. Yet, Europe in particular offered abundant evidence of how this had come about...and the results. So I thought, *Here, EEF, lies opportunity for a great public service on your part!* I put a month of whatever free time I could find into researching foreign transport policies at the AAR library, then put together an outline of the kind of mission I felt could work. I then caught a train to Philadelphia—to the EEF's stately old townhouse office on Chestnut Street—and went over the plan's details with Barnes. He liked it!

The next step was getting approval from the full EEF Board: How would they react?

At this stage, I decided I had better read in Handly Wright on what was going on. To my surprise, he liked the idea, too! More than two years had passed since the featherbedding campaign exploded across America, and our PR activity had receded to a holding action. Handly therefore felt that the unique study of nationalization I proposed would be timely and helpful to both the industry and America...*and* that now was as good a time as any for me to take off.

As for the EEF Trustees, I had noted earlier that this select group included the influential chairman and CEO of the Sante Fe Railroad. So, Handly and I read him in on the idea, too. The result: A couple weeks later, the phone rang and there was Hampton Barnes. The Trustees had approved our plan! I was now to become one of those rare, rare EEF Fellows....

Perhaps you've noticed that there's one key person in this chain who had not been informed of anything so far: Inger. She was left out purposely. I didn't want to disappoint her in case the wheels came off my explorations. I was also a little apprehensive about her reaction to traveling abroad at this uneasy time. A promising new president—John F. Kennedy—had just taken office in the USA. And he was having his hands full: The Soviets had launched *Sputnik* in 1957, and a shocked US was now adding a heated space race to the arms race. Fidel Castro had taken over in Cuba, putting International Communism right on our doorstep. One of our U-2 spy planes had been shot down in Russia, setting the stage for shrill, prolonged denunciations by Krushchov. And in distant Vietnam, French rule was falling apart under concerted attack by communist rebels (but that was *France*'s problem, not ours, *n'cest pa?*).

Putting all these tough portents aside that evening after work, I broke the news to Inger.

"We...we're all...going to Norway?" she asked in total disbelief. She looked at me searchingly.

"Not only that. We're going to the world!"

"No, no, *du kjelltring*! Yes, one big rascal—that's what you are. It's all a joke! You've got to be kidding...."

So I had to go through the whole chain of events again, baring each detail from my first contact with Barnes...with Inger constantly interrupting, probing with new questions, trying to reassure herself it *was* true.

When the truth finally got through, Inger was torn with a wrenching shudder. She burst into crying, then let out a shrill laugh, then fell to doing both at once. Torrents of tears streamed down her face. This time, though, they were tears of relief, of hope, of expectation. Then the smiles broke through:

"I'm going home!" she shouted in unrestrained joy, smothering me in a deluge of kisses.

Yes, it *was* true. Fifteen years after she had sailed for America, Inger was finally going home for a real stay, proudly, with her one-time-seaman husband and two sons in tow—just as she had always dreamed of doing.

Chapter V

The sea again—the restless, limitless, timeless, all-powerful, uncompromising sea.

On a cool night bedazzled by a full moon, Inger and I wrapped ourselves in a blanket and stretched out on a deck loungechair which we had dragged to the lee side of the *Oslofjord's* housing...and traced a shimmering moontrail off the starboard stern across the rippling North Atlantic to the distant horizon...then followed the phosphorescent wake of the ship back toward the America we had left a few days before. It was a night of pure magic.

After eating far too much from the ship's groaning *smorgasbord* (nevermore! Inger vowed), we put Jimmy and Erik into their bunks in our 4-bed, crowded cabin and stole away from the other passengers. Now, we found ourselves immersed not only in a night to remember but also in a melodic mixture of muffled sounds of dance music coupled with the distant rumble of the ship's engines. Occasional wisps of diesel exhaust drifted past from the stack high overhead. The ship rose and fell slowly on long sea swells, rocking us as gently as babes in a mother's arms.

"Feel better now, sweetheart?"

Inger needed no elaboration to know what I meant. "Was just daydreaming I had died and gone to heaven. Want to know what it's like?"

"Like this?"

"A lot! Actually, it's a surrealistic kind of place...all lit up by that golden moon and silvery reflections from those dancing waves. And inhabited by one other person. Know who?"

"Salvador Dali!"

"Nope...*another* magician. He's a guy I met long ago on a ship.

Remember the *William B. Travis*? And our gun turret...where we first fell for each other—literally! Well, this guy turned out to be a real hat-trick artist—he waved a wand and turned himself into a factory worker, a lowly student, a powerplant engineer, a magazine editor, a railroad flack, a Washington hack and, now, a world-traveling Eisenhower Fellow. Don't you ever settle down? Or give up?"

"Ah...but haven't you heard? Quitters never win and winners never quit. Besides, I know someone else who never quits. And that's why you just hit the jackpot!"

"*Jo, jo*...the trouble is, though, that jackpot isn't going to cover all those fancy travel expenses you're planning to rack up. You...we...are heading for bankruptcy!"

It was then I told Inger the rest of the story behind our travel plans...which amounted to a veritable modern flying carpet. These called for us to spend the whole next year studying transport systems and related government policies in 25 countries, from Ireland through Europe to the Soviet Union and out through the Middle East to India. We would set up our base in Norway (where else, Inkie!) and travel for up to two months at a crack, returning afterward to base to catch our breath, write up our notes, etc. Meanwhile, a swarm of letters had gone out from the AAR and EEF to US ambassadors, transport ministers, railroad chiefs, academic authorities and in-country EEF fellows. The rails were cleared—for a ton of work! It was now only a matter of getting moving, and this dream-voyage on the sleek *Oslofjord* was the first step forward...to Norway as our first target.

There were other goals I wanted to tie in, too. So Inger and I met with Russell Moore, president of Simmons-Boardman Publishing, and worked out a contract for a book to be written on our findings. Moore's company also published the industry's flagship magazine, *Railway Age*—so the book was a natural fit. Our intention was to tackle the monstrous job a book posed by writing a chapter on each major country we studied, right afterward. I also wanted to check in with the US Information Service wherever we went to see how well the US was doing in the worldwide propaganda war versus the communists. Our trip into the USSR, the last leg of our long journey, promised to be decisive in this regard.

Our mission wasn't supposed to be all work, however. Hampton Barnes had stressed that we should also get to know as much as possible about each country and each people we visited — their traditions, customs, culture, etc. Well, that took little urging! And that's where local EEF fellows who had been to the USA could be especially helpful. Without such grassroots contacts, how could you get to know the over-all context surrounding and conditioning your selected study area? Or how to promote real understanding among peoples? Or even, by reverse osmosis, come to know better your own country...and yourself?

Inger's financial worries were allayed by none other than Handly Wright. When he found out how modest EEF's hotel and meal allowances were (fortunately, all direct travel outlays were covered)—and that we would have to set up another household in costly Norway—he somehow arranged for AAR to put me on half-pay. (Thanks, Handly!) We then rented out our house in Bethesda to a Canadian Army colonel and his family [who took immaculate care of the property—unlike what many other homeowners experience when renting to certain other peoples assigned to Washington embassies].

By now Inger was getting stiff from the chill winds whirling around the deck, so proposed we try some dancing. Great idea! After all, we had decided to cross over by ship to have, finally, some real free time together. A sort of mid-marriage honeymoon—despite having two children in tow. So we got to dance and hold each other tight—tighter than usual to steady each other against the ship's rolling—the first time since our evening in Baltimore ages ago. The orchestra lulled us along, playing selections from Broadway musicals—from *My Fair Lady*, which had opened in New York five years before, from *West Side Story*, which had opened four years before, and from *The Sound of Music*, which had opened two years before. Great pieces from great musicals! Even an opera fan like Inger had to admit that each musical had some intrinsically fine melodies, all fitted ingeniously into a solid story line with solid impact.

Now 38, Inger was a crowd-stopper on the dancefloor, attractive in both face and figure. An action-filled life had kept her body in the lithe, supple shape that a model would envy, despite the difficulties of child-bearing. When anyone touched on this, however, Inger turned dismissive, saying she had been lucky to get a sound physique to begin with...and still luckier to live an active outdoor life throughout her growing-up years. (Truth be known, she *had* to be outside: Mamma wouldn't let Inger bring her pals into the house; they disturbed the peace re Pappa and his singing...and, worse, they tracked in DIRT!)

Inger could not so readily dismiss her face, however. Nature may have given her the features but, as only I knew, she had *earned* the expression. Years of uncompromising effort, deep thought and struggle had etched fine lines of sensitivity and understanding onto her once-smooth features. Even so, the radiance had now begun to return to her big, wide smile. I was immensely proud of my wife. And despite inevitable differences on almost everything—differences ranging from minor to heated to hilarious—we retained immense respect for each other...and remained immensely in love.

Besides reading and playing ping-pong, checkers and monopoly with the boys all through the voyage, Inger and I set aside an hour each day for me to learn Norwegian. And what a struggle that was! The vocabulary wasn't so difficult, even though there seemed to be countless dialects and a strange cleavage between *Nynorsk*, an amalgam of dialects spoken in the hinterland, and *Riksmal*, the Dano-Norsk tongue spoken by the better educated in Oslo—or, more accurately, on the city's westside. The tough part was the division of nouns into "et" and "en" words and the myriad declensions that followed, plus vowel sounds that seemed utterly unutterable. AND the sing-song melody of the sentences. The boys, who had naturally absorbed all these language tricks from their mother, laughed uproariously when I tried to pronounce *oel* [for ale] or even Paasan.

Having taken three arduous courses in German at Wayne, I concluded that Norwegian was somewhat closer to English—especially in the straight-forward flow of sentences (praise be!). The Viking settlements in the British Isles a thousand years ago had made sure of that. But I also fell to interspersing German words when I tried to speak Norwegian. And, as Inger assured me, this would hardly make me a hit in a land which remembered all too well the horrors of the Nazi occupation.

On a misty morning in early September, the *Oslofjord* sailed through a swarm of islands and on into the old Hanseatic trading city of Bergen on Norway's west coast. A mood of vibrant expectancy pervaded the passageways. Inger and I packed and chatted with our fair-haired boys (they *did* have fair hair!), who whooped and hollered about the year ahead, with Erik (now 7) getting so worked up he had to be put back in bed. Next door, an elderly passenger who had not seen Norway since emigrating to America 40 years before, was crying uncontrollably. And another oldtimer named Axel, embracing a bottle as though it were his last friend, was begging a ship's officer to let him remain aboard and return to New York City: Coming home was simply too much to bear.

Out on deck with the others, I was absolutely enchanted by this special view of Inger's homeland—by the craggy islands we swept past, the brightly painted houses graced by red-white-and-blue Norwegian flags, the wholesome-looking people waving from docks and boats, the ship whistles and harbor bustle, the pungent fish odors, the shifting fog streaks that revealed glimpses of towering mountains ahead. Then, suddenly, a grand thing happened that engraved the moment forever in memory: Over the ship's loudspeaker boomed the recorded song, "Naar Fjordene Blaaner" [when the fjords turn blue...with flowers...in the Spring]. And who was the singer? Erling Krogh. Pappa himself! His stirring tenor soared out over the harbor, reverberated against the mountains, stopped all talk and brought tears to eyes. Then, as the song ended with "Hoorah for mitt brave, mitt kraftige folk!" the whole ship erupted in a giant, rumbling shout of joy. And my dear wife almost went into orbit!

Inger had arranged for the four of us to disembark in Bergen and travel by train over the mountains to Oslo, all in order to show me and the boys more of her native land. It proved a case of love at first sight. We stayed overnight at the Terminus Hotel near the railroad station, walked the winding streets, visited the wooden 13th Century market buildings, watched live fish being "dressed" for dinner, took a cable-car up to Floeyen and looked far out over the magnificent harbor and gleaming fjord. We then strolled back into the damp, moss-covered hills, where life seemed at its beginnings...with plants struggling to gain a foothold in the rocky soil before the onslaught of Winter. And for this one rare moment in Bergen, it wasn't raining!

Next day came our train ride on *Bergensbanen*—the railway that led us on a winding, weaving trip along crystal-clear fjords and through dark forests, countless tunnels and snowsheds, to Voss. Then came a boat trip on the Sognefjord, which cuts in through precipitous mountains 114 miles from the sea. I was speechless! And Inger was delighted at my reaction. We stood in biting wind at the boat's railing while I stared at the ice-blue waters, the looming granite ridges laced with slender waterfalls and ghostly cloudtrails brightened by sporadic sunbursts. Here, I felt, was one of nature's crowning creations—a thing of not just beauty but with inner soul. And isn't that what makes Norway singular? Its nature has *soul*. And that's what makes Inger singular, too, I now knew: She *really* has soul.

Next came a rare moment of truth, hitting like a sharp slap in the face. How in the name of God, I wondered, could Inger, who had grown up with all this natural splendor, have withstood the dirt, disorder and depression of Detroit's slums? And all the struggle and hardship she had experienced? I shook my head in deep sadness. I hadn't understood anything....

At Flaam at the head of the fjord, we stayed in an immaculately clean Fretheim Hotel, where I wrestled most of the night with my featherbed-like *dyne*—not knowing whether to sleep on it, under it or inside it. All to Inger's vast merriment. The next morning it was onto another train for what a railfan would surely consider one of the world's great runs—the Flaamsbane.

Termed by Mimbo "the little train that could," this turned, twisted and clawed its way from sea level to mountaintop—providing breathtaking scenery, sharp curves and steep grades and a timeless example of engineering ingenuity. At Myrdal we limped off, relieved to get back onto solid ground. Here, under sharp, clear air and the blue-white gleam of eternal snow, we caught the *hurtigtog*—the express train—coming from Bergen on the final leg of the trip to Oslo.

As the steel wheels clicked along over steel rails, my thoughts turned again to this land of Inger's. She was an inseparable part of its magic. So, too, were our sons. And perhaps, with an open heart and diligent effort, and by the grace of God, I could absorb some of its grandeur, as well. For Inger had given me not only a new world of music but also an extra family and an extra country—and I wasn't going to dismiss that good fortune lightly.

On the platform of the station in Oslo stood a beaming sister Grete, and at the Kroghs' we were greeted with miles of smiles, *smoerbrod* and akvavit, and a swirl of breathless babbling in norsk—all interspersed with bursts of English for the enlightenment of the *utlending*—the "furriner." Who could fail to like such in-laws? As I had found out before, Mamma was a vibrant, natural enthusiast, and Pappa mixed an air of authority with unhideable warmth behind twinkling eyes. Grete remained a great pal from 'way back in our rough Detroit days, and brother Erling, a tax attorney, proved to be an expert on virtually everything involving the Norwegian state—which came in mighty handy in my transportation research work.

Later I met a seemingly endless row of aunts and uncles and cousins—opticians, doctors, artists, businessmen—a veritable cross-section of Norway. Handsome, good-humored, dedicated people. This included cousin Arnodd, who, with wife Aase, couldn't do enough to help us settle into our new life. Oddly enough, what really struck me about these relatives, though, was that if they spoke English—which most did—they could move right across the Atlantic and pass for Americans.

Norway itself also struck me as very American—maybe too much so. Similar products lined store shelves, though at shockingly higher prices due to the pocketpicking Value Added Tax [now 25%]. People dressed casually...with many of the young looking like bums (purposely?). And in entertainment the same bummy-looking people were going hog-wild on rock, jazz and rap—the louder and more discordant, the better. Worse, the press seemed to lionize them, lavishing all-out coverage on their aboriginal antics at one music "festival" after the other (which often turned out to be more in the line of narcotics, alcohol, and sex fests).

For a music lover like Inger, such performances resembled nothing so much as sideshow barkers stomping out war dances for a ragtime rabble of simian escapees from the local zoo. They made her wonder, *to what extent does this mess in modern music reflect an equal mess inside modern man?*

I also found out about an odd Norwegian/Danish "law" known as *Janteloven*. This bit of blantant tyranny toward outsiders is designed to silence and put them down by decreeing that...*You shall not believe you are anything...or that you know more than us...or think you are wiser than us...or better than us...or can teach us anything.*

"Can the people here be *that* inhospitable?" I asked Inger.

"Better not try to find out!" she answered. She then reminded me of the poem I had written for her at Wayne, called "The Strangers," and added: "Outsiders have a bad time everywhere, even in America, *ikke sant?*"

I noted one difference, though—small but revealing. When you went out walking in America and met others on the way, people usually smiled and nodded and sometimes said hello. Not in Europe, though...where you seldom got any greeting at all.

Inger proudly introduced me to an extra-special friend from early childhood, Eira (and husband Kjell) Damsleth. Eira, intelligent and keenly interested in current affairs, had gone to school with Inger, and probably knew her better than even the Kroghs. Including Ink's free-wheeling conduct in the classroom. Eira once showed me a funny verse she had written in grade-school about her pal...that set me howling with laughter. It went like this:

Inger is a little lamb, who likes in school to sleep.

So though her hair is white as snow, she IS the class Black Sheep!

My own normally quiet reserve must have surprised such friends and relatives. Aside, they asked Inger where were the brassy, swaggering traits portrayed as American in film and song...and by so many tourists? And the flashy clothes? Could the portrayal be wrong? Or was I some kind of oddball? Well, Inger already knew the answer to *that!*

Inger proceeded to give the boys and me a close-up look at her hometown. We rode the remarkable *trykk* up to the famed Holmenkollen ski-jump and on to *Nordmarka*, which makes up four-fifths of Oslo's total area and sports miles and miles of woodland trails [every one of which Inger and I eventually came to hike, including the long, wet, rocky *sti* to distant Kikut].

We visited the Vigeland sculpture-park and beheld raw human

emotions wrought in myriad heavy, squat stone figures that impressed with their power but resembled nothing so much as American football players. (What a difference from Carl Milles' elongated, graceful scuptures in Stockholm!) Then came the mammoth, startling monolith—120 intertwining figures reaching frantically toward the sky. Inger told of this being under wraps for many years when she was young...and of the massive howl of protest that went up when it was unveiled.

We saw more raw emotions portrayed in Edvard Munch's paintings, both in the city and at his home at Asgaardstrand, partway down the sailboat-filled Oslofjord, which runs 60 miles south to the Skaggerak. And what could have more impact than his "Scream"— the tortured portrait of modern man crying out his misery in an eerie, blood-streaked sunset scene?

All this made me stop and wonder, how could a nation with no more people than, say, Philadelphia have produced such world-renowned giants as Munch in painting, Vigeland in sculpture, Ibsen and Hamsun in literature, Grieg in music and Nansen and Amundsen in polar exploration? Inger's answer was that all were products of the fervent nationalism that swept the country in the 1800s...and which finally forced Sweden in 1905 to grant Norway its independence. All these world-class achievers felt the need to assert themselves as part of a singular national identity. She *knew*, for Pappa was part and parcel of that spirit, too.

By some miracle, Mamma had been able to rent an apartment next door to theirs on Kirkeveien, up from Oslo's bustling westside section of Majorstua. This was old familiar territory for Inger, who had grown up, gone to school and romped her way all over Majorstua...right up until she left for America. The boys were then enrolled in Marianlyst Skole, in the same area, and we waited for a ton of homework to fall on them. It didn't. Inger finally had to admit that things had changed since she went to school. As in America, discipline in the classroom was falling apart, and academic standards had lightened up...considerably. The Dewey approach to education had crossed the Atlantic, and "motivation" was the new rage. Another new rage was the inane 10-year-old US television programs being shown on NRK, the national network—inane yet hypnotizing and time-hogging. In the

Norway! Back in her native land, Inger waves from the deck of a coastal steamer in Norge's inspiring western fjord country, and (below) she shows her family the wonders of Nordmarka, the vast area of forest, lakes and trails on the north side of Oslo.

process, learning results for the bulk of students had "progressed" to a state of free-fall.

The stage was nevertheless set for Inger and me to proceed with our study mission. I contacted the Norwegian government's Transport Ministry and found that a new planning and coordinating section had just been set up, headed by scholarly, cooperative Robert Norden. Together, we came up with a solid overview of the country's problems and policies, which were by no means minor. For here was a land of notoriously tough mountainous conditions, where construction and maintenance of roads and railways were both difficult and extremely costly. Small wonder the nation relied heavily on coastal shipping to tie its 1200 miles of strung-out sections together. With Inger helping as translator, I also interviewed the head of *Norges Statsbaner* (the national railroad) and Transport Minister Trygve Bratteli, respected stalwart in the Labor Party, which had been ruling Norway for the past 40 years.

Finally, we felt we had gotten our first test case pretty well "in the bag" and could move on to the Continent. Our short-range plan called for us to proceed to Denmark, the Lowlands, Great Britain and Ireland, France and Spain...then return to Oslo for a Christmas break before taking off for India and working back through the Middle East. One elderly church-going "Tante Gudrun" was hired to take care of the boys, under Mamma's watchful eye.

Shorn of child burdens and feeling much more mobile, Inger and I then boarded the DFDS overnight ship for Copenhagen and booked in for a week at the Hebron Missionhotel. It was glorious to be alone again (even though Inger never forgot the boys for one moment and was telephoning Oslo daily). And there was no place like cozy Denmark for "cozying up" to each other. Here, as elsewhere, the US Embassy staff went out of their way to be helpful (with research, contacts, etc). It seemed that someone bearing the magical Eisenhower name commanded red-carpet treatment—even in the bold new era of the Kennedys. We also benefited greatly from the warm international brotherhood among railroaders; they couldn't do enough for us, including free—free!—trains trips wherever we wished to go.

It's strange, what stands out in such a varied journey:

• In Copenhagen, Mamma's birthplace, it was advanced city planning integrating rail and road facilities to move people efficiently while preserving the old city center, which Inger loved dearly from countless earlier visits. And throughout Denmark, it was the singular feel of prosperity and wellbeing. Here is truly a land of milk and honey [and high cholesterol?].

• Great Britain was in an uproar over a report by Sir Richard Beeching, called in from Imperial Chemicals to trim down British Rail and stop the system's disastrous losses. When I asked him how he could possibly withstand the vicious attacks on him in Britain's notorious "yellow press," he replied: "No problem at all! I've simply stopped reading the papers."

• Our other host, a British Transport commissioner, insisted we get away from our work and visit York—which gave us a chance to live again through an exciting page of history. For here was a city founded by the Vikings and christened *Jordvik*—later Anglicized and sent westward to become (New) York. Here also landed the last Viking armada to invade the British Isles—in the fateful year of 1066. This army was defeated by the English right before the English army itself, worn further by a forced march all the way to Hastings on the south coast to intercept an invasion by the Normans, was defeated by these grandsons of Vikings.

• The Commissioner further told Inger and me at an endless lunch at his London club: "If there is ever peace in the world, the English-speaking peoples will have to bring it about. [Inger argued that the Scandinavians should be included.] That's why America and Britain must always stick together. We're America's bridge to Europe. Use it!" [That's happening, too, both politically and economically—as US firms focus investment in the UK, building on friendly soil to get inside the EU.]

• Then came Oxford, where we immersed ourselves in learning under its Gothic towers...and Stratford on Avon, where we walked the medieval streets with the ghost of Shakespeare—whose *Falstaff* was converted 200 years later by Verdi into a rollicking opera, which we were lucky enough to see at Covent Gardens. Finally we journeyed back to ancient Egypt through the British Museum's Rosetta Stone, which fascinated Inger with its code to hieroglyphics...and its unlocking of so many mysteries of those beginnings of civilization.

• In Ireland we met two transportation information directors who more than lived up to the Irish reputation for hospitality—Tim Dennehy in Dublin and Bertie Ryan in Belfast. They provided an unforgettable picture of the Emerald Isle...yet it was hard to understand how, with such people of good will as these, there could be such bloody religious/class clashes in Northern Ireland — which never seemed to end.

• Holland provided a big surprise: A rail system making money! (The same with Switzerland.) Actually, we found the Dutch running one big intercity passenger network at an amazingly efficient, high-speed pace. Passenger trains were monopolizing the system by day, with freight trains getting a "highball" only at night.

• In Paris we met the recognized giant of the industry: Louis Armand, head of the International Railway Union and deemed one of postwar Europe's "three wise men" because of his earlier role as head of Euratom (the European Atomic Energy Community). Unlike the many pessimists in and around railroading, Armand exuded confidence in the lines' future. The key: Railroaders must come up with a firm picture of the railroad the future *could* bring, then convince politicians and the public to give them the freedom to achieve that goal.

• And who could fail but be enthusiastic about this wondrous city on the Seine? As a first visitor, Inger was enchanted (I had been here during the heady days of liberation toward the end of WWII)...even though our hotel room on the Rue de Richelieu was compressed against a sharply indented roof, with cooing pigeons as would-be roommates, while the building itself was being held erect only by leaning on its neighbors. All the same, the location had grand virtues: Only a block away was the Louvre, with its priceless *Mona Lisa* and *The Winged Victory.*

• And did Inger's French ever come in handy! I pushed her forward to deal with the local citizens as a fellow European, which she did with amazing good humor—triggering good humor on their part. Can it be that even those Frenchmen who know the English language go out of their way to avoid speaking it?

• Spain's Praha art gallery in Madrid stood resplendent with elongated El Greco paintings and their light-streaked, probing eyes. Then there was the battle-scarred castle, the Alhambra, looming high above the Tagus River at historic Toledo—a reminder of the ruinous civil war of the late-1930s and the grim rehearsal it provided for the combatants of WWII.

By mid-December, when Inger and I sped north toward Norway on the Scandinavian Express, we had met hundreds of Europeans, walked holes in our shoes through cathedrals, museums, castles and ruins, and stared so long at carved ceilings that we developed permanent kinks in our necks. Europe as a whole presented a radically different view from the one I beheld from dockside, and which Inger lived through, during the war years. We found it amazingly dynamic, with a new spirit of hope and daring in the air. The idea of "Europe" was slowly taking hold, bridging balkanized borders, and US-aided continental production and mass marketing were spurring rising living standards. For better or worse, the new Europe was rapidly becoming increasingly like America.

Overshadowing this bright scene of revival from WWII's ravages, however, was that ever-threatening colossus to the east, Soviet Russia. The Cold War reality of possible communist take-over, though seldom mentioned, never strayed far from thought, among politicians and citizens alike...with many simply throwing up their hands in the face of constant communist pressure and crying "better Red than dead." Still further submerged in thought was the constant threat the Soviets posed of atomic annihilation. Yet, America's atomic power held Russian expansion in check, right? We found that enough Europeans, though battle-scarred, still cared enough to resist defeatism, create a strong defense on their own, and build a new life.

Only among Germans did we find open discussion of such life-and-death issues. Germans knew all too well that their longed-for national reunification rested squarely on the outcome of the East-West struggle. Russia, meanwhile, played constantly on Europe's memories of Nazi horrors past and its fears of a resurgent Germany to come—as though the present communist horror was somehow less odious to those forced to live under it, and as though the masses of people trying to escape to the West were somehow at fault—

they, not their communist jailers.

Language problems and cultural barriers obviously remained deeply embedded in the new Europe, with realists admitting it would take generations to bridge them. Once, eating in an off-the-beaten-track restaurant without my interpreter (Inger), I ordered what I thought was wiener schnitzel from the menu but, instead, got a big helping of baked brains. (Inger allowed that eating them just might have helped my thinking!) We witnessed a similar fate befall an Englishman on a train diner: Using many gestures, he tried to talk a waiter into giving him his bill after eating; instead, he got a whole new dinner.

Shopping produced few bargains. Except for handcrafted items and artwork, US products and their prices proved largely unbeatable. Perils also lurked here and there in buying pure junk. At a Spanish bazaar, for instance, Inger questioned whether a pair of table-tongs she liked was actually silver. "Absolutely!" trumpeted the merchant. He seized a metal stamp and hammered the sterling symbol into the tongs and said proudly: "See, pure sterling!"

The three days it took to travel by train from Madrid to Oslo provided a great chance to retrace our trail and see much of Europe again the easy way—through a train window. We wrote up our notes and finished our analysis on Britain's transport dilemma, which we decided would be the first chapter in my book. But, mainly, in a happy, homecoming mood, we simply relaxed. We had been on the go for 10 weeks and were dead-tired of traveling—worn down from hassling with hotel clerks, ticket agents, porters, waiters and different currencies and languages. So much so that we no longer saw things clearly, absorbed little of what we saw and retained little of what we absorbed. Yet, shouldn't travel be fun...not a drudge? It was truly time to call a halt.

As our train steamed into Germany, two splendid things happened: A cleaning crew swept through our car like a fresh breeze, and a serving crew came aboard with real coffee That dark stuff we suffered through in France and Spain was now a thing of the past—but so was that delicious French morning chocolate. The coffee brought a blissful look to Inger's face. Now she knew she was nearing home.

We pulled into Oslo in a driving rain, which almost washed away the bright lights and decorations in the streets and the brave pre-Yule spirit in this land of Christmas.

"Where's the snow?" I wanted to know.

But Inger was in no mood for joking. Her seventh sense, I decided. And sure enough, we found at our apartment all our careful arrangements for the boys in tatters. Tante Gudrun turned out to be a lazy lout who neither cleaned nor cooked...and had long since been dismissed by Mamma. She and Grete had then taken turns boysitting...but had not told Inger: They didn't want to shortcircuit our travels.

Inger was outraged. She fumed and stomped and hollered...then hugged and kissed everyone. We resolved to make better arrangements next time.

In the meantime, I stood by the window, watching the grayest, wettest, raggedest, gloomiest clouds I had ever seen skidding across the rooftops of Oslo. Would I like to live here? Inger had once asked. *Huh-uh*! Not today. And just then a fleeting picture came to mind of a lone man in a sinking sailboat being picked up in a storm in the Bay of Biscay. He had sailed in December from Norway and was bound for Spain, the AP reported. Why? Because, he said, he wasn't ever, EVER going to spend another Winter in Norway....

Christmas! Here that meant 10 days of celebration while the whole country ground to a standstill. The Kroghs planned to spend this Yule at an old *pensionat* or country inn some hundred miles north of Oslo— as they had for years. Inger buttoned up some travel appointments while I finished another chapter for my book, then all four of us joined Mamma and Pappa on a train-trip to the crossroads village of Eina.

Now we saw a different Norway—a picture-postcard Norway. Snow set in as the train chugged beyond the city. Soon it was a foot deep along the tracks, then two and three feet deep. Great evergreens stooped over with their arms laden with snow. It piled up on roofs, fences, cars, on the rosy-faced kids on sleds. It covered everything with a thick white blanket, creating a hushed silence, a veritable Winter wonderland.

At Eina station, our pensionat's heavily clad host greeted us with a booming voice and packed us into his ancient Volvo. Then, reading us in on the latest local news, he drove slowly over the newly plowed, narrow, winding road to his big farmhouse at Paalsrud. It was three o'clock in the afternoon, cold and dark—nearly the shortest day of the year. Yet, the bright lights twinkling through the trees heralded a warm refuge, a grand revelation of days gone by. For here was the old Norway, one that no tourist could hope to experience. And one that Inger, sounding like a wounded Valkyrie, said was rapidly disappearing. The reason: People like Paula, the elderly hostess who toiled long hours in the kitchen and in running the place, were themselves disappearing. And no one—and certainly no one in presentday Norway—would ever again put such personal effort into running a pensionat of such boundless quality.

Paula greeted us all heartily. With a special warm embrace for me...since, she said, I was the first American ever to visit Paalsrud. And as she told Inger in her inland dialect, she would consider me a real-life stand-in for the many members of her family who had emigrated in the 1880s...and disappeared in that great land beyond the sea

Chirstmas in Norway! During a crosscrounty ski trip on the shortest day of the year, Inger and I came across this inspiring scene outside a kolonial *(grocery store) at a remote crossroads. Inger paused long to admire the glowing tree, for here suddenly appeared a uniquely heartening symbol of peace and good will in a darkening world.*

and under the western stars.

That week overflowed with good food, camaraderie, crosscountry skiing, Pappa's singing at the local church and a lot of fiddling and stomping (dancing, they called it) on New Year's eve. And still the snow fell, in huge flakes that drifted lazily onto the courtyard and adjoining barn and overloaded small trees and created weirdly twisted animal and human shapes. Trolls seemed to lurk around every turn of our ski trails—which Inger took with effortless, rhythmic ease while I lumbered along in a sweat. And the *stillness* in the deep woods! It seemed as though the whole world had stopped.

But, alas, it hadn't. All too soon came the time for me to depart on the long flight to India. Our plans called for me to work my way alone back through Iran and the Holy Land and to meet Inger in Istanbul. Yes, my wife actually turned down going to all these exotic places! She wanted, in short, to make sure all went well with Mimbo and Erik. From Turkey, we would then journey together through Greece, Yugoslavia, Italy, Switzerland and Germany...back home.

In New Delhi, the hotel claimed it had no record of a reservation for me, then dispatched me to a shoddy, shaky place in Old Delhi where weird jungle noises filled a nervous, sleepless night. I managed to contact a couple of grand Eisenhower Fellows, however, and got my mission underway. Yet, even that went partially awry; by eating and drinking like the natives, I contracted dysentery, which came to hound me long afterward.

Like millions of Indians, I crowded onto trains of the British-built railroad and found it *the* subcontinent's workhorse carrier. In fact, as India's first big industrial organization, it had been used for a hundred years to introduce Indians to evolving technology and administrative systems. Like most developing nations, though, India was having a hard time following up new construction with adequate repair and maintenance. (In fact, when railroaders everywhere have to pinch pennies, R&M suffers the first cutbacks. And while that might save the day financially, it takes its toll on operating safety.) Development also got tied up repeatedly in reams of red tape...which Indians seemed to equate with management sophistication. And even those Indians who spoke English often appeared to have limited comprehension of the language.

Yet, the deepest of all impressions I carried away from my two-week visit was the enormous contrast between the riches of the Maharajahs and the grinding poverty among the many. This showed up particularly in the pink marble city of Jaipur, with its bejeweled palaces. As well as when January rains flooded the low-lying, tightly packed hovels in Delhi, turning vast areas into quagmires. Right afterward, freezing weather set in, and many froze to death in the streets. In still further contrast was the big Republic Day (January 25) celebration in Parliamentary Square. Here, massed thousands cheered as Army regiments marched to the slow, somber cadence of Mahatma Gandi's favorite hymn, *Abide with Me.*

How can Westerners really grasp such a world? Or help it solve its problems? Population numbers alone are staggering. As Inger pointed out, all of Scandinavia had only some 20 million people. India alone at that time had over 20 times that number [and was rapidly moving toward the present 50 times]. In addition, there was the rigid caste system that made US racial barriers look downright mild in contrast. Plus chronic Hindu-Moslem religious clashes, as in Kashmir.

After India, Inger and I came to the conclusion that the best way—perhaps the only lasting way—to help developing nations is to help their own people help themselves. As the Eisenhower Exchanges, for one, are doing. Through massive educational exchanges and intensive on-scene basic training programs—in food cultivation, building skills, health care, sanitation and elementary education. AND in the encouragement of political/social systems that give the creative energies of individuals a real chance to assert themselves. Sad to say, much government-to-government aid (including World Bank and International Monetary Fund help) seems to invite corruption and wind up in too few pockets and too many Swiss bank accounts.

When I boarded the airplane for Iran, I must have looked pretty ragged from dysentery attacks, for the hostesses went out of their way to make me at ease. Here were real, live fellow Americans and a small bit of the USA halfway around the world. I collapsed... and slept so soundly they had to half-carry me off the plane in Teheran.

Here in the land of Darius and Xerxes and now the Shah, I was met by a colonel in the US Army Transportation Corps, who had been alerted to assist in my mission by his commanding officer in Washington. He took one look at me, said, "Gee, you sure look green around the gills," and sped me to the local hospital...where copious doses of sulfa got me back on my feet in two days. Then it was off to the Caspian Sea with the railroad president in his private railroad car. The German-built route wound high, high up over the 14,000-feet Caucasian Mountains. The ride was breathtaking! During WWII, my fourth Liberty ship had docked at a desolate place at the head of the steamy Persian Gulf called Bandur Shapur...and unloaded huge aerial bombs on railcars bound for Russia. And now I got to see the other end of the line 895 miles away. Here, glum Soviet troops, descendants of our erstwhile wartime allies, eyed us silently, suspiciously. We did not linger long....

Discussing US railroad labor problems, one Iranian rail leader startled me by saying: "If your bosses want to see real featherbedding, come to Iran. Twice a month, on paydays, scores of people the railroad's never employed show up here to collect checks. Pure and simple political pay-offs! How can we ever make money that way?"

Arriving next in Beirut, I checked in at the Alumni Club of the renowned American University overlooking a serene Mediterranean, and began discussions that would take me across Lebanon into Syria and Jordan and eventually Israel. The overriding topic: Israel—or, as all the Arab people I met put it, "the intractable problem of Israel." PLUS the even more intractable problem of the displaced Palestinians. Whose children, shunned by their host-country neighbors, were growing up in the barren desert...rootless, purposeless, with hatred in their hearts and an unquenchable thirst for vengeance in their heads. A vast incubator for terrorists.

I heard of no plan, no proposal, no program that would address this issue, this deadly political cancer. And none of the Arab peoples I met, except in Lebanon, seemed willing to entertain any thought of an accommodation with Israel. Their "solution": Israel somehow had to disappear or be blown off the map. Israel, in turn, kept the pot boiling by constant resort to its *Old Testament* eye-for-and-eye doctrine—by retaliatory raids on its neighbors for any terrorist act or threatened act.

And Lebanon, the one oasis of reason in a vast desert of rigid positions, disintegrated. The Holy Land had become a killing ground. And you got the feeling that the worst was yet to come....

Clearing Damascus and Amman, I walked (read *ran*) past machine gun nests on both sides of the Mandelbaum gate, arrived in Jerusalem and finally had a chance to drink in the timeless wonder of this harsh, sun-scorched land that has spawned three major religions. I walked the *Via Dolorosa* and visited the Tomb, the Mount of Olives, the Wailing Wall, the churches. It was inspiring. Yet, the shameless commercialization around most of the holy places was revolting. I finally found a bit of the sacred mood I had sought among some gnarled old olive trees in the Church of the Garden of Gethsemene. Here I sat for a long time, trying to capture something of those far-off times that Jesus knew...and the things He experienced during His short life on earth. A song I had known as a boy growing up in America's "bible belt" then crept into my thoughts, and I found myself softly singing,

I come to the garden alone...while the dew is still on the roses....

Israeli officials could not do enough to assist in my work, and I had the run of their land, from Haifa through Tel Aviv to Eilat on the Red Sea. Since they were dependent on US aid for a third of their imports, it was hardly surprising that they were eager to make a good impression. Even so, I felt they had every right to be proud of what was being done to make the desert bloom and fashion a viable nation in the strife-ridden Middle East. It *was* impressive!

However, I also found that Arabs everywhere deeply resent America's aid to Israel. As a newspaper editor who has lived and worked in America told me in Lebanon:

"It robs you of your objectivity and, in effect, makes you a partisan in the Middle East—on Israel's side. So you can't be an honest peace broker. Ever hear of America taking *our* side? No US President would ever dare! The Jews' lobby and their friends in the news media would crucify him the next election. Even so, we find it hard to comprehend a foreign policy that favors 2 million Jews while alienating 100 million surrounding Arabs. But it isn't a real foreign policy at all, is it? Just an extension of domestic politics...."

Seven weeks had now passed since I left Norway, and I was missing Inger. It was with genuine joy, therefore, that I boarded an El Al flight to Istanbul to meet her at the train station. And there she was! One stand-out blond in a vast crowd of brunettes. She had ridden trains for four long days from Oslo, and had stories to tell: Like her roommate who was smuggling wristwatches into Turkey, and had them lined up on both arms all the way to the shoulders. And the hushed negotiations in the car's corridors, followed by "secret" pay-offs to border guards as the train crossed into Bulgaria.

We got a room in a hotel overlooking the ship-filled Bosporus, with Asia Minor sprawling in the background and the great dome of Aya Sophia's Cathedral on our right, and I laid out some surprises: A pearl bracelet from Iran, a necklace and aquamarine earrings from India that reflected the blue in Inger's eyes, sea-green and maroon silks from Lebanon, Holy Land carvings from Israel. Inger was *shocked* at my extravagance. But all was paid for out of money I had saved from my living allowance during the long trek from India. I had never been able to give my wife much of anything. Yet, who deserved it more? Or showed nice things off better? Even so, I had to be careful in my choices. Inger abhorred gaudiness and ostentatious display. Her philosophy was that if you've got it, you don't need to flaunt it; and if you don't have it, flaunting won't help.

"You've robbed a bank!" she exclaimed.

"No, no," I replied, trying to keep a straight face. "They were bought at big discounts through the people I worked with."

"Well, I can't accept them. No one gives away discounts like that without attaching a lot of strings."

"But you've got to. You can't send them back through customs. They'd be confiscated. And you wouldn't want to throw them away. You wouldn't...would you?"

Gingerly, ever so cautiously, Inger picked up the bolt of maroon silk, eyed it closely, felt it carefully—then, more boldly, spun out several yards and draped them around her like a sheath... and soon went dancing and laughing around the room like a child.

"Don't do one more thing to it, Inkie. Just cut it off and wear it!"

And that's just what she did back home...to the delight of everyone (women, too?).

Inger communes with some beauties of ancient Greece at the magnificent Acropolis in Athens during our year-long (1961-1962) study of transport systems from Ireland through West Europe to India and Russia—a mission sponsored by the Eisenhower Exchange Fellowships, set up in 1953 as an enduring international-problem-solving tribute to Ike. This also gave us a chance (below) to visit Ireland's lovely Lakes of Killarney.

After a couple days of attending to almost nothing except each other and some sightseeing, we took a shaky train to Ankara for talks with Turkish transportation officials, then returned and boarded an ancient German "rust bucket" for Izmir and Athens. And there beheld the magnificent Acropolis. Here, you could almost feel the presence of those everlasting teachers of us all—Socrates and Plato—even though 2,400 years had passed. But Greece, as Inger reminded me, was also home of the first Stoics, who taught us the virtues of the simple life, of self-denial and self-discipline—lessons the West seems to have long forgotten in its headlong abandon to the heady lures of affluence.

At the ruins of Delphi, Inger tried to get whatever oracles were still hovering around to help us divine our future...but no luck! Like the waterfowl in Bryant's poem, we would have to continue relying on our internal guidance system (remember?). We then caught a train to Belgrade—a long, slow, rocky ride through ragged mountains and past impoverished villages where bony dogs barked at us intruders and black-clad women tended the fields—remote, difficult places untouched by the modern world.

Yugoslavia was one of our key study targets. We especially wanted to see how a communist country, especially one outside the Kremlin orbit, was handling its transport problems—so as to prepare ourselves better for our look at Russia itself. Still, the most potent impression we came away with here in the Balkans was a comment by one of Tito's officials, an EEF fellow, who was asked by Inger why so many societies are now experiencing so much internal disorder, riots and public demonstrations.

"All over the world people are rising to their feet," he said in an unbeatable crystallization of the primary human urge of our time.

"In the former colonial countries, yes...but how about in Yugoslavia?" Inger responded.

"Yes, here, too—as you'll one day see."

"And in the Soviet Union?"

"Absolutely! And in the United States, too...."

Boarding the famous Orient Express, we headed next for Venice, shifting from the gray Balkans to the vibrant, refreshing world of Italy. Inger promptly fell in love with this amazing, incomparable city of gleaming canals and gondolas—just as I did with Florence, and both of us with Rome. And who wouldn't? No landscape is more colorful than Italy's. Here is the grandest of grand operas. And everywhere are reminders of great artistic achievements and of empires that rose, ruled, then fell. [Have you read Gibbons, America?]

Everywhere, too, are the "banditos"—waiters who gleefully added the serial numbers of checks onto bills and cab drivers who not only gave us the ride of our lives but also quoted life-threatening fees. All done with a merry Italian smile: "Oh, I'm so glad you caught that error!"

Not surprisingly, perhaps, we also found Italian transport policies in a state of near-anarchy, with railroad operating losses among the highest in Europe. All in vivid contrast to what we found nextdoor in Switzerland—where railroading was a model of efficiency. And how, asked my perplexed wife, do the Swiss manage to live in harmony with three main nationality groups speaking three different languages— German, French and Italian—while the rest of Europeans barely tolerate each other? And sometimes not at all?

The ready answer we got is that Switzerland has a decentralized governmental system—a federal state—that allows the maximum of regional autonomy, so that each ethnic group pretty much runs its own affairs. Significantly, the different groups also largely stay put in their own enclaves, mixing little with each other. There's a simpler answer, though: They're all *Swiss!*

The calendar now showed it was April, and Inger was intent on getting me back to Norway for a last crack at crosscountry skiing. But, first, we had to cover another major study target: Germany—whose castle-studded Rhine valley is the most important single transport artery in Europe. Here, on each side of a river laden with waterborne commerce is a doubletrack railroad, with autobahns crisscrossing the area. One competitive challenge! Yet, we found the railroads meeting this test well, reflecting the over-all picture of a nation doing well. One EEF Fellow, however, felt this was an illusion: That constant increases in union-inspired pay and benefit demands, coupled with constant increases in government social benefits, would eventually raise German production costs so much that German products would be priced out of world markets. And thus would end the "economic miracle" that had made it possible for West Germany to absorb 13 million political refugees fleeing to freedom from East Europe. [And now economic refugees from Turkey, the Mideast and North Africa.]

In Berlin, we came to feel what life is like living in the middle of a volcano. We also joined everyone in the West in grieving over the horror of the wall that East Berlin had begun to erect the Summer before—and which had already claimed the lives of many trying to scale it. Inger called it a 155-kilometer monument to the abject failure of communism. And as though to rub in the point in no uncertain terms, West Berlin had erected a huge sign facing east: *Freiheit kennt keine maurer.* Which amounted to another unbeatable crystallization of the primary human urge of our time: FREEDOM KNOWS NO WALLS!

[One year later, President John Kennedy was to give the Kremlin clear notice of Western solidarity with this island of freedom in a sea of savagery when he declared, *"Ich bin ein Berliner!"* And 27 years later, President Ronald Reagan used the same platform to issue his blunt challenge to the Russian prime minister: "Mr. Gorbachev, tear down this wall!" And the wall did come tumbling down—along with the whole wretched Soviet system.]

At the US embassy in Oslo, the public affairs director had good news. It had taken nine long months, but the Soviet Railroad Minister had finally replied to AAR President Loomis' letter...and indicated he would be glad to have Inger and me visit Russia and see in person their "glorious achievements" in transportation. So, against all odds, there it was—one of our foremost objectives...in sight! I let out a long *whew!* Professional visits to the USSR were still a rarity (except for certain Western "liberals" who, innocently or otherwise, prostrated themselves before the communists and allowed Kremlin propagandists to use them blatantly). Only a short time earlier Intourist had begun to operate, bringing in a handful of foreigners. And Inger and I were clearly something more than mere tourists.

Right now, however, Inger was *rasende* [furious] over the mention of liberals, dupes, fellow travelers—anyone who swallowed the Communist Party mythology while ignoring the cold reality of its brutal implementation. She contended it wasn't a political philosophy at all but, rather, a plot by a handful of radicals and thugs to seize and wield power and enslave everyone else. In effect, one power system that ignored the needs of the masses—the czar and Russia's old aristocracy—had been replaced by another that cared even less...yet deceived many by making a noisy *pretense* of caring. In most places in the West, the Party was no problem, she felt: You knew where the members stood; they performed like puppets whenever Moscow pulled the strings. It was the non-Party-member Party-line swallowers—mainly duped academicians, social theorists and journalists—who were the real danger. It seemed that the more informed such people became in their specialized fields, the more naive they became about the real world. And Norway, for one, had far too many of that stripe (the USA, too?). Their goal was to build a socialist state—not by violent revolution but by gradual change—law by law, bureau on bureau, control upon control, handout on handout and (oh, yes!) tax upon tax upon tax. The more gullible public, led to believe they would be getting something for nothing (a free lunch!), listened in wide-eyed wonder as these social engineers played their pied piper's song. Evidently, few had read, or cared to read, the alarm sounded by Friedrich von Hayek in *The Road to Serfdom* or the devastating account of government run amok in Ayn Rand's *Atlas Shrugged*.

More currently, Inger was also worried over the imminent prospect of entering that closed world behind the Iron Curtain. Scandinavians had long lived under the shadow of the Russian bear, and, to her, that vast police state to the east looked at once forbidding and foreboding. So, with heartfelt reluctance, she said:

"Look, Jimmy, if one of us has to go, why don't you...and I'll stay behind. I'm thinking of the boys. You never know what might happen once you're in the communists' hands. There's no way out. All kinds of accidents can be arranged. And there's nothing that anyone—not even all of America—can do about it."

Well, I was secretly uneasy myself, especially over my intention to dig into Soviet propaganda methods. But I also felt that we could never know what this threatening system was really like, or how to cope with it personally, unless I, at least, saw it close up, face to face.

Entry date was set for August 1. This allowed time for Inger and the boys to visit Sweden and Finland with me (via express train to

Stockholm and ship to Helsinki) while also providing a chance to talk with more railroaders and government officials. In Stockholm, we got a surprise: Ike himself was there! And what an honor Inger felt it was to meet the hero of Norway/Europe's liberation. We spoke briefly about the Eisenhower Fellowships, the recently founded Peace Corps (President Kennedy's monumental accomplishment) and other aspects of people-to-people diplomacy, which Ike was strongly promoting. The President then saw our Erik standing nearby—now a slender, light-haired boy of eight, with soft eyes and a mischievous smile, and clapped him on the shoulder. Always afterward, that became known (and shown) as Ike's good-luck touch.

In Helsinki, the evening before my departure for Leningrad, an exuberant Finnish Eisenhower Fellow named Pluto and his wife kept us up until 4:a.m. eating crayfish, drinking aquavit and dancing. Yet, there they were again at the train station to see me off...at 7:30 a.m.! Inger, fearing we would never meet again in this world, bid a tearful goodbye...and I turned my attention to the great unknown ahead.

But was the Soviet Union really that unknown? After numerous stops for customs, immigration, agriculture and police checks, my train finally neared Leningrad and there, silhouetted against the setting sun, stood a veritable forest of TV aerials on the housetops. Proving the foremost importance of internal communication—tightly controlled, of course. Soviet leaders were exerting desperate efforts to keep Western news and information from getting through to their people. So much so that they thereby proved this to be the real Achilles Heel of the whole sorry system. They also carefully limited and spoonfed only bits of information to outsiders about their own land, keeping the external picture of conditions within the USSR almost as distorted.

Still, I found big holes in the controls. For instance, railroaders received virtually everything published abroad on their industry—as did almost all other industry and professional groups. How else could each stay abreast, not to mention ahead? And much "dangerous" general information came in along with the technical. Also, despite mighty jamming attempts, the Voice of America and Radio Free Europe *were* getting through loud and clear to many, many. So, myriad contacts with the outside world, coupled with the system's need to give many an advanced education, were gnawing away at the very foundations of the communist colossus.

A handsome Russian marine engineer I met on the train to Leningrad confided he was reluctantly returning home after two years' work in a Swedish shipyard. He spoke excellent English, which he termed *the* language of the world maritime trade. As for the harassment we got from all the government inspections, he startled me by joking:

"You'll get that everywhere here. It's the only fun these bureaucrats have. And I can assure you, the USSR is one giant bureaucracy." [Inger would have said that's nothing new: In Norway, the social democrats were rapidly achieving the same goal.]

"Have you read Pasternak's *Dr. Zhivago?*" I asked.

"Yes, in Sweden...in English."

"What did you think of it?"

"Basically a true story. It's a book the authorities should never have banned. It pointed out how cruel life here used to be—and everyone knew that anyway."

"*Used* to be?" To that I got a noncommittal grunt, then continued: "I thought it was banned because of its emphasis on individual freedom?"

"Yes, well, perhaps that was it...." And with that the engineer turned silent and stared out at the shifting landscape where far-out-numbered Finns had fought massed Russian forces to a standstill in the murderous Winter War of the late 1930s.

In Leningrad [which was destined one day to resume its old name of St. Petersburg] I toured the czars' old Summer palace and saw a treasure-trove of art, much of it Western, at the famed Hermitage. I then boarded the overnight Red Arrow for Moscow—a roomy, beautifully appointed train with comfortable beds—but also with men and women mixed indiscriminately in the same sleeping compartments. And into my room (another coincidence?) came a young, bright English-speaking passenger—Gregor, a former Russian now living in Australia. After some opening pleasantries, he turned on his portable radio, hung it from the central chandelier (drowning out possible listening devices), and quietly began to hint at meetings he would be holding at various places inside the USSR "with people who despise

Communism."

Well, this proved too much (read *hazardous*) for me...so I switched to the weather.

But, no, that didn't prove a safe subject, either. For hadn't Soviet agriculture reputedly suffered horribly from 45 years of bad weather? (Not to mention from Stalin's killing off 4 million farmers in a vicious, incredibly ill-conceived/backfiring campaign to collectivize agriculture.)

Next morning in Moscow, I was met at the train station by a wiry, jumpy little man in a worn, oversized suit who said he had been delegated by the Railroad Ministry to help me "in any way." This was followed hard on by " please, just call me Vic" and, most important, I suspected: "Got any cigarettes?" Gruff and likable, he related that he had spent many years in Paris and London on minor diplomatic assignments (which I assumed to be KGB work). He next checked me in at the Leningradskaya Hotel, where he spent two whole hours talking openly and longingly of those wonder-days in the West. All the while mooching freely my cigarettes! (I had given up smoking eight years before but had brought a few packs along as gifts.)

But what would I like to do in the USSR? Vic wanted to know, jolting me by stating: "You're the personal guest of the Soviet Railroad Minister. [One of the most powerful men in the country.] He has assumed responsibility for you...so you can go wherever you like and do whatever you want."

I was tempted to ask to ride the Trans-Siberian on its 6,000-mile route to Vladivostock, but felt I should be making better use of my three weeks here. So the plan Vic and I worked out called for a week of talks and visits to rail facilities around Moscow, a lengthy train trip to Tbilisi via Stalingrad [where the German invaders suffered a devastating setback in February 1943, which, along with the earlier Allied victory at Alemein in Egypt, turned out to be the turning points of WWII], an air flight to Kiev to visit that big rail operating center, then another train trip back to Moscow for wind-up meetings before flying home. Intourist got into the act, too, occasionally providing attractive sightseeing guides, who offered embarrassingly canned replies to all questions about the USSR—

unlike the amazingly open and direct railroaders.

"Do you have a radio?" I asked one carshop foreman.

"Nyet!" he replied in a frank comment on the USSR's notoriously poor apartment construction techniques. "Don't need one. I just use my neighbor's 'way down the hall."

More canned comments were served on the train to Tbilisi, where I was invited to join in a typically Russian dinner (heavy!) in the diningcar by a fellow passenger who was born in Brooklyn and taken back to Russia as a boy by his parents—and who, I concluded, could not possibly be another coincidence. I was being watched! Or maybe safeguarded? But there were also real people to meet: Like the elderly schoolteacher I stumbled against in the corridor. When he found out I was an American, tears filled his eyes, he cracked my ribs with a wild bearhug, out came a bottle of vodka...and I had to tell all I knew about that wonderland unimaginably far, far away. And this after 40 years of hate-America propaganda!

More tears came when a Russian woman in Kiev told me about the long German siege and starvation of Leningrad, where she had fought as a soldier right alongside the men. But it wasn't Communist ideology they fought for. It was *Russia!* The ordinary Russian's love of country is absolute and unequivocal (no less than the American's for America?). Yet, the Kremlin shrewdly used this to the hilt, equating Communism with that love of country...and reaping the benefits.

Women were also found working alongside men throughout industry. In Tbilisi I ran into two all-women maintenance-of-way crews wielding picks and shovels—hard, dirty work out in the open, under raw weather conditions. This reflected the loss of some 20 million men in WWII—a loss with staggering consequences for the USSR's future. Can you imagine Western women working like that? Well, they did at least once, Inger would have pointed out: All across America during the pioneers' century-long push westward and along the frontiers...as depicted in Rolvaag's classic book, *Giants in the Earth.* They were the real hero(ine)s in the "manifest destiny" saga.

On the ground and in talks with experts like the Soviet Deputy Railroad Minister—Vladimir Gavrilov, a heavy-set, quick-witted, tough-sounding administrator—I discovered that a superrailroad of awesome proportions was in the making across this land of double the USA's size. The standout fact: With one-third of US trackage, Russian rail was handling *double* our freight load and *ten times* our passenger traffic. This was due heavily, of course, to the poor state of highway development. And the Soviet air system was built largely for military, not civilian purposes. As in India, however, it was also clear that the entire system was suffering from inadequate repair and maintenance. Yet, as WWII proved, it's amazing how much intensive service can be squeezed out of panting locomotives and creaking rolling stock! Interestingly, Russian track gauge—the distance between rails—is 3 1/2 inches greater than the 4' 8 1/2" found in the rest of Europe and the US. This makes for roomier cars but it was also raising hob with cross-border traffic with Europe, which had to be reloaded in both directions.

Asked about worker productivity—a constant concern in the USSR—Minister Gavrilov fixed me with a measuring eye and said: "We have a special law for loafers—it's off to Siberia!"

(Was he thinking of me, too?)

Actually, a host of benefits was being used as work incentives, proving that all the breast-beating about a classless society and an equal sharing of production results is strictly a myth. Surprisingly, the rail system was also making a profit; its high rates made it an indirect tax collector, with the excess revenues returned, of course, to the state treasury. This kind of pricing was purposeful for another reason, too, Mr. Gavrilov said:

"When an enterprise makes extra money, it can provide better facilities and services, and everyone is happy. BUT the public loses respect for enterprises that operate at a loss." [Oh, if only the deficit-ridden US railroads and US government could both take note!]

An inside look at the Soviet "agitprop" machine in action was provided that August 18 when Vic escorted me through 10 lines of armed guards in Red Square to watch Khrushchev pin medals on two cosmonauts whose space vehicles had been circling the earth the week before.

We wound up some 20 yards from the reviewing stand outside the Kremlin walls, which were festooned with flags, slogans, balloons and even a model spaceship. The "maximum leader" spoke interminably about this great Soviet achievement, indicating again and again that "we will bury the West." Loudspeakers all over Moscow blared out his remarks, and that night fireworks filled the air. A fantastic show! But was it all meant to divert the masses' attention from the system's failure to provide even the meanest necessities of life? You got the feeling that *this* "god" really had clay feet.

Vic also announced that railroad officials planned to hold a farewell dinner in my honor the next evening in a private room at a leading restaurant...but added in a low voice: "But for god's sake, Jim, don't drink too much...." He vanished before I could ask what he meant.

Many of the people I had worked with attended the gathering, along with two beady-eyed men I had not seen before. There was round after round of toasts with straight vodka. To peace and friendship! they howled. Toasts were also hoisted to me and my wife, to the USSR, to Khrushchev and Presidents Eisenhower and Kennedy, to the railroads, locomotive "drivers," yard workers, etc. While everyone guzzled, however, I sipped—much, I noted, to the two strangers' consternation. The party finally broke up with bear hugs and heartfelt farewells. Emphasizing anew the vast, vast gap between the icy Soviet rulers and the warm Russian people.

Arriving back in my hotelroom, I heard almost immediately a knock at the door...and outside stood the two strangers from dinner, one of whom introduced himself as a Tass reporter. They wished to record an interview with me. Fine, I said, the light now dawning on what Vic meant. It was a difficult moment. But then I remembered the advice PR counsellors give to people when going in for a TV or other news interview: *Regardless of what you're asked, find ways to get across the message you want people to hear.* The questions came in a rush—all pointed at getting my impressions of the wonders of Russia's railroads AND Communism. I talked, rather, of the great things the *US* was doing in transportation—of high-speed train developments and automated switching yards, of our rapidly expanding Interstate Highway System, of new air traffic control systems and the recently opened St. Lawrence Seaway—and of our priority efforts to promote peace and friendship around the world. With Russia, too. And I extolled not the Soviet system but the wonderful people I had met everywhere...and the hunger they expressed for news of the outside world. An obviously disappointed "reporter" and his (KGB?) assistant shortly departed.

Early next day, I unloaded my remaining cigarettes and other extras onto a grateful Vic, embraced him as a true friend and clambered aboard an Aeroflot jet for Copenhagen. A dizzying kaleidoscope of people, places, events and impressions whirled through my head. What revelations! It was as though a bright light had broken through into a long-locked, dark basement. If a social/political system is to be judged in its truest terms—in its impact on the human spirit—then, I felt, I had just witnessed the ultimate disaster. Indeed, here was one right out of hell. A system built on fear, hate and suspicion. You survive by burying your real self and wearing a false front. You get ahead by ratting on your neighbor. What a way to live!

I began to write down what I had experienced, setting aside my transport mission and concentrating on the US-USSR propaganda war. This worked itself into such total concentration that I became completely unaware of traveling. With Inger's shrewd subsequent help in rewriting, we came up with an eerily predictive article which ran as a cover story and for an unprecedented seven printed pages in the June 1963 issue of the *Public Relations Journal*. It also got a lot of attention within the US Information Agency, partly because of this lead:

The Free World is winning the cold war but hasn't sense enough to know it. Worse, we are not doing what it takes to pin down the victory; as a result, it may slip right through our fingers.

The article covered the Kremlin's PR campaign vs. its own people, as well as its propaganda clash with the forces of freedom around the world, including that in the more vulnerable countries Inger and I had visited, then went on to state:

I am convinced that freedom's lines can not only be held in these areas but also ultimately pushed forward. How are these miracles to be achieved? The answer lies both in maintaining space and economic superiority and in using to the hilt the greatest weapon in freedom's arsenal—freedom itself. The answer lies in a concentrated, determined assault on the mental Iron Curtain dividing East and West—in challenging Khrushchev and the whole Kremlin hierarchy to an all-out duel of ideas—to an ideological war that can eventually sweep away the walls of the Soviet Bloc's closed information system and let the

Russian people civilize and humanize their masters.

[And so, eventually, the Russian people *did*!}

I was jolted out of my intense concentration by the Aeroflot jet's wheels hitting the runway at Kastrup Airport. Still lost in that other world, I straightened up and looked around in disbelief: I was back in the Free World! Back in the familiar, relaxed world of Scandinavia!

A smiling Inger was there, too...jumping up and down and waving wildly. No new Soviet citizen, this! She would have been the first to join Voltaire and Jefferson anytime anywhere in declaring "eternal enmity against every form of tyranny over the mind of man." Suddenly through my mind flashed her favorite quote from Henrik Ibsen:

Up here on the mountaintop there is freedom and God. Men do but grope in the valley.

Well, I had just seen enough groping to last a lifetime.

We fled into each other's arms. "Oh, Jimmy, you're back! You're back!" Inger cried in complete abandon, finally leaning back and looking at me as at someone returned from the dead.

And that's just the way I felt.

Chapter VI

Wherever Inger and I traveled during our year-long comparative study of transportation systems in the score of countries we targeted, we found, paradoxically, that in those nations where railroads were experiencing the most severe difficulties, the lessons to be learned were the clearest. So we called our resulting book *QUEST FOR CRISIS—A World-Ranging Search for Clues to the Transport Future.*

Sailing back to the USA on the sleek *Oslofjord*, I spent the better part of each day whipping the book manuscript into next-to-final shape, with Inger acting as Supreme Critic and rewrite editor. The trip also gave us a wondrous chance to catch our breath and reflect on our year abroad. A lifetime of experiences had been crowded into 12 eventful, wearing, enlightening months. All of which Inger put into her unique brand of perspective in these words:

"That's why age cannot be taken as a yardstick of wisdom. Most people simply live the same year over and over again their whole life."

That was certainly not true of this year. As predicted by the EEF's Hampton Barnes—the very soul of good will toward others—while seeing peoples overseas, we had learned much about ourselves. And while seeing other nations, we had learned much about America...and Norway. The year also underscored for us the limitations on any one person's ability "to grasp this sorry scheme of things entire," as *The Rubaiyat* puts it. Further underscored were the limitations on the human race's creative achievements. We were struck everywhere by how few cultural concepts and basic art forms mankind had developed over the ages...and how much copying and adaptation has taken place since. It was odd, too, how peoples of different nationalities become increasingly similar as they become more educated—and how the less-developed often tend to live up to the stereotypes associated with national origins.

Personally, I was happiest of all over what our year abroad had done for Inger. The onrush of new experiences had dulled the edge of tragedy that only a mother can feel over the death of two children. Like her harrowing shipwreck, this had not been forgotten, I knew—just shoved back into the recesses of the mind. But now, at least, she seemed better able to cope with its memory. She laughed a lot and tackled daily challenges (including me!) with a lighter spirit and renewed energy.

Arriving back at the AAR, we got a royal reception. As we traveled and learned, I had been sending back memos that later became chapters in my book—and they *had* been read! But I also noted that Handly Wright had loaded my desk with piles and piles of postponed work. (What else could you expect?) The Law Department assigned one of the association's best lawyers—Harry Breithaupt—to go over the ms. with me and make sure my free-wheeling policy interpretations accorded with current law. This, I'm sure, he found fly-specking drudgery...but never once complained about it. (Thanks, Harry!) Inger and I then sat down with Publisher Russ Moore and decided on the book's layout and illustrations and publicity plans. (We naively thought publishers actually made an effort to publicize their products!) Finally, incredibly, a half year after returning, we found ourselves holding a handsomely bound volume of 22 chapters on 223 pages of glossy paper—our *Quest for Crisis*.

We weighed the book, smelled the fresh ink, leafed through the pages and felt their thickness, stared holes in the type and photos (many of which we had taken ourselves), turned it over and over and minutely examined all six sides.

"Think anyone will ever know or care about how much work went into this six-by-nine-inch monster?" I asked Inger.

"Or, more important, think anyone will ever buy it?" she countered.

"Yes, *you*!"

"*Du, da*! I knew there was a hook in there somewhere!" Inger paused, thought a moment, then said: "The real question, though, is, will anyone *act* on its conclusions...AND policy recommendations."

"Yes ma'am, they've got to...'cause I'm putting you in charge of PR—of making sure exactly that happens."

"*Fannen!* [The devil!] I think I just swallowed another hook...."

We did get the feeling that the book proved worth the money EEF invested in it. For instance, it made crystal clear the "why" railroads are in such trouble almost everywhere—an understanding of which America or any other country would find crucial to coming up with solutions. In a word, that primary reason is *change*. And the railroads' failure to adapt to change is due primarily to that old bugaboo: *Politics*. As the book states in chapter 22, "Bright Trail to the Transport Future":

The 20th and 21st centuries have brought an accelerating technological revolution, vast economic growth and the development of useful new forms of transportation. Railroads everywhere had to make drastic internal changes in order to adapt to these new external conditions, both in reshaping plant and operating methods and in competing for business.

But governments, reacting largely to local political and labor pressures, have largely blocked these changes—especially an essential flexibility in pricing, in merging operations and in reducing light-traffic lines and stations and unneeded manpower. Yet, if a nation is to get the most out of its railroads, it must allow them to go on making these changes and to coordinate more closely with other carriers, particularly in handling transferable container and "piggyback" services. Above all, it must treat all carriers alike when it comes to regulating, taxing and aiding them—so that each, in competing with others, will operate on a level playing field and become as good as it can be...naturally.

Mainlining thus becomes the key to, the shape of, the railroads' future. The iron horse on steel rails is unbeatable in handling large volumes of people and goods between population and production centers. Simply put, the more cars per train and the more trains per track, the more efficient railroading becomes, and the more effective in competition. In fact, if a nation had no railroads, it would probably have to build them from scratch specifically for this purpose—as we found

Russia and India doing. And in public policies making mainlining possible lies hope not only for railroad survival but for full-blown revival.

As to whether government take-over of railroads is desirable, our study found no real support for this feckless approach. Why? Because nationalization of once-private railroads in Europe did nothing whatever to solve the carriers' basic problems. Its major effect was simply to shift responsibility for rail losses from private owners to taxpayers—and, worse, to delay solutions interminably while the public picked up a mounting bill for operating losses. Louis Armand put this most clearly during our interview in Paris:

"Government take-over is pointless. It solves no problems—merely transfers responsibility for them. Europe's experience shows how badly this can work out."

Perhaps our book would have driven this crucial point home more clearly if it had been entitled *The Wreck of the Railroad Nationalization Myth*. For a wreck it was, wherever tried.

[The US history of Amtrak underscores how poorly politics mixes with railroading. From its advent in 1970 as a semi-public corporation designed to take over the railroads' problem-ridden intercity passenger operations, Amtrak has been forced by congressional pressures to maintain train services in certain districts even though these produced few customers. (To find out where, note the membership of Congress' two Interstate Commerce Committees.) Politicking thus never allowed Amtrak's structure to be *rationalized*. The result has been chronic operating deficits—which have required equally big annual federal (taxpayer- financed) subsidies.]

Inger took her assignment as the book's PR chief seriously—exhaustingly so. Numerous speaking engagements for me around the country were arranged over the next two years—events that seemed to surprise audiences, for we made them as much a world-ranging travelogue as a policy learning process. Using my trusty Kodak Retina, we had taken scores of color-slides during our peregrinations. These were shown first to the EEF staff in Philadelphia right after we returned to the USA, with me providing the "voice over" about each pictured country's transportation approaches. The reaction was so enthusiastic that we decided to package the combination for our barnstorming appearances elsewhere. Sad to report, however, this sometimes involved projectors that froze up or bulbs that burned out at critical moments, torn screens, sunlight shining directly on the pictures, etc. (Don't ever even try it!)

Working further magic, Inger and railroad PR staffers got considerable "ink" and radio/TV interviews at these events. Lengthy articles appeared in key publications:

U. S. News & World Report carried two full pages analyzing our findings.

The Washington Star picked up our book's entire chapter 20, "City Traffic Snarls: Where a Train Can Be a Car's Best Friend." This surveyed actions that big European cities were taking to coordinate rail and road approaches to transport problems, both within the city and along urbanized corridors (like that between Washington and Boston). The *Star*'s Sunday Magazine also carried one of our byliners.

Rotarian and *The American Legion Magazine* likewise ran major pieces on our urban transport findings.

The National Transportation Defense Journal printed all of Chapter 19, "Russia Reaches for Superrailroads."

Nation's Business ran most of Chapter 1 under the title, "England's Plight: Warning to US Transport."

Railway Age picked up the Louis Armand interview (Chapter 15) under the heading, "Global Effort Called Key to Railroad Survival."

In a different category, a scholarly (heavy, heavy) paper we wrote, "International Trail to Tomorrow's Transportation" won a Gold Medal from the Pan American Railway Congress.

So the message *was* getting across!

[A unique postscript to the book: Years later I got a note from that Grand Old Man of publishing, Alfred A. Knopf, inviting me to talk over an idea he had re *QforC*. Excited yet puzzled, I beat it to New York at Inger's instigation and found that Mr. Knopf had read the book, liked it, and wanted to know if I would be interested in updating it for re-publication—this time by his own company. *Yes, indeed!* I replied...but then asked who would cover the considerable expenses such a project of new travel and research would entail. *You!* he rejoined. End of conversation. End of idea. End of project.]

Meanwhile, there were trains and trains to ride, with Inger and the boys reveling in the chance to see America again as "deadheads." We could get free railroad passes, all right, but could not generally ride the best trains. However, Mimbo, now in his 'teens, showed sheer ingenuity in poring over railroad timetables and coming up with intricate connections all over the country. Using the train window as a magic moving picture screen, Inger and I thus came over the next few years to see great steel mills reddening the night sky over Pittsburgh, miles and miles of lush cornfields across a Midwest dotted with silo-ed family farms, "tank towns" on lonely prairies shimmering in noontime heat, winds rippling through reed-filled marshes in Georgia, bountiful orange groves in Florida, "darkies" spilling out over the steps of shanties in Alabama, a full moon eerily lighting the vast cattlelands of Texas, giant cactuses silhouetted against a crimson sunset in Arizona, the blue Pacific pounding the edge of the continent in California, dense forests lighted by mountains of snow in Oregon, Glacier Park and the immense grasslands and Big Sky reaches of Montana.

An annual favorite for our whole family was an Easter-time trip to Mexico City via the B&O to St. Louis, the Mopac to Laredo and the Mexican National Railways to destination. It was three days each way, with only two days there...but, as aboard ship, it provided an unbeatable chance to get together without telephones and homefront hassling. Two adjoining bedrooms would be reserved, with the wall between opened up to form one large unit with four beds. You then relaxed to the car's endless swaying and the clicking/humming of wheels on rails, to the mournful sound of train whistles at intersections, to good food in the diningcar and to incomparably courteous Pullman porters [who sadly became increasingly sour as more and more trains were discontinued]. What a life! We didn't know it then but we were riding along at the very end of a fantastic century-long era of great trains.

It was the Golden Age of her life in America, Inger said later with no little nostalgia.

Another aspect of America that really enthralled Inger was that greatest of our natural treasures, the National Parks. When Jimmy rounded 18, I went to our Maryland congressman, the intelligent, warm-hearted Gilbert Gude (who subsequently showed his intelligence by shifting from politicking to heading up the Library of Congress' Legislative Reference Service), and got him to recommend our son to the Park Service as a Summertime trail-crew worker. Mimbo wound up at the Rocky Mountain National Park at Estes Park, Colorado — and, subsequently, at Glacier National Park in Montana. Then, when Erik got old enough, he went into the Forestry Service in Vermont. Inger was overwhelmed with joy, and not just because her sons had these tremendous outdoor jobs. *We* got into the act, too...spending much of our Summers at the boys' posts, hiking over miles and miles of mountain trails, with their radiant flowers, lakes and waterfalls, clear air and inspiring vistas.

For me, it was grand to see my wife getting to know America better than most Americans. And what has impressed her most? Our TREES! She loved the palms, the magnolias and moss-festooned oaks in the South, the 4,000-year-old sequoias in the Sierras (which can only be beheld with the deepest reverence), the huge elms framing the White House, the poplars towering over the beautiful Dupont Winterthur estate in Delaware, the lavishly yellow/red-painted panorama of the Appalachians in Autumn and the quivering aspens reflecting golden sunlight among the dark evergreens of the Rockies.

Rangers in the Sequoia National Park tell the story that these monarchs of the forest, however huge and seemingly strong, one day simply tilt over and crash to the ground. Even at times when there's no wind, snow or rain. Why? Their roots weaken and finally give 'way. Well, Inger latched right onto this, fitting it into her fear that Americans are forgetting and neglecting their national roots — their unique history and resplendent traditions — in favor of an almost total obsession with the clamorous present and the dubious lures of the unpredictable future. So what happens when a whole nation neglects its roots? Like those sequoia monarchs, it *crashes!* She liked to quote Harvard's George Santayana in this regard:

Those who cannot remember the past are condemned to repeat its failures.

Inger's America came to mean more than its geographic reaches. It was the *spirit* of the people that really intrigued her. They exuded *hope.*

Here, anything seemed possible. Things might be bad today *but just you wait until tomorrow!* America was no finished product; it was a *becoming,* a *process*—an awesome movement of people from everywhere toward a God-only- knows-what kind of future. Inger was discovering the awesome secret underlying America's dynamism—the miracles that can be achieved when people are given opportunity to learn, work and rise through a fluid social structure and become whatever their vision and abilities allow. Even the monumental Union Station right off Capitol Hill, she noted, captures the essence of the American spirit, for it was designed by a man who said:

Make no small plans! They have no magic to stir men's blood....

Inger decided one day to put her knowledge of her new country to work—as a Washington tour guide. This came about when the Norwegian Embassy called one day and asked if she could show the Capital to a group of travel agents from Oslo. *Of course!* she said a little too fast—realizing later that this would require reams of *specific* knowledge...and she'd better get crackin' in putting it together. But wasn't that what I stood there ready to help do? That first tour came off a bit rough, but it led to many more with both Scandinavian and German groups. These became a bit more polished...as Inger got into the swing of things.

I accompanied my wife on one of these tours and found she did some tall stirring of her own. People arrived from abroad filled with fear and trembling over the horror tales they had heard about US crime, drugs, urban decay and chaos. A first stop in New York City only heightened their apprehension. But then Inger took them over in Washington and miraculously reassured them with her common sense, openness and honesty. *And* warm, relaxed, personal style. It was amazing: My wife was a natural public speaker, a born actress!

"Did you ever think of going in for a stage career," I asked that evening at home.

"Oh, *that* again!" she laughed merrily. "Sure...doesn't every teenager have such dreams? But Pappa would have none of it. He didn't want me to live such a life. Or go through the tough times he had experienced. I think, too, he feared I would self-destruct. So, instead, I became a clown. Like now...."

And *smack!* I got a quick kiss in reward for my interest.

Remarkable mood changes occurred in the tour bus under Inger's talk ("off to the right you'll see...etc" and "here on the left...etc"), interspersed with Q&A sessions. The Danes soon wanted to know where they could get some beer. The Norwegians asked about entertainment possibilities. And the Swedes took careful notes. And even though few left as true believers, they at least came away with the feeling that modern America might not be so bad after all.

Not that Inger was the kind to paper over the USA's complex problems. (Hadn't she run head-on into many herself?) However, she considered these defects to be remedied, not irremediable wounds leading to death. She knew how strenuous effort can radically transform an apparently hopeless personal situation. And that America as a whole has a fabulous capacity to do so, too, and regenerate itself...despite all the damage our politicians sometimes seem intent on inflicting on the nation and its economy and culture. Above all, she was repelled by whiners and complainers...and regularly brought them up short by asking not what they thought should be done about problems but what they intended to do about them *personally.*

Our new era's rampant concentration on *self* especially bothered Inger. People, she felt, should find out enough about their selves to cope with their selves, then get away from their selves as fast and as far as possible. And by that she meant their "greedy, graspy, uncaring, utterly self-centered selves." She believed people must ally themselves with something bigger than their selves and live a pervading sense of responsibility to *others*—to family, friends, community, the nation, the world. She believed that the growing stress on self-centeredness and self-fulfillment is a centripetal force, and that the inevitable end of accelerating self-emphasis within humans, as in physics, is inward collapse. Comparing the situation to the universe, astronomers would say that people are digging themselves into *a black hole.* And then, Inger stated sadly, comes the final irony:

"The modern psychologists, sociologists and teachers—all the "social engineers" who preach self-fulfillment rubbish—then get full-time employment at fancy salaries treating the victims of their preaching."

Meanwhile, *national* problems seemed to be piling up, too. The horror of President Kennedy's assassination in Texas hit us all like a giant club. How could such a monstrous thing happen in America? Inger pleaded to know. To a man so full of promise, and to a nation so much in need of that promise? The loss came just a year after he had guided the world through the Cuban missile crisis, which under any other leadership could have blown us all sky-high.

[In the current age of worldwide terrorism, with the USA its principal target, one wonders what the outcome of a similar crisis would be today if the instigators were Muslim fanatics. Our Russian adversaries, like us, wanted to go on living, after all...and pulled back from an atomic abyss at the last minute. But what do you do with people who *want* to die...as martyrs? People who murder and maim and then believe, grotesquely, that this will get them a royal reception in Islamic heaven? And that the more "infidels" they can destroy, the more royal their reception?]

For Inger, the Cuban missile crisis was a grim reminder that every moment of every day military people on both sides of the Iron Curtain sit with their fingers on atomic triggers—waiting, waiting. [Today, too!] Who could ever know when a miscalculation or accident will set off a nuclear holocaust...and all life on earth would end? All the more reason, she felt, to try and try and never, never stop trying, to bridge the yawning gap between the Kremlin and the West—even in face of the rigid, uncompromising, chilling Stalinist attitude: *Never apologize, never defend, never retreat. Attack! Attack! Attack!*.

Overnight, the nation found itself governed by Lyndon Johnson, a Texan, a shrewd "old Washington hand" and a different kind of president. Drawing on his storied Senate experience, LBJ proved a wizard at pushing major legislation through Congress, like Medicare [which, though grandly conceived, would eventually threaten bankruptcy to the whole national "safety net" system]. He also steered Congress into approving vast new US military aid to South Vietnam, where, by the peak year of 1969, over 540,000 American fightingmen would be involved in deadly jungle warfare. [And you know how that turned out....]

Then there were mounting race problems. The Summer we returned to America, Martin Luther King led a nationwide "Freedom March" on Washington...and gave his inspiring "I Have a Dream" speech at the Lincoln Memorial. US blacks were truly rising to their feet. And the nation—especially the South—was having a hard time adjusting to the new reality.

King also spoke at the National Cathedral high up on Wisconsin Avenue overlooking the District, and Inger and I heard him there in the monumental building's gothic surroundings. He urged a national dedication to the pursuit of equality. (Inger would have urged a companion goal: The pursuit of *quality*). This was no ringing oration like his sermon on the mall. Instead, he talked *reason*. He appealed to the privileged, the propertied and the powerful, many of whom sat right before him, to lead the way toward fulfilling the American dream "that all men are created equal." For shouldn't society's leaders *lead* in this tough integration battle? Instead of retreating into the finest neighborhoods and insulating themselves against societal upheaval? As Inger commented, you seldom hear of change in such a fundamental emotional area arising from the masses. They might respond, sure, but *someone* has to stir them up. Someone has to *lead*.

Inger and I had closer-at-home problems, too. The boys' education in this new land probably concerned her more than anything else. From kindergarten on, she watched teachers and their classroom conduct like a hawk, visiting them often to urge tougher lessons, more homework and tighter student discipline—for Jimmy and Erik no less than others—and letting the teachers know they could count on us to support these approaches. Reactions were mixed. Some treated Inger as an ignorant foreign meddler; others as a fresh breeze in a dank cellar. Meanwhile, disorder in the public schools was rising...and learning declining.

What to do? Inger wasn't about to give up on her aim of making our sons into four-dimensional human beings...even if our society as a whole seems to have long since forgotten that this was the grand goal of every thinking person since the Enlightenment. And in case what she meant had slipped my mind, she enthusiastically reminded me that a 4-D person has *knowledge, cultural awareness, spiritual depth* and *an abiding concern for others*. A truly developed human being!

"Okay, Inkie," I said, "you've told us what a person should *become*. Now let's see if you can tell us how we got where we are—

what's gone into *making* us what we are?"

"Ah, but that's a whole new college course!" Inger responded, shaking her head over my baiting her. "The short answer, though, is that each of us is the product of all our yesterdays—PLUS the yesterdays of our forefathers."

"Oh, oh...better steer clear of *that!*"

She went on to say that what we are, and what we hope to become, seemed to her to work together like the two sides of a 2-by-4. The 4-D's represent one side—tomorrow. Another 4 represent all those yesterdays. Thus, she said, all of us stand today as the product of the genetic structure inherited through our parents—our *genes*—as well as the *oppdragelse* or raising received in our home, our *experiences* in life, and the *education* we've had pounded into us. Like by a 2-by-4! She noted, too, that Americans don't like to emphasize genetic inheritance in analyzing personal development problems; they flail away, instead, at the other three factors. As though this is the more democratic thing to do!

Inger spent a year visiting private schools in the Washington area, finally settling on what she thought would be a tough, no-nonsense Quaker education at Sidwell Friends School in the District. Jimmy readily passed the entrance exams. Then, a year later, Erik, reeling from a couple harrowing weeks of our personal tutoring, also made the grade. In time, we discovered that Sidwell wasn't as tough as we had hoped. But it *was* better.

So now, I moaned, I had to pay college-level tuition costs while the boys were still in grade school and highschool. Inger, however, was unmoved. What better way for parents to use their money than for their children's education? she asked. *What* money? I wanted to know. My wife tossed her pretty head and strode away. No words were needed: I knew what *that* meant!

Well, maybe the school's extra cost was worth near-starvation, after all. Erik seemed to thrive in the new classroom climate, and went in for an oddly mixed devotion to classical music and physical training. In time, he became a stand-out track star, winning several grueling cross-country meets—cheered on by a wildly excited Inger running alongside at the finish line.

Jimmy, meanwhile, showed a remarkable penchant for taking the most obstreperous positions on issues and defending them with the most detailed argument—not only against fellow students but also, unfortunately, in his youthful exuberance, against teachers. Somehow he survived, however, with everyone agreeing that here, indeed, was a natural lawyer-in-the-making. He finally graduated with honors and, after visiting numerous schools with me in tow, moved on to top-rated Haverford College outside Philadelphia.

With its ivy-covered graystone buildings and parklike setting, Haverford *looked* grand...but here as elsewhere, Vietnam and the spreading LSD/ marijuana/drug mania was raising hob with life on campus. Jimmy knew exactly where Inger and I stood on drugs and drinking. We had talked this out at home (and with Pastor Luffberry at St. Paul's Lutheran Church on Connecticut Avenue), so the boys understood fully the grave dangers involved and would, we hoped, choose to do what was truly in their own interest. Even so, Inger and I were amazed to find Jimmy dressing neatly, getting his hair cut regularly and championing the most conservative positions at his ultra-liberal college. And, boy, did he ever have it tough!

When a notorious drug-use advocate was invited to speak on campus about the alleged wonders of LSD and other "mind-expanding" drugs, Jimmy tried to organize a boycott of the speech. Failing to get more than a handful of students to go along, he phoned us, complaining bitterly. Inger was alarmed. So off we went to the US Bureau of Narcotics, where we got an armload of materials, then traveled to Haverford and, with Jimmy leading the way, talked with the school's dean and president. Young people taking drugs were winding up in psychiatric wards and jumping off buildings. It wasn't their young, fragile minds that were being expanded; it was the graveyards.

What would this college do to avoid such tragedies? we wanted to know.

Well, we got one limp reception. Yet, the officials did finally decide to issue a formal statement opposing drug use on campus and, at our insistence, invited a spokesman from the Narcotics Bureau to speak, too. The result: Whereas most students turned out to hear the drug advocate, few attended the anti-drug session. Which is about what you might expect, no? In any event, we ourselves did *try*...hard. And our children witnessed this firsthand...and *they*, at least, got the message. Which proved anew that actions communicate much more clearly than words.

Also proved was that family life is one formidable challenge— maybe even more so than pursuing professional careers (though the former is too often short-changed in favor of the latter, with calamitous results). Inger's view, repeatedly and aggressively expressed, was that *THE HOME AND FAMILY ARE EVERYTHING!* Home, she said, was the one and only sure refuge the boys would ever find in an unstable, uncaring world—the one place they could always turn to for help and comfort on an enduring basis. The boys heard this so often they turned it into a ditty, sung loudly and far off every key known to man. That got Inger laughing so hard she broke up in a stream of happy tears. Thus did this fabulous woman-in-our-lives prove daily that a good sense of humor is probably the most important ingredient in a happy marriage. For marriage is filled with friction, she often said...and humor is the oil that keeps the whole relationship from overheating and burning out.

[Or is a happy sex relationship the most important? Or should one simply say: *Assuming* a good sex relationship, a good sense of humor is the most important...etc, etc?]

The pounding children's minds took from TV and other forms of communication in our modern society was considered no laughing matter, however. Long before Haverford, Inger pointed to my seafaring days and lamented that too many people go through life like a ship without compass, rudder or anchor—no sense of direction and no values to anchor themselves to when storms come up. Small wonder you see so many shipwrecks! So we warned the boys to be on guard against today's Media/Entertainment Complex, which only aggravates these conditions through both subtle and crude influences on the psyche. [Remember the previous reference to the Complex? It's in Chapter 3.] For instance, just as news people emphasize the divorces rather than the happy marriages and disasters rather than happy events—because bad news *is* news—so most entertainment plays up the abnormal, the sensational, the perverted. Why? Because that's what gets attention.

That's where the money is! With the normal, the traditional and stable thus getting short shrift from Media Complex drumbeaters, young people especially come to feel there's something wrong with tried-and-true values...and are driven, willy-nilly, to seek out the new and extreme—however wrong *they* may be—in order not to be deemed "square", old-fashioned or out of touch.

Well, Inger was having none of that. TV was singled out as Culprit No 1 (for there it stood right in the middle of the livingroom!). She needed no polls, tests or "depth research" to tell her what kind of impact TV's frequent airing of sex, crime and violence has on children. She *knew*. You saw it firsthand every day: Impulses poured into people, but where was the outlet for the emotions they stirred up? For outlets *will* be found—and you may not like the result. As for research purporting to prove the opposite, this was roundly dismissed as blatantly slanted or dishonest attempts to push a commercial or partisan point of view. [The same goes for today's Internet.] She was further appalled by the way TV cameras bored into the very souls of people caught in tragedy; program producers made public sport of private grief, threatening to make modern peoples incapable of feeling anything at all. Topping it all off, giving yourself over to TV and becoming a "couch potato" seemed to Inger to completely flatten out the human personality, turning people into veritable zombies.

And those TV ads! A half-dozen continually popped up, clamoring for attention, after each couple minutes of programming...hawking a happier home and love-life, improved eating and drinking and appearance, better health, taste and smell, a more comfortable car, etc, etc. All constantly intruding on the consciousness, fragmenting attention and threatening to create a nation of nitwits. And what about your paying for all these offerings of the Merchants of Desire and Discontent? Don't worry! Other ads promoted the easy availaility of credit cards...allowing you to join the millions saddled with a growing mountain of credit-card debt. All of which led to Inger's decision to watch no more TV programs with ad interruptions; this meant few programs, indeed—not a bad solution at all! [The ad stream proved just as profuse in Norway BUT there, at least, the ads were usually grouped at the beginning/end of TV programs, not at all points between—so you could flee from the intruders the moment they showed up.]

Well, Inger had a name for television trash: *Trashevision.* And there was a name, too, for the sex-and-violence products being churned out by Hollywood producers, who, scrambling to pull people away from their home video sets, were out-trashing Trashevision. Their giant-size contribution: *Giant-Screen Trash.* [And what should people now call internet trash?]

This led to a decidedly unpopular homefront ruling: No movies except those cleared by the censors (Inger and me). And as for Culprit No.1, it was decreed that the boys could watch TV for one hour each school day, two hours a day otherwise. This produced torrents of protests, wheedling and pleading. Especially from Erik, who, I believe, could have spent the rest of his life watching "Star Trek." But Inger made it stick, saying "either that or the TV goes." It stayed...and so did the ruling.

The boys didn't give up all that easily, though—not by a long shot. They tried to use our nextdoor neighbors, the Ericksons, with their four children, to show how unfairly they (Jimmy and Erik) were being treated. To no avail! Inger headed them off by conspiring with Kate, a slender, amazingly helpful lady from England with an iron will, to present a common front. So *det var det!* [that was that] as Inger's doctor cousin in Oslo laments every time one of his patients dies.

We marveled at how fate had brought us such grand neighbors. By purest accident, we moved into a new house in a new neighborhood and, there, right nextdoor, Inger found a permanent, ever-loyal friend in Kate—just as earlier, on Chase Avenue, she had been similarly rewarded with Dottie Breedlove and Edna Sprague...and, still earlier, at the Woodacres Apartments, with Mary Anne Hodge and Nancy Hudson. [Is everyone so fortunate?] So, while Inger thought *herself* lucky, I could think only of how lucky the others were to have found a friend in Inkie. For here was someone who, once a person had proven himself/ herself worthy, would do anything for that person. She never, never knowingly put others at a disadvantage or took advantage of their friendship—despite the common American assumption that "well, that's what friends are for." And she had the absolute, unshakable loyalty to friends that only a Viking in a longboat could feel for his shipmates, or a US

Marine for his fellow Marines.

At the AAR, I found myself working closely with that grand boss, Handly Wright, on a major new railroad campaign seeking equal government treatment of all carriers. Borrowing a leaf from the Whitaker & Baxter PR book, we put a lofty name on our goal: "A Magna Carta for Transportation." There were all kinds of materials to be produced, and the whole AAR by now looked to me to do this kind of demanding work, with my brain frequently working things over all night long when I should have been sleeping. All this to Inger's distress—not to mention my own! But that's what happens, she said, when you *do* and *produce* rather than just talk, like so many others in my field. Unlike the anti-featherbedding effort, however, this one didn't seem to be getting anywhere. And it wasn't just that the truckers, airlines and water carriers weren't about to give up their public policy advantages...and were ganging up on us.

Did the fault, Inger asked innocently, echoing Shakespeare's *Julius Caesar,* lie not in the stars but in *ourselves?*

A revolutionary thought! In truth, railroading was an old industry beset by old ways of doing things, including its lobbying tactics. Decades of tight government controls had bludgeoned its leaders into a cave, where they seldom dared to stick their neck out. They simply weren't up to fighting public battles by using the pressure tactics wielded so effectively by the newer carriers or the "activist" groups—despite the lessons of the anti-featherbedding campaign. They sent well-groomed, polite lawyers up to the Hill to make gentlemanly presentations to sleepy Congressional committees—who then *really* slept...and largely ignored their case. While opponents ran rings around them. So we found that our latest PR train was spinning its wheels and slipping badly as it tried to move the industry up a steep, steep Washington hill.

An unexpected PR ally turned up one day, though...within the AAR itself: Dr. Burton Behling. An expert on political economics, Burt was brought in from the Library of Congress to become our economics vice president. His broader outlook made him a breath of fresh, bracing air. Since I had been working precisely in his field at Whaley-Eaton—reporting on the pocketbook impact of politics—I found him endlessly informative and inspiring when I tackled speeches, articles, etc...and we became close friends. His wife and Inger, too. It was he who put me on to an analysis by a marketing authority that stated clearly one of the railroads' self- inflicted wounds in these singular words:

Railroads let others take customers away from them because they assumed themselves to be in the railroad business rather than in the transportation business. They were PRODUCT-oriented instead of CUSTOMER-oriented.

In other words, running trains wasn't the end-game at all: The end-game was *filling up* those trains...with passengers and freight shipments. And how do you do that? By giving superior service with superior equipment at competitive prices. This the newer carriers did...and grew and grew and grew, while you-know-who languished.

Interestingly, Hollywood almost fell victim to this same brand of marketing myopia that laid the Iron Horse low. Movie producers apparently thought they were in the business of making films for theaters...and almost went under when TV came along. Finally, however, they joined the enemy and began producing films for TV, too. And the money rolled in once more.

Railroad marketing problems were further accentuated by a freight rate structure designed for the days when the lines had a virtual transport monopoly across the country. Prices were set at "whatever the traffic will bear." And high-cost goods bore the highest rates, while bulk shipments got much lower rates—and sometimes below-cost rates. When trucks came along , this neat balance was totally upset by their undercutting the profit-making rail rates and skimming the cream of high-rated traffic right off the top, leaving the lines with lower-rated freight and forcing them into repeated appeals to the ICC to raise these. It was truly like taking candy away from a baby—or, more accurately, like stealing his club from a slumbering giant.

[News coverage of freight rate cases struck me as a classic study in terminology. Few ever wrote or talked about freight rates; it was always *high freight rates*—as though the three words were welded inseparably together...to the public's ever-lasting detriment, of course.]

One good thing came out of the new PR campaign. To give our advertising extra bite, we hired one of the nation's best photographers to spend a week shooting action photos of modern railroad operations around the Northeast. He came back with stunning shots of trains in blurred action that seemed to run right off the page, eye-catching wide-angle views of automated yards, stark silhouettes of "gandy dancers" at work on rights of way. *Grand*! said Inger...but, now, she asked, after their spectacular use in ads, do these treasures just go into a musty file? No way! Handly and I got our heads together and came up with a booklet for distribution to the media, thought leaders and public officials...and we called it *Railroads Unlimited!* So those speeding trains continued to run right off the pages in a much more enduring format.

A "headhunter" phoned one day and gave my career an unexpected boost. The Aerospace Industries Association was looking for a new PR director. Would I be interested? Sure! But I was also reluctant. Inger, too; she didn't even want to think of my leaving such a fine place as the AAR, and such fine people. But why not hear what AIA had to offer?

So I met with the group's president, and negotiations heated up to the point where I decided I had better alert my boss, since I didn't want to leave him hanging out on a limb IF things panned out. For Handly and I worked in tandem: He made the policy decisions in concert with our PR Advisory Committee, coordinated with other AAR executives and kept our budget "sold" to the Board, while I developed materials and worked with PR staffers on day-by-day operations.

How to break the news? I decided I would do it at the distinguished Metropolitan Club, with its long diningroom overlooking 17th street...where, by coincidence, Handly and I were to discuss personnel matters over an already scheduled lunch. When I mentioned the head-hunter and his offer, Handly's normally pleasant expression gave 'way to a deep frown. He reared back in his chair and fixed me with a glassy stare. (I never revealed this secret but, anytime he felt uneasy or threatened, his eyes lost their sharpness and turned downright glassy; meaning *you better watch out!*)

No problem this time, though. Handly posed a couple questions, looked out the window for a long moment, then asked me to delay responding to AIA for a week—leaving me thinking, *well, that was that!* It developed, however, that he simply didn't want to tip his hand. For he went to AAR President Loomis, both went to the Board of Directors and, suddenly, I found myself no long Assistant *to the* Vice President but Assistant Vice President. An EXECUTIVE! Inger was astounded over the change in our fortunes. Twenty years had passed since her meeting with that lowly seaman in the far-off North Atlantic...so maybe, she decided, her crazy decision to join up with him wasn't so crazy after all.

And, most important, now we got to ride even better trains!

[About Washington clubs, news people here like to tell a self-deprecating joke...to the effect that people with money belong to the Metropolitan Club, people with brains belong to the Cosmos Club—and people with neither belong to the Press Club!]

Fate continued to work in strange ways—one day boosting you up, the next day slapping you down. It reminded me of a woodland scene in the Blue Ridge Mountains that I once tried to paint: It was supposed to show a trail winding through the woods, with the unseen sun off to the right-rear providing backlight for two hikers (who just happened to be Inger and Erik). Alas, the finished product didn't come off at all: It was plain dull! But where are the shadows? Inger wanted to know. Ah, hah! So in went dark streaks from the treetrunks to the lower left...and, amazingly, right before our eyes, the whole scene came alive!

Yes, dear Jimmy, Inkie said, just as in life, if you don't experience the dark, how can you ever come to know what light is like?

Some dark streaks were, indeed, looming on the horizon. Major changes were occurring in the rail industry (many of which I myself had been promoting). Mergers were making the biggest railroads bigger. These, in turn, felt they should be handling their own affairs more directly...and relying less on joint action by the many lines through their association in Washington (the AAR). These harbingers of trouble got brushed aside, however, when an invitation came in to me to join the PR directors of Europe's railroads in a seminar on the rail carriers' PR policies. The place: The beautiful resort area of Montecatini, Italy. What an invitation! If there were one place Inger and I wanted to see again after all our traveling, it was Italy. And, suddenly, here was a golden chance to do so. Handly's response? It was generous but enigmatic: "Go ahead. Better do so while you can."

Was there something brewing that he knew but wasn't telling?

As might be expected, Inger and I took the long way to the meeting—via Norway—and got to ride a couple of Europe's finest trains again, all the way from Oslo to northern Italy. There, we met many of the people who had contributed so greatly to our earlier policy mission ...but, this time, in gracious surroundings and under supremely relaxing conditions. One of these men was the conference leader—the PR chief for the Dutch railroads—who opened my eyes to an unusual fact of PR work in the USA with these words:

"You Americans are lucky to be able to use *America* in appealing to public opinion. The word, I mean. You can talk about the United States—just as we in Holland talk about the Netherlands—but that's a geographic entity. *America* is something else. The very word appeals to the soul. It resounds with echoes of a grand past…with hope for the future...with freedom and equality and opportunity…with the dreams of millions of struggling immigrants. We have nothing like that in Europe."

"But can't you use *Europe* itself?" I asked.

"No, that doesn't work at all—not like *America*. Not yet, anyway. We still have too many fences, too many internal rivalries and petty jealousies. One day perhaps...in the far-off future. But that's assuming EU is successful in promoting peace and better living standards."

Special thanks, then, should go to that daring Italian navigator and mapmaker of 500 years ago, Amerigo Vespucci. Because of him, we've come to know the two big Western Hemisphere continents as North and South America—not North and South Columbus. And think of Irving Berlin! A genius in using the speech of everyday people in his lyrics, Berlin wrote his grandest song around the rousing words *God Bless America*—not *God Bless the United States* or *God Bless the USA*. And at the AAR we seldom talked about US railroads. It was almost always AMERICA's railroads, which conveyed quite a different *feel*.

Before the meeting at Montecantini, I had prepared—with Inger's people-oriented, over-the-shoulder input—a talk which bore the title, "A Public Philosophy for Railroads." This summed up the case on reshaping the lines' operations to emphasize service to the public in everything they did, and underscored the basic importance of effective PR action to their future. Upon our return, Handly sent it out to the industry's PR forces with a must-read note. I was puzzled: Why should he go out of his way to be so magnanimous toward me? I soon found out.

Dan Loomis that Fall announced his retirement and was simultaneously replaced as AAR president by a tall, taciturn Pennsylvania road maintenance-of-way engineer who had become president of the Long Island Railroad (a line of somewhat dubious reputation to all living along that system). The new president, a newcomer to Washington, was soon running over cliffs in his brusque dealings with officialdom. He clearly needed PR help. But what was his attitude toward our field? This he displayed when he asked that a speech be written for his use before a shippers' group. It was no big occasion. I put a draft together and sent it to his office...and, boom! it came back with a cryptic note: "Re-do—no punch!" Turned out he wanted humor—lots of jokes. So I got together with our Dr. Tom Sinclair, a veritable repository of quips and quotes, and inserted a selection into draft No. 2. Boom! This came back, too. Seems what the new chief really wanted was bedroom, bathroom and barroom jokes. So, against any PR man's better judgment, these were, indeed, inserted—but the News Service was told to lay off any public distribution of text, press releases, etc.

The new president shortly moved to retire Handly and install his own PR director—a move that Handly seemed to expect. So the industry's PR Advisory Committee was called into session and asked to endorse his change: This was to be his own PR man from the LIRR. And what did these PR directors from the major railroads do? The unthinkable! These grand people whom I had long worked with, *skaal*ed with and rode the rails with—who had never disagreed with their autocratic bosses on much of anything—*rejected* the new president's pick...and, instead, amazingly, shockingly, recommended me. They urged that *I* become the AAR's new vice president of public relations.

A grand gesture of respect and camaraderie! Inger called it.

But also a death sentence, I moaned—my stomach churning, my eyeballs turning red and my nerves in tatters. I felt down and out...for the count.

The situation had a Kafkaesque, nightmarish quality about it. It was impossible for me to succeed to a position which the new president had opened up specifically for someone else.

I also felt it would be difficult—maybe impossible, too—to work with a new boss under the circumstances which my industry peers had posed. So, my rail career derailed in mid-journey after 15 eventful years, I decided I had no alternative but to resign. Inger, however, wisely stopped me cold...virtually on my way to the front office.

"Without a job, you're a nobody," she said. "You have no bargaining power. Employers think that because you're out of work, there's something wrong with you—NOT with your last employer. Much better to grin and bear it...*and* the new VP. And start looking around on the side...*quietly!*"

Ol' pal Joe Keeley of the *Legion Magazine* agreed but put his advice more succinctly:

"Don't...do NOT!...*never* leap until you see where you're gonna land."

The new president showed some understanding of my situation, in any event. I asked to see him shortly after this debacle since, to add to our difficulties, word came that my father had just died in Detroit. [Mom died while I was out of touch deep inside Russia.] Dad had contracted a bad case of bronchitis and his Christian Science wife wouldn't call in a doctor or provide simple medicines like antibiotics...so, despite being a strong, youthful 72, he literally coughed himself to death. Dad always wanted to be buried next to his own father in the lonely, windswept hilltop cemetery on the north side of the Ohio River overlooking Huntington, W.Va. Inger and I needed a week to get to Detroit, move the casket onto a train, travel with it to Huntington and make local funeral arrangements. The new president readily granted my request. He told me his own father had recently died and expressed sincere sympathy. He then added that he understood I was "disappointed" [and how!] over the staffing change in our PR department, and declared:

"If you want to get ahead, Jim, do a good job. Let people see that you're worth promoting...and they'll respond. That's the way to do that. Yes, *that's* the way to do that."

Startled, incredulous, I just stared. *But, Mr. President,* I felt like saying, *what the hell do you think I've been doing the past 15 years?!? Who did all that work on the anti-featherbedding campaign? Who spent a year reporting on foreign transport policies? Who's now spearheading the Magna Carta PR effort?*

Ever after, when something happened that required the most obvious kind of reaction, Inger and I would say: *THAT'S the way to do that.* It was the new boss's signature statement.

Job hunting must be one of the worst forms of torture known to man, especially when you're 44 years old. I immediately ran head-on into the sad fact that few wanted to hire someone that old. So there you stand—too old to get a job but too young to roll over and die. Ah, but doesn't experience and ability still count? The answer is *yes, but*—a very big BUT. Over the next two months I got two job offers from well-meaning friends who wanted me as their aide (meaning I would do the hard work!): One was the PR vice president of the mighty Pennsylvania Railroad—the other, the chief speechwriter at IBM. In both cases, though, my would-be boss and I found out, unbelievably, that I was already making more money than those hiring me. The answer, of course, was for my friends to use this cockeyed situation as an opportune way to get a big fat raise for *them*—but, alas, they feared to exert such leverage.

A big break then came in the form of an invitation to meet with one of the nation's largest PR firms, A Public Relations Company (APRC).[1] The firm wanted to overhaul its Washington office and was thinking of me as THE guy to do it. Why me? The back-story proves you better be good to the mailroom boy, for you never know when he'll become your boss. A regional railroad group had hired APRC years before to rally public support for governmental policy changes in its area. The rest of the industry didn't like the APRC activist-like approaches, however, so the AAR was compelled to steer clear of involvement. I never felt this included personal help on my part, though. I admired what APRC was trying to do on behalf of the railroads (wasn't every other alert group in the country using public pressure on government the same way?). So whenever the APRC account executive assigned to

---

[1]APRC is not the actual name of the firm. The name has been changed, as publishers often say, "to protect the innocent."

the rail group or his associates came to me for information and other help, I gladly provided it. And, now, obviously, they hadn't forgotten....

Inger and I met with APRC executives at their offices near the East River in New York—particularly with the firm's heavy-set, smart, authoritative, personable-yet-not-sticky Chairman, who never spoke except with the utmost confidence in his viewpoints. We liked what we saw, even though we noted several shifty-eyed types hovering in the building's wings. And we liked especially the idea of working with the firm's roster of 40-plus blue-ribbon clients—mainly big corporations and associations—and becoming deeply involved in their Washington policy problems. Here was truly a much wider stage to act on!

Employment terms were then hammered out. I had ferreted out what APRC was paying the outgoing Washington office manager— darn little! Yet, Inger cautioned against our asking for too much more. So we wound up suggesting that APRC match my present salary, with The Chairman promising (in writing) to add on another $5,000. after one year, assuming all went well with my stewardship of the Washington office. This was fine with me, for I didn't mind facing up to the additional challenge. What I failed to understand at that time was that, whatever the salary level you get in such a firm, *you have to earn it yourself*...either by bringing in new clients or by creating new charges against present clients. And this requires convincing a lot of tight-fisted people that *your* services are worth the extra $$$$ they must shell out.

The system is downright Mephisthophelean. And *that* I came to learn...soon enough!

Arrival at my new office on the second floor of the National Press Building was set for March 16. Before, though, some loose ends had to be tied up at AAR—ongoing projects, of course, but also the matter of severance pay. The new PR VP was plenty irritated about my leaving; it meant that he himself would have to go to work instead of smoking his pipe and blowing smoke rings all day. As for vacation pay, if I had stayed on till June 1, I would have received four weeks' full pay. But it was now March, so New VP lit up (his pipe), quibbled, backed and filed and quibbled some more. My years of all-out service evidently meant nothing to him. Nor did those lush severance packages executives were getting elsewhere. His attitude: *Too bad*! So I told him to forget the whole issue and walked away, never to meet again.

[Harking back to my seafaring days, I came to put the scoundrels I met in life—and they were not few—into three categories of scoundrelness, depending on their "merits": Bastards, dirty bastards and filthy bastards. Inger didn't like these terms at all; in fact, she couldn't stand any kind of obscenity. Even so, she had to admit it was sometimes necessary to call a spade a spade—not to mention a mouse a rat.]

The boys in our mailroom developed their own method of showing their displeasure at the change in PR leadership. As you know, there are two ways to abbreviate "association"—*Assn.* and *Assoc.* People sometimes got carried away, however, and used *Ass.* So, in all cases where mail was addressed to "The Ass. of American Railroads," it went as straight as a prairie rail-line to the new PR chief!

March 16 is a date we came to remember well, for I'm right now looking at a handsome pen set that my new employer presented with that date inscribed on the mounting. But light years more to the point, it was also the date of the My Lai Massacre in Vietnam...and, though the news was suppressed for a year, it finally sent the US anti-war movement off like a rocket. That same month of March, President Johnson announced he would not seek re-election. Then, on April 4 Martin Luther King, the shining advocate alongside Mahatma Ghandi of peaceful pressure for peaceful change, was shot down in Memphis, Tennessee...and fires broke out all over the nation's capital. From the Press Club on the 13th floor of the Press Building at 14th & F Streets, NW, ominous columns of black smoke could be seen wherever I looked. This in America's national capital—in *Washington!*

There was no question about it: I had one helluva tough new job on my hands....

Chapter VII

Vice President in Charge of the Washington Office, APRC.

Oh, what a nice ring that has! said Inger.

Yes, but if you listen closely, I responded, you'll notice it's giving off a somewhat hollow sound.

The problem, obvious from the first day behind my new desk, was that this wasn't ever meant to be a cushy PR executive position, where subordinates do all the work while you drift around glad-handing important people and enjoying long lunches. Not at all! You, James, are going to be a *working* executive. Or more accurately, a working stiff.

Right off the bat, the nation's race/urban crisis began bringing frantic queries from clients into the office about what the Federal government would now do...and how this would affect business and APRC clients, in particular. Phones were ringing. People were dashing in and out. The whole place was jumping. Meanwhile, I had to get my bearings. Where was everyone going? And what was I supposed to do to help people get there?

The position was, by nature, centered in the eye of a hurricane of sorts. On one hand were over 40 client companies, including myriad client executives at their headquarters and their Washington offices. Plus the APRC account executives (AE) assigned to these clients and the half-dozen top executives at APRC-NYC, who divided up the roles of account supervisor (AS). On the other hand was the great sweep of Washington that I was supposed to relate these clients to, depending on the individual needs of each—Congress, the Executive departments and regulatory agencies, the big lobby groups, the Washington press, "think tanks," etc, etc. And to accomplish all this I inherited a staff of three professionals, a secretary and a receptionist/typist.

It was a ticklish situation, rife with possibilities of stepping on sensitive toes. For instance, you never, never contacted a client without going through the APRC AE and/or AS. And if a client happened to contact you directly, you turned around promptly and informed the responsible APRC people. *Coordination* was the name of the game. All this because *money* was the ultimate game. Each of my office's three PR pros was required to come up with at least 40 hours of chargeable time against clients each week. Me, too. This meant we had to have the best of all possible relations with the AE's, since it was they who approved all actions and resulting charges from all of APRC's half-dozen branch offices, including that in Washington.

So I set out to get acquainted (well!) with these 40-plus PR people, as well as with their AS's (no pun intended) at APRC-NYC. This called for an initial week at New York City headquarters for meetings and briefings on who's-who and what's-what at all the clients.

Besides long talks with The Chairman (also known as "Chair") and The President (a.k.a."Prez"), I went over the firm's myriad internal operating details with a genial, soft-spoken "nice guy" who was executive vice president in charge of APRC branch offices (a.k.a. "Exec") and who was to be my main contact with headquarters. Besides sitting down with most of the AE's, one by one, I then met two standout "department" chiefs: The attractive, sharp-witted head of our radio/TV department, plus a clever wordsmith who had written a handy stylebook and who served as no-nonsense copy editor for all materials distributed to the press. The latter bestowed an autographed copy of his book on me, urging attention to all its commands. I weighed it carefully, not quite sure whether to embrace it or discard it. I was used to the *New York Times* stylebook...but you've got to adjust, no?

Clients, the AE's told me, hired APRC for many separate reasons—and shelled out their money accordingly. Most came in during emergencies (product problems, community unrest, strikes, government pressure, etc.), the same way you go to a doctor when sick or to a lawyer when sued. Afterward, they often stuck around for general counseling as a backstop to their own PR efforts. Others wanted help with the financial/ investment community. Another needed help with product promotion and marketing. One client was unique: APRC people served as the company's entire PR department, with their offices inside corporate headquarters.

It was revealing that no one, however, had hired APRC specifically to get help in Washington. I got the distinct impression that the Chairman and crew were all looking to me to change this situation. Quite an order!

I also wasted no time getting to know each client's Washington rep. At Inger's suggestion (smart gal!), I then made get-acquainted visits to many of our competitors, including the local head of the country's leading PR counseling firm, Hill & Knowlton. This PR executive struck us as being in the impression business. That is, he would meet a client at the airport with his chauffeur-driven limousine, whisk him/her into a meeting with a congressmen on the Hill and an assistant secretary downtown, then have dinner at some fancy restaurant peopled by Washington *kjendiser* [celebrities]. And, oh, was the client ever impressed! Public opinion or governmental action seldom if ever got changed in this process...but that didn't seem to matter.

One thing that did matter was that heavy anchor of required client charges. This was draped around my neck like the rail featherbedding campaign albatross. And... surprise!...I found myself spending most of my time on APRC business, which was *non-chargeable!* The Chairman, who owned over 90 per cent of the firm and ran it not just for fun, took the blunt position: That's *your* problem, Jim! And if you don't solve it, it's *farvel! adios! sayonara!*

Well, we had one weapon: The Washington office published a weekly newsletter that went to all APRC people *as well as* selected client executives. This was right down my alley (remember my tour with the *Whaley-Eaton Newsletters*?), and I proceeded to upgrade its style and content—telegraphing to one and all that big changes were now afoot in the Washington office. In it we could mention the host of reports coming out of GPO, Congress and private organizations...and chalk up modest changes against clients who requested these. Press placements, personal client services and queries for government information were also coming in regularly over the transom from AE's—which I channeled to staffers to help them "make their hours." Sadly, though, all this left *me* sitting high and dry, earnings-wise, wallowing on the shore like a boat after the tide has run out.

It's a strange crisis that doesn't contain opportunity, however hard to detect. But Inger detected it! She wondered out loud what an executive at a major company would want to know about the many new national problems pressing in on business...and the kind of information he would need to adjust to them. And shouldn't APRC be providing this kind of guidance to him and other clients? Yes, absolutely! The Chairman agreed...*go to it!* So Inger and I began by listing the insistent demands for change arising across America and focusing on Washington action centers:

• Environmental activists were gaining expertise and clout in pressuring government to legislate and enforce reductions in air, water and ground pollution.

• Consumer activists were mounting major campaigns for safer products, meaningful warranties and a fuller, franker flow of information to the consuming public.

• Race groups were stepping up pressure for education and employment equality, minority business aid and a greater share of our vaunted economic system's benefits. (Blacks were also cashing in on new political leverage in the big cities, where their concentration was giving them control over both City Hall and many urban congressional districts.)

• The women's liberation movement was clamoring for better positions and equal pay for equal work. (Women, too, were gaining political and business clout, finally using the voting power accruing to their numbers—more than half the population—and pressing their role as dominant consumers and major stockholders.)

• Antiwar groups were mounting wider forays against defense contractors and demanding a "reordering" of national priorities.

• Bombings and violence were being increasingly used by homegrown terrorists to disrupt business as well as the whole society. (Inger abhorred these tactics; yet one of their rallying cries that struck a chord with her was what they called the spreading "depersonalization" of American society that was coming with accelerating technological change. She thought *dehumanization* was a more fitting word.)

In short, our trouble-shooting indicated that old living patterns were being shaken...*hard*...and that business managers trained in production, finance and marketing were having one difficult time operating on this tough new public battleground. *And* an even worse time responding to its Washington implications and pressures for broad new levels of government intervention. Graduates of the Harvard Business School and its imitators simply had no case studies on dealing with this inside-out operating environment. It was hard for them and their lawyer cronies to grasp that the first thing Washington thinks of when issues arise is *the state of public opinion*...and how people will react to a given position. This seemed almost the *last* thing businessmen considered. The result: A gradual, inexorable expansion of government and a whittling away of the private enterprise system. Indeed, the very survival of business was at stake. Not to mention the survival of the nation.

Overdrawn? Inger and I didn't think so. That June, Bobby Kennedy was gunned down in Los Angeles. Coming on top of the assassination of Martin Luther King (*plus* that of President Jack Kennedy earlier) and the growing Vietnam mess, the nation went into shock. Public confidence in our system went into free-fall. And confidence is the ultimate X-factor in the economy's entire functioning. We feared that activist pressure, unless kept within reasonable bounds, could lead to unmanageable demands being placed on the nation's productive system, with pyramiding costs and taxes leading to accelerating inflation, loss of world markets and disruptions in the way people work and live. *The center cannot hold,* Irish poet W. B. Yeats warned in another context.

The result could only be still further governmental intervention and take-over of private functions—and Inger and I had seen what that could lead to overseas. Forceful action was clearly needed to calm the situation and restore people's beliefs in our country and its institutions...and Inger and I hoped to contribute our small bit to reaching that goal.

Many of these points were summed up in a speech I was cajoled by The Chairman into making to a communications conference in St. Louis. Groping around for an arresting title, I turned to Inger...who had just been reading Alvin Toffler's jarring book, *Future Shock*. Why not call it what it is? she said, pinning down the obvious in her own perceptive way. How about *Washington Harbingers of Future Shock...?* As it turned out, the talk was widely reprinted—without a doubt largely because of this title.

With Inger using her librarian talents to dig up materials and pinning down the top authorities in each of the major issue areas we had listed, I proceeded to write a lengthy analysis on each, beginning with consumer action developments. This took the better part of a week for each—three days for talking with sources and sifting through the mountain of materials Inger had gathered, a day for writing and a final day for rewriting with Ink's help. Besides the normal information contacts, this got me closely involved with the Urban Coalition, the League of Cities, NAACP, the Public Affairs Council and virtually every major trade association and lobbyist in Washington, plus think tanks like Brookings and Heritage.

We churned out six of these major-issue reports at the rate of one per month—each roughly equivalent to a *Fortune Magazine* article but with more pointed, *useful* information. [How much really useful information do you get from regular reporting?] Before doing these, I got a dozen of APRC's most active clients to agree to contribute X hours in payment for each. This not only solved the horrific problem of "making hours" but it also established myself (and my silent partner, Ink) as *the* source clients could turn to for inside information in pressing issue areas. (Actually, the information wasn't very "inside." But who else was compiling and personally interpreting it for such a select readership?) As a result, requests for help and invitations to meet with client managements at their headquarters started coming in.

Even the doubting Chairman began to take notice. He started visiting Washington regularly, with the two of us beginning the day with a 7:30 a.m. breakfast meeting [can anyone possibly be alert at such an hour?]. This took place in his rooms at the Carlton Hotel on 16th Street, a couple blocks from the White House. The main topic: How to turn APRC's new Capital visibility into new clients (AND new $$$$ for The Chairman). And *that* I had no ready answer to.

Isn't that your bailiwick, Mr. Chairman? I asked. No answer. Pleasant, productive meetings, they were...where I came to understand that this subject was one *very* serious matter.

That sweltering month of August, Soviet forces invaded Czechoslovakia and put an end to the brief "Prague Spring" and the Czechs' longing for freedom from communist oppression. It was Hungary all over again ...and Inger and I reacted with the same sense of anger and frustration. Acting almost on instinct, she and I walked across the street from my Press Building office to the stately old Willard Hotel and joined the press team working on the ground floor there to elect Richard M. Nixon president. Yes, *Nixon*! By the sheer magic of not giving up, he had resurrected himself from his dramatic defeat by Jack Kennedy in 1960 and the subsequent setback in his run for governor of California...and was back in business at the same old stand. Inger didn't like my involvement in the 1968 campaign any more than she liked politics and most politicians. But looking at Vietnam and the explosive worldwide Cold War scene, we felt there *had* to be a change in US leadership.

As it turned out, my own contribution to the campaign, made on Saturdays and a couple hours on scattered evenings, was immeasurably minor. It consisted mainly of putting my feet up on old, beat-up desks at the Willard and shooting the breeze with "the gang." Yet, that's how I came to meet Nixon's communications guru, the immensely able, likable Herb Klein, and numerous others who would shortly be big names around Washington.

Next came the inevitable: When the Nixon-Agnew ticket romped to victory that Fall, I was asked if I would like to join the new team in trying to manage the unmanageable—the Federal government. It was an idle question in a way. As Inger knew all too well, the more informed I became, the more my views on public policies had been shifting gradually toward the conservative side. (It was also farewell to my radical views from Wayne!) My new-found pals agreed that my overseas experience and interest in propaganda warfare made me a natural for the US Information Agency. Nor would that magical Eisenhower name-connection hurt. But, alas, in my home voting district of Montgomery County, Md., Inger and I were registered as "declines"—meaning we had declined to state a party preference.

An *independent!* Upon this revelation mouths flew open among my erstwhile partners in politics. Talk ceased. Throats were cleared. The ceiling was carefully studied. Handshakes were exchanged. And Inger and I left the beloved Willard and returned to my APRC offices.

Another postscript: In 1971, Dr. James Fletcher, the distinguished head of the University of Utah, came to town as the new Administrator of NASA, the US space agency. He wanted a PR professional to serve as Assistant Administrator for Public Affairs...and political affiliation didn't matter. So Herb Klein arranged for the two of us to get together. We met twice: Once to hear his ideas on NASA and how communications could contribute toward its goals, the second time to tender my withdrawal.

"Why?" asked a surprised Inger: "Aren't you interested in tackling important challenges? And isn't NASA important?"

Well, that wasn't exactly the point. Despite the worldwide excitement the year before of Neil Armstrong and the other astronauts landing on the moon, neither Inger nor I could bring ourselves to be all that interested in space exploits. And still can't. We were, and are, much more concerned about the acute problems here on earth. And feel taxpayer dollars should be allocated accordingly.

John Gardner and his Urban Coalition soon gave us an unusual chance to express that concern. The National Advisory Commission on Civil Disorders (the Kerner Commission) had issued a report in 1968 showing the nation to be badly divided between the races—one part white, one part black. A year later the Coalition and others came out with an analysis on what America had achieved since in terms of eliminating discrimination—a report called simply "One Year Later." By coincidence APRC's Chairman became president of PRSA that year, so the information director of the Coalition, Brian Duff, got in touch with me to see if PRSA and APRC could combine with the Coalition in a public service campaign to publicize the report. Many meetings later, I found myself named director of a national task force based on Washington and New York and including both national and local elements of the involved organizations—one monstrously complicated coordinating job! But it somehow came off. Solid materials were prepared and personally placed with editors across the nation, capped off by a news conference spectacular at the National Press Club featuring John Gardner and other national leaders. Press coverage exceeded all expectations.

Everyone, even The Chairman, seem impressed. Especially since his powerful inaugural speech as PRSA president urged everyone to join in building bridges across the nation's ominous race divide.

Great! my ever-questioning wife exclaimed...but did all this activity do anything to promote real racial integration?

Well, after all the long, hard days I had put into this effort, I felt like choking her. But the honest answer was, *no, not so's you could notice*—at least not right here and now. Overcoming ages-old discrimination seems to take ages. [Now, 40 years later, you can see that demonstrable progress *has* been made. And more is on the way?]

Inger's views on race, like everything else, were affected by her feelings...and particularly by two extraordinary black people in our lives—Maggie and Marie. Each in turn had been engaged to help once a week with housework and the boys, and their sensitivity and compassion made them the closest friends. Inger loved them! Maggie, rotund like the pancake flour's Aunt Jemima and with a smile as big as South Carolina (where she hailed from) entered the picture first. When Erik, at age three, first saw her, his eyes grew wide and he said in awe, "Maggie *moerk*!" [Maggie's dark!] But what a feeling of security she gave us all. And what is more important to children? Like Inger, the boys grew to love her over the next 12 years...until the day she returned to her Carolina home to minister to her family and neighbors *as a minister*—with our aging blue Plymouth as Inger's farewell present.

Deeply religious, Maggie proved a veritable angel in helping Inger pull through the loss of our two babies. After the second death, I helped Maggie out the frontdoor with her "tote" and stopped to watch her going up Ogden Court to the bus stop. Her head bent, shuffling along in dark clothes under dark skies, she looked the ultimate symbol of sorrow. With her deep sense of empathy, she was, in fact, experiencing Inger's sorrow almost as much as Inger herself. *Bless you, Maggie!*

Then came Marie, who for years became the indispensable aide to Inger in preparing the most delicious foods and serving at the many dinners we began holding at home for clients, government officials and news people. Truth is, she helped make my wife a true Washington "hostess with the mostest." Both Marie and Ink fit into their roles perfectly. (The dinners were fun, but oh, what hard work!) When Marie's daughter got married later in suburban Maryland, Inger and I attended the wedding—a big one—with our white faces the only ones in sight. Inger, however, was truly color blind. She hadn't grown up in our part-white, part-black society and didn't have one iota of racial prejudice. She judged people strictly on their merits...as Marie and Maggie came to know so well.

One incident that endeared Marie to my wife occurred during an evening with friends and neighbors...when Pappa sang a number of songs, accompanied by Mamma on the piano. Marie had music in her soul, and was *enthralled!* And never stopped saying so.

Inger's parents returned to Norway a short time later, along with her, to celebrate Pappa's 80th birthday, which became something of a national event. Erling Krogh had been singing for over a half-century and had performed in every town and village from one end of the land to the other...and had come to occupy a special place in people's hearts. But it wasn't just operatic roles that did this; it was his singing and recording of hundreds of Norwegian folk songs and popular melodies that really endeared him to the nation. He had become to Norway what Jussi Bjoerling was to Sweden and Lauritz Melchoir was to Denmark. Only more so. For while those two became better known *outside* their countries, Pappa had become better known *inside*. And what counts more? Yet, the celebration was perhaps too much for Pappa; two months later he died of a heart attack, and the great voice was stilled forever.

[Not in his records, however. They're getting scratchy, but Inger now sits with glistening eyes, more enthralled than even Marie was, and plays them on all occasions...and often on no occasion at all. I knew she was not just hearing and feeling Pappa's singing; she was actually *there* beside him. She was, is, and always will be...his admiring fan No. 1. What a daughter!]

On the tomb of a pharaoh of ancient Egypt are carved these words: *To speak his name is to make him live again.*

So it became with Pappa. He had a sure, calming touch...and even at her Ornery Troll orneryest, Inger became gentle as a lamb around him. She cited him so often as *the* authority on every conceivable thing that, when anything came up, we would ask jokingly: *Fortel oss, Inger, hva ville Pappa ha sagt om dette?* [Tell us, Inger, what would Pappa have said about this?] So now I also wonder as I write these words that make him live again, *Hva ville Pappa ha sagt om denne fortellingen?* [No translation needed!]

The APRC Chairman had some of the same sure touch as Pappa. When he talked PR, I listened with both ears...whether it was during our private sessions, around clients or at staff meetings. Inger, too, begin to take notes. It now became, *What would The CHAIRMAN say?* He made sense out of a field that was filled with public misconceptions. Not even business executives who hired PR counseling firms seemed to grasp what PR could do for them—not to mention what it could *not* do. Many thought PR was simply press agentry or slick image-making. Others considered it in league with the world's oldest profession (!). Still others felt they could plunder their firms and hatchet employees, stockholders and customers at will and then use PR to whitewash their foul deeds. Carl Byoir, a no-nonsense pioneer of PR, long ago set such people straight in these blunt words:

You cannot whitewash a manure heap; the smell WILL come through.

Trying to explain the often inexplicable to others, Inger and I harked back to Colonel Henry, Al Beatty and Handly Wright and combined their wise comments with The Chairman's and came up with these guideposts through the public relations forest:

• *Do well and make it well known.* This is the simplest PR formula of all. Yet, how hard it was to get across to many executives the essential point that doing well has to come FIRST!

• Robert Burns perhaps said it even better: *Oh wad some Power the giftie gie us...to see ourselves as ithers see us! It wad frae monie a blunder free us."*

• Or you could paraphrase Ralph Waldo Emerson's warning: *What you are speaks so loudly I cannot hear what you are saying.*

• PR is like shooting an ingenious gun at the public: The kick back against the shoulder has as much effect as what comes out of the muzzle. It's main effect is thus often *internal*—within the organization seeking to practice sound PR. In short, there's no easy way to reap public understanding and support. You have to *earn* it. And you earn it by putting your own house in order and making sure your actions accord with the public's interest. That's the tough part, we tell people in trouble (who seldom like to hear such advice). The easier part is something PR people can then handle—*communicating* the new reality.

• "Preventive PR" is the best medicine. That is, PR should be in on the take-offs as well as on the crash landings. And if it is, there'll be fewer of the latter.

• Talking to the public is like speaking to a passing parade. He who decides to rest on his laurels—his past achievements—soon finds he's not getting across to the new contingents coming along...and steadily loses ground in terms of public awareness and support.

• Modern communications is a message madness—like living in a steel drum, with all kinds of people banging on the lid. Your message must be made unusual, dramatic or appealing—or *delivered* dramatically—to have any real chance of getting through and achieving impact.

• Communications is a two-way process. If adequate steps are not taken to "put yourself in the other guy's shoes" and elicit receiver response or feedback—and to reshape your communications accordingly—your efforts can be as futile as sending signals into outer space.

• In controversies, don't allow opposition forays to control strategy. Flagrant errors and distortions should be corrected...but remember that responses often merely give accusations and errors wider circulation. Pursue your own goals and mobilize your friends and allies—and if you have enough and can mobilize them effectively, you can virtually ignore your enemies.

• The ultimate Chairmanism: Never give free advice; it's simply not appreciated. *Charge* for it! If people have to pay for advice, they listen carefully. And the more they have to pay, the harder they'll listen...and the more likely they'll be to *act* on your advice.

• And perhaps most important of all: PR isn't something you buy like a new machine or an office building or put on like a mask. It comes out in the way you *behave*—in what you *are* and what you *do*. It's a personal and organization philosophy—a way of life. *Live it!*

Public relating in Washington is different from any other place,

Inger and I found out from my first job here. Not only because you're often dealing with government and matters of broad public interest, but also because you're surrounded by one of the most sophisticated and aggressive press corps anywhere. Chances for falling on your face are unlimited!

Washington also operates much more on *perception* than on fact. [Like PR?] Here is a whole smorgasbord of smokescreens, red herrings, mirrors and sleight-of-hand tricks. Here is *the* place that defies a basic law of physics—where sound truly travels faster than light. Indeed, politics—America's *real* national sport—is probably the purest perception game of all.

At the request of the PRSA Counselors Section, Inger and I wrote a paper on this subject which begins with this take-off on Julius Caesar's immortal commentaries:

All Washington is divided into three parts regarding public action in this wonderworld: Government, special interest groups and the communications media. And while popular attention focuses on government leaders as the major agents of Washington action, capital insiders know it is, rather, the INTERACTION among these three elements that leads to the big decisions.

We went on to raise this warning flag:

It therefore follows that those who would influence the course of the Washington drama must deal with the TOTAL cast of characters. Yet, especially in the case of business, lobbying year after year gets the emphasis (and the money). And each new year sees the private enterprise system a little closer to total government control than the year before.

It has always struck us as downright weird that executives simply cannot seem to grasp the fact that government issues are seldom decided on their objective merits but, instead, on the basis of their political implications and their interplay with public opinion. *And* that they must deal with such issues accordingly. Our paper concluded with a general, absolutely essential rule:

If you cannot build a convincing case that what you want is in the public interest, FORGET IT!

PR seldom gets credit for this aspect but, at its best, it is an unusual, useful, needed problem-solving mechanism. Inger and I have been called into many crisis situations, where you must, first, analyze the nature and causes of the crisis (which often differ from what those who are involved *say* they are), then come up with a plan of remedial actions on the clients' part, coupled with a decisive communications program targeting these actions at crisis centers. Developing creative materials, administering the program, making essential arrangements and contacting people are other essential parts of such an action program. Oddly enough, though, in doing all this, you also develop a wonderfully constructive and rewarding problem-solving approach to everyday problems—to life itself. *Thanks, PR!*

So how do you put PR guidelines to work in a major problem area? We got a chance to show that in 1970 when the US Information Agency, then directed by Frank Shakespeare, called to ask if I would be interested in joining a USIA inspection team as a "public member" on a mission to Sweden. It was a difficult time. Olaf Palme, that nation's prime minister, was denouncing the USA day after day for our involvement in Vietnam...and stirring up worldwide opposition. That we were trying to stop communist take-over of that country, and possibly others in Southeast Asia, apparently didn't get across to him. Yet, the mission's main concern was the state of public opinion *within* Sweden itself, and the ways USIA was dealing with that.

Would Inger like to go along, too? What a question! She had already packed our bags....

The USIA team of three senior officers spent the assigned two weeks at the US Embassy in Stockholm while Inger and I visited editors and non-government organizations around the country. We wanted to get a feel for how people at the grassroots level felt about America and our policies. And what we found, surprisingly, was that Palme wasn't all that popular inside his own country. In fact, he seemed to be getting more attention outside the country than within... and there remained a big reservoir of good will toward the US. Even so, we came up with a long list of recommendations urging more emphasis on people-to-people contacts to shore up resistance against Palme's tirades—through Swedish-American groups, labor unions, business and trade, etc. It was another case of recognizing that while nothing overt could be done about the trouble-maker himself, a lot of good could be done about mobilizing friends as an offset.

It was also a treat to visit Sweden again, plus old railroad contacts like Svenska Jernvagar's Malcolm Bjoerkman, stay at the cozy Esplanade Hotel on Strandvagan, tour Stockholm's colorful waterfront and ride SJ's superlative trains. Most Norwegians, I've discovered, consider Swedes stiff and formal. Yet, Inger and I never found them anything but receptive and helpful—as they were this time, too.

Danes, we've also discovered, are considered pleasant on the outside but hard as granite inside. As Inger's Mamma could well tell you!

And how do Swedes and Danes look at Norwegians? As people who are friendly, naive, somewhat out of date...and with a wide wild streak. This allegedly comes out in the way they drive (think head-on collisions), charge down skislopes, race speedboats, drink until all bottles are empty, etc. And now that they're swimming in high-priced oil, they're labeled "the blue-eyed Arabs." Yet, terrorists they're not!

Back in the USA, I got a call from the USIA's Shakespeare indicating he would like to discuss my report. Ah ha! I thought—maybe Inger's and my efforts would do some good after all. But what was Frank mainly interested in? My feelings about the personnel at the USIS post! Specifically, who was worth promoting. And that's how my brief fling at diplomacy ended. The public affairs director and cultural affairs adviser got our warm recommendation—and that, we trust, helped boost them a bit up the career ladder.

Vietnam! A foreign name, a distant place, hell on earth for those who fought there, one of the darkest, saddest chapters in American history. And now this horror was coming to rest right on our doorstep. Jimmy graduated from Haverford and was accepted at Georgetown University Law School, one of the finest in the country and, fortunately, located in Washington. He had a fairly high draft number, but the threat grew daily that he would be inducted into one of the Armed Services and sent to that jungle hellhole. Inger, like US mothers of vulnerable sons everywhere, was appalled at the prospect. Which is putting it mildly. And even more so since Erik was graduating from Sidwell Friends Highschool and was coming up for the same fate. Both were over six feet tall, strong, healthy and *eligible....*

Meanwhile, this national nightmare was bringing death and injury to thousands. It was literally tearing our society apart and injecting a strain of poison into the bloodsteam of our relations with other nations. America had stuck all four limbs into this disastrous tar baby, and the Kremlin could hardly contain its glee as we struggled in vain to pull loose. Inger and the rest of us bled over the deaths being suffered and the torment this brought into thousands of homes across the country...and over Washington's hapless approach to getting out of this quagmire.

Unlike the highly vocal segment of the public that came to dominate national debate on Vietnam, Inger and I felt that America *should* take up this struggle to prevent communist enslavement of more millions. Hadn't we seen firsthand what that meant? In Poland, Hungary, Czechoslovakia, in Russia itself? I for one also believed that once committed to battle, we should do what's necessary to *win*. As a wartime merchant seaman, I saw Vietnam as essentially a supply war, and argued openly for a total blockade of Haiphong and all other ports in the north and destruction of all vulnerable transport facilities up to the China border. Why not stop the pipeline of communist war materiel at its source, NOT with our soldiers' bodies at the southern end? Why not make it as difficult as possible for the communist killers to kill?

Obviously, we weren't winning any popularity contest with such views. People countered that such actions wouldn't really stop the flow of supplies southward, and a blockade might lead to an atomic war with Russia. We considered both arguments a lot of bunk, along with the liberals' view that Hanoi's leaders were benign unifiers of a tragically divided nation. We re-echoed Churchill's long-ago warning that communists respect only strength and *the will to use that strength*. I also felt a deep moral issue was involved: That if America is to ask *any* American to die for a cause—in effect, to have the world end for that one person—then the whole nation should be prepared to take the same risk, by blockade or whatever.

As things turned out, nothing like this was ever done...while the flow of war supplies southward from China and from the Soviet Union through Haiphong became a torrent. Inger agonized endlessly over the downhill course of events. Had she abandoned her own country and raised two sons in this new land only to have them die in some desolate jungle half a world away? In a god-forsaken war that no one seemed to understand or support? She talked and talked with Jimmy and Erik, who, like everyone else, understood nothing of what was going on. Then came the day of relief: President Nixon and Foreign Secretary Henry Kissinger finally took everyone off the spot, using massive bombing of the north to force Hanoi into a "settlement."

[Within two years, the communists tore up this agreement and took over South Vietnam, leading to the mass exodus of "boat people"—mainly to the US. Ironically, this has proved the one prize worth winning in an international catastrophe second to none. Including Iraq?]

The uproar over Vietnam within the USA, focused as it was so heavily on Washington, perversely enough strengthened my role with APRC...for all eyes turned to our political leaders' actions. (Hints of the Watergate crisis were also being turned up regularly by the *Washington Post* and getting wide attention.) I found ourselves handling a barrage of client questions relating to government, as well as responding to numerous invitations to make presentations and compete in getting new clients. This created a need for more home entertainment (another load on Inger!) and this, in turn, led us to move from our split-level house in Bethesda to a larger, more distinctive house a mile away...in the Kenwood area of Chevy Chase.

Inger considered entertaining at home the absolute bane of working in Washington: It was not only hard work; it was also nervewracking. You put together a balanced list of guests—then, almost invariably, someone had to drop out because of a political crisis, leaving a big hole at the dining table. Or politics entered along with the guests. One night Herb Klein came to dinner, then spent most of the evening on the telephone in the familyroom trying to straighten out a White House problem. On another occasion a sprinkling of snow forced cancellation because our house was located on a slippery incline (in the Capital, as nowhere else, the slightest precipitation ties traffic up in knots). The lesson: Don't become a Washington hostess!

Parties with friends and neighbors were a lot more fun. These included Inger's inner circle at the Norwegian Embassy, plus correspondents assigned to Washington by Oslo's *Aftenposten* and NRK,

Norway's national broadcasting network. These events were further enlivened when first cousin Liv Krogh Midttun came to town with husband Harald, the Embassy's new press attache' (who later became ambassador to the Philippines), along with friends Else and Bjarne Grindem, Maritime Attache' (later ambassador to Saudi Arabia.). Other enliveners were Edward L. Beach (Capt.USN-Ret.), author of *Run Silent, Run Deep*, and his striking wife of Swedish descent, Ingrid, and ex-US. Navy officer Bob Weiss and wife Ingrid, a mathematics wizard (that's right!) from Chile, who was now running the Montgomery County, Md., school math programs.

Dinner with such wanderers was pure Scandinavian Design. Festivities began with a drink or two (invariably *strong*), followed by seating at the table and a *velkommen til bords* [welcome to the table] greeting. After good food with good wine came a *takk for maten* [thanks for the food] speech by the man "lucky" enough to occupy the guest-of-honor position next to the hostess. Then came coffee with cookies and chocolates in the livingroom, followed by more drinks. And more! The whole event often ran into the wee small hours, doing absolute violence to both diets and the next day's work schedule. But complaints were few!

Beautiful Kenwood turned out to be a wondrous refuge from work-a-day turmoil. Here were classic colonials and big graystone houses from the 1920s and 30s, set among 100-year-old oaks, maples and poplars, with winding lanes graced by Japanese cherry trees which each April burst out into a panoply of blossoms rivaling those on the Tidal Basin. Kenwood had the unique charm and character of a real neighborhood—a square mile of quiet and grace in a shrill, traffic-scarred world. (What a change from our Detroit beginnings!) We had long admired the area...and now, acting on the spur of a special expense allowance from our employer, we swallowed hard, mortgaged away our lives, and bought a three-story Federal-style brick house backing up on forested parkland. Or, as Inger put it, we bought the trees and the realtor threw in the house.

The need to host visiting clients also led us to reserve a box for four at the Kennedy Center. No work, this! Now, every week for two years we attended concerts and heard Anton Dorati conducting the

Washington Symphony Orchestra. Beethoven, Brahms, Dvorak, Mozart, Copeland, et al, became household names and gracious friends...to Inger's endless delight.

These personal events were played out against galloping news developments. Spiro Agnew (a neighbor at Kenwood) resigned in disgrace as Nixon's vice president and was replaced—portentously for me—by that solid Congressman from Michigan, Gerald Ford. Arab oil producers cut production 30 percent, precipitating long lines at gasoline stations. In Inger's former homeland, the first oil wells were drilled in the North Sea, portending vast new wealth for a country once the poorest in West Europe. A striking new operahouse opened in Sydney, Australia...and a big musical hit opened on Broadway: *Song of Norway*, based on the life and compositions of Edvard Grieg.

As for our Washington PR work, a typical example emerged when a pipeline company faced the prospect of Congressional action on a bill that would freeze it out of competing to provide natural gas in the Northwest. APRC was hired, leading to a campaign in the three affected states to alert the public to what was happening—*and* to stop the bill's sponsor from proceeding. This grassroots effort was directed on the scene at local newsmen and thought leaders, as well as at the client firm's suppliers and customers. Resulting press coverage was then focused on Capital centers dealing with the pending legislation. The happy outcome: The proposal died in committee.

The lesson this case provides is that Washington lobbying must realistically be viewed as the tip of a spear that stretches back into all 50 states and 435 Congressional Districts, with public opinion support the indispensable power needed to drive the point home. Inger and I never forgot, either, that the shortest route to a government official often runs through a Congressman's office, while the shortest route to a Congressman often circles all the way back through influential people in his constituency. As for the news media, we've also found that the best way to get wire service coverage of a Capital development is often through contacting a member newspaper far afield, while the best way to get an association to move may be through a key member company.

The Northwest pipeline case led to a personal break. One of the involved clients was the CEO of a Texas-based oil company. We became such close friends that he signed up his company as a separate APRC client, much to The Chairman's joy...for this meant that another big annual consulting fee came in to fatten up our firm's bottomline (Chair's, too, naturally). The CEO also figured in a humorous incident in Houston. I flew in one day to discuss some problem and, after a lengthy meeting, he suggested I look in the mirror before we headed for lunch. And there I beheld *red blood* all over my white collar! (From shaving while half asleep.) Oh, said he when I, red-faced, apologized, *I thought that was part of your PR presentation!*

Acquiring new clients elsewhere proved almost impossible. With Inger's help, I put together what we thought were persuasive presentations and competed year after year against other PR firms in a score of major instances where groups were seeking Washington PR help. One Washington-oriented client signed up—and I became Account Supervisor on top of my other duties. Otherwise, PR consulting firms seemed to be chosen by clients on the basis of internal politicking and personal contacts. In one case, an association's PR director told me confidentially afterward that the selection committee wanted to hire me along with APRC but was overruled by an executive who had personal ties to another national PR firm.

This shows how dumb people can be...for the wise know that success on a new program depends far less on the PR firm you hire than on the *person* the firm selects to run your account.

Failure to attract new clients began to my surprise to take its toll in my relations with The Chairman. He had evidently hoped that the overhaul of APRC's Washington office would produce more clients and more revenues and profit. In short, enhancing APRC's own external image and strengthening ties to existing clients wasn't enough to offset the rising cost of my services. One strategy we tried led to my talking with leading Washington law firms—key actors in any combined lobbying/PR campaign. The main result: I met a lot of interesting people! Charles Rhyne, Nixon's personal attorney outside the White House, put it best: Such decisions are really not made in Washington but, rather, in business operating centers in New York and Chicago and elsewhere. A Washington law firm and a PR firm are then often hired as part of the over-all effort. The railroad anti-featherbedding campaign was a standout example.

The Chairman didn't seem to want to hear that answer. He sent a memo proposing another approach to Capital insiders—which made no sense whatever to me or my staff or Inger. I phoned to discuss the matter, but his secretary said he was "in a meeting." Reminding me again of how remote my branch office—even one as important as Washington—was from the maneuverings at NYC headquarters. So off went my own memo outlining what I thought was a workable approach to his proposal. This triggered still another Chairman memo stating how disappointed he was to note that I had "purposely misinterpreted" his proposal. *Purposely.* A big word! As Inger said, you have to get inside another guy's head to know he's doing anything purposely—and not even a clever character like The Chairman could manage that trick. It thus became painfully obvious to both of us that my days at APRC were being numbered.

Before the anticipated ax could fall, however, a series of incidents occurred that might have gone right into a Hollywood B-minus movie. For instance:

• An APRC-NYC Group Vice President (*grope* would be more descriptive) came into my office one day and complained that a client company wasn't getting enough press coverage in Washington. (This echoed the envisioned position of the firm's President, to the effect that any time APRC was having trouble with a client, it was generally due to "lack of publicity.") When I tried to explain what could be done to make the Washington press react better to the client's drab handouts (which Grope himself churned out) this humorless individual, thin and prickly as a strand of barbed wire and known as an expert in organization tactics (meaning how to undermine colleagues while promoting yourself), slammed his briefcase on my desk and demanded "action."

Action? Okay! Without a word, I rose to my feet, came around the desk toward him (beady eyes bulging in alarm, he back away and raised his briefcase up like a shield) and walked right past and out of the office to the Press Club...where I spent an hour reading newspapers. When I returned, he was gone, leaving me thinking that such an affront would never have happened in those halcyon days when everyone thought I was The Chairman's "fair-haired boy." This was totally erroneous, but that's how his attention was *perceived.* And believing is seeing...right? Inger's conclusion: Those days were gone forever.

• APRC landed a big new client—a group promoting highway repair and maintenance (meaning more Federal $$$$ was being sought for this purpose). The account was to be based in Washington, and an ex-Marine was appointed AE. Trained to take the offensive, he looked over my office suite and *demanded* the spacious corner room overlooking F Street—now occupied by my Second-in-Command. I refused, citing staff morale...and suggested instead other Press Building space. Well, this incident ricocheted all over NYC headquarters, creating a whole row of enemies. (Ironically, my Second wasn't worth the uproar; a former Capitol Hill staffer, he had made an art of doing just enough to keep from being fired...but no more, regardless of need.)

• My oil company friend then contributed to the gathering storm...completely innocently. Since his firm had hardly used APRC services in the year since becoming a client, he called to say he was withdrawing. We met and negotiated, instead, a continuation...at half the normal APRC retainer fee. This seemed to me a great outcome. Not to The Chairman, though. He was upset that I had acted on my own, without bringing him into the talks. He thought I was becoming "too damn independent," as a headquarters pal informed me confidentially.

• Right out of the blue, memos appeared on my desk from two of the AEs I had been working most closely with over the past six years, complaining that I was overcharging their client companies. I had always thought of these two as decent guys, and it did, indeed, appear that they were acting under orders...for the memos were addressed to the two accounts' AS—the APRC President himself. It was a low blow. It indicated clearly that the animals in this PR menagerie that Inger always considered a rapacious zoo were now baring both teeth and claws—and that Prez had been assigned to build a case for my dismissal.

But hold your horses, Prez! Someone's got to solve the "Trouble Light Case...."

Before the expected internal storm broke, a distress call came in to me from a client company's top lawyer asking if I could join him in a meeting with counsel from other national retail chains to discuss a major problem they were having with the Consumer Product Safety Commission. Seems that a trouble light (the bulb in a wired cage that mechanics use to light up an area undergoing repair) had been found to be defective and might electrocute users...and CPSC was demanding that people owning the thousands of these already sold by retailers across the nation be alerted to the danger. This meant the whole nation had to be informed, and the CPSC, acting on its information director's weird recommendation, was asking the big retail chains to pay for doing so through three successive nights' commercial messages over three major TV networks.

I found everyone in a state of shock. How could a government bureaucracy order such a costly approach? What kind of precedent would this set for other product recalls? The lawyers asked: Could we PR people come up with an equally effective, cheaper alternative?

Yes, I assured them, we could...and would! I met with the AE and Prez and APRC-NYC staffers, and we came up with a plan to create news releases, radio tapes and TV clips on the situation...and to blanket the nation with these. CPSC didn't like this approach at all, and called client reps in for hearings, at which I was the main witness...for the issue came down to an overriding question that only communication pros could address:

What constitutes adequate information dissemination across the entire nation?

This case kicked off in early June and ran through August, occurring alongside mounting nationwide turmoil over an asinine burglary of Democratic Party offices in the Watergate Building on Foggy Bottom (appropriate name!). *The Washington Post* had sunk its teeth into this morsel of a story and wasn't about to let go, for ties were being turned up daily that led all the way to the White House. The half-year-long ordeal was inflicting hard blows on the nation's soul...for here was evidence that people at our highest leadership levels were flouting moral values and breaking faith with the public. Worse, by the time each new detail was magnified and amplified endlessly by the news media, the cacophony was deafening. As Inger said, life in the hard-hammered hollow steel drum was getting unbearable. When Richard Nixon's resignation and replacement by Gerald Ford came in August, it was with an almost audible nationwide sigh of relief.

Meanwhile, the Trouble Light Case was tying up my Washington office...and much of APRC-New York. However, despite these national information efforts on behalf of our client and other retailers, the CPSC sued to force compliance with its own communications demands, and the case wound up in Federal Court for the District of Columbia. (Inger joked about visiting me in jail.) Using newspaper clippings and return "use cards" from broadcasters, my staff prepared maps of the US showing in red, blue and green dots where our news stories and broadcast materials had appeared. This was to be Exhibit A in the showdown in court.

Another revealing Grade B-minus movie incident intruded during this crisis. Inger, knowing I had to work one evening, came downtown so that we could have a late dinner together at the Press Club. Before going upstairs, however, I made a call to the APRC-NYC manager of our reproduction/mailing department to ask when the latest batch of news stories on Trouble Light would be sent out.

"Hi," I said in a friendly tone, "this is Jim Sites in the Washington office...."

I got no further: He burst into tears!

"I'm a married man," he cried, "and I got two children...and bills...and...and I can't afford to lose my job."

My god! I thought, *what's going on up there!*

I consoled him, hung up and turned with baleful eyes toward Inger, tuning in from my office sofa. Her conclusion: The Chairman was having nervous fits over the Trouble Light Case and was telegraphing his anxieties to the whole staff. With me cast in the role of *bete noir.* For if APRC lost the case and came off with a big black eye, how many present clients would that scare off? And how many new ones would never sign up?

Early next morning, I phoned Prez, told him about the incident and said that if I could not depend on him and the New York office for support in this case, I would have to withdraw. That sent him into near-panic.

"No, no, no, NO!" he blurted out in alarm. "Everything's fine here. We're supporting you all the way. A hundred percent. No, *two hundred!* Just hang in there!"

Inger's reaction: "He wouldn't lie to you, would he? Oh, no, of course not! It's just that they'll say anything to keep you hanging in there. With the *real* hanging coming later...."

When the case opened up in the courthouse in DC in late August, I again found myself the key witness...going over our campaign, explaining in detail what the maps showed and winning surprisingly sympathetic response from the judge. It was obvious he didn't like CPSC's precedent-setting approach. The second day on the stand, he asked me a leading question: Would the group I represented be willing to cooperate with CPSC in making a special new TV film of the dangerous trouble light? Of course we would, I responded. So did the attending CPSC officials. The judge then proposed personally taking an action that amazed everyone:

He himself would follow up by calling the major television networks and ask them *to air the film as a public service.* Amazing!

Exactly this sequence of actions took place. Over the Labor Day weekend, our new TV clip was aired repeatedly by NBC and ABC (CBS turned down the judge's request). And APRC was hailed throughout the business community and the PR world for a great victory over government bureaucracy. *Now*, we thought, The Chairman must be smiling from ear to ear.

Hardly! The second day after the holiday, the new Exec supervising branch offices appeared in Washington, and fumbling in embarrassment for the right words, informed me that I was fired. *Fired!* No explanation. No phone calls from Chair or Prez. No thanks for my six years of all-out effort to put APRC on the Washington map...and APRC-Washington on our clients' map. No fare thee well. Just plain old *fired.*

All of which must surely prove that truth *is* stranger than fiction.

Inger's response was Classic Inger: "You've just been dealt a signal honor—a great favor. You had no business being in that zoo anyway. You should have cleared out long ago. Be glad you're free!"

"Yeah, that's easy to say," I responded. "But six years ago, I wondered if anyone would ever hire a guy 44 years old. Now, six years later, I sit here wondering, who's ever gonna hire a guy who's 50? Those six years were wasted—thrown away—gone down the drain!"

"Oh, c'mon, James!" retorted Inger. "You've learned volumes about national issues and even more about working in Washington. And think of all you've learned about human nature!"

"Thanks! But no more of that, *please*. I think I've learned enough." I saw at a glance that I would have to expand my category of scoundrels to include some new, extraordinarily devious types.

Inger also pointed out that I had to consider not only the mess I had *fallen into* when I joined APRC but also the mess I *escaped* when I left railroading. A surviving friend at the rail association reported that in the year after I left there, the ax fell all over the AAR, and its celebrated PR department had been slashed from 38 people to 6. To *six!* So that's why the new AAR president and PR VP were brought in! It wasn't just an RIF or reduction in force; it was *slaughter*. A bloody business I'm *very* glad I missed out on....

On September 8 President Ford pardoned Richard Nixon, sparing the nation the bitter agony of another long-drawn-out uproar over Watergate. Leaving me wrestling with the question, would Fate now pardon me, too? For here I stood, abruptly reduced from what Inger derisively called A Big Man Downtown to a low, low new reality: The Outcast of Poker Flat.

Readers deserve some postscripts at this point:

• That year's November issue of *The PR Journal* carried a comprehensive bylined article about the Trouble Light Case by Dr. Ray Hiebert, chairman of the Communications Department at the University of Maryland. When the piece was still in galley-proof form, the magazine editor, apparently seeking to ingratiate himself with APRC, showed it to one of the firm's NYC executives. And this worthy (!) proceeded to remove all references to the guy who had carried the whole load during the grueling battle. I was simply *deleted*. Rubbed out. I became a non-person. Dr. Hiebert raised cane with the PRSA president over the editor's tampering with his byliner: The editor was summarily dismissed.

• Speaking about the case at a US Chamber of Commerce closed-door seminar shortly after my own dismissal, I found myself sitting at the conference table opposite The Chairman, who, acting as though nothing untoward had ever happened between us, told me that the former APRC Exec had died of cancer. I was truly sorry, since Exec had always struck me as one nice guy. Chair went on to praise Exec for expanding the firm's profits greatly by a simple change in accounting: Instead of billing clients for the pro-rated *salary* of people working on their accounts, Exec had recommended billing them for *employee cost*—that is, for salary PLUS 10-to-15 % for life and health insurance and related fringe benefits. Much more revenue was thus generated, increasing APRC's (The Chairman's) profits.

Well, I must have looked shocked, for this was *exactly the proposal I had made much earlier* after learning of APRC's peculiar former accounting system at a NYC staff meeting. Exec had evidently stolen the proposal I made in a memo to him and made it his own. (Some Nice Guy!) And I had a copy of my memo to prove it. All this meant, ironically, that even during the painful half-year I was being set up for the boot out the door, my proposal was further lining The Chairman's pockets.

I asked Inger whether I should send Chair my memo. *Absolutely not*, she said. First, if revenge is the objective, I could forget the whole thing; revelation wouldn't harm Exec the slightest: He was dead. And, second, it would do *us* no good, either, since, happily, I was now on the outside looking in. Also, she added, you'll benefit anyway by never, ever letting such a thing happen again. [It hasn't!]

• In time I received in the mail an APRC check for slightly more than $6,000—the amount I had accumulated from six year's hard work under the firm's "profit-sharing" plan. This was supposed to supplant an employee retirement plan. But that was a hopeless hope. Inger figured that at this rate, in 30 years I would pile up the vast sum of $30,000. [and you know what kind of retirement you'd get for *that*]. Five years earlier I had worked up an employee pension proposal with an acquaintance who specialized in such matters, and memoed this to The Chairman via the Exec. This was followed a year later by a more refined, cheaper proposal. Both were ignored. Why? Obviously, such a plan would have raised internal costs and narrowed the firm's net earnings. Yet, something more important was involved—which Inger and I couldn't know. But The Chairman did....

• The answer came years later when the news broke that APRC had been sold for many millions of dollars to another communications agency—sending The Chairman off into retirement a very rich man. This cleared up many of the mysteries behind my dubious experiences at APRC: Chair was holding down internal costs and pushing for new clients and new revenues not just to fatten up the firm's bottomline...but *to increase the sales value of the company.* And why not? After the founder's death, Chair had made it *his* company. And if, in the process of building up its value, some of the profit came out of the hide of his employees, isn't that what the system encourages people to do? Didn't Adam Smith say in his classic *An Inquiry into the Nature and Causes of THE WEALTH OF NATIONS* that if, under *laissez faire,* everyone pursues his own self interest, society as a whole will benefit?

Sad to say, Smith's dictum evidently did not include benefits for APRC employees. Could he possibly have been wrong?

Inger had a lot of fun at my expense over the $6,000 check: "So this is what...in your blinding brilliance...you gave up a fat railroad management pension plan for! And now here you sit at age 50 with nothing—*nothing!*—for retirement...except this lousy $6,000!"

She reminded me (I needed no reminder) that I had spent nearly four years getting shot at as a merchant mariner during World War II and had come out of that ordeal with no veterans benefits of any kind. And now no retirement, even though Congress had recently passed a bill requiring employers to provide "portable pensions" for employees after five years on the payroll. Unfortunately, I had left the AAR *before* the bill was passed...so I missed out on that, too.

Inger said I reminded her of that character in the L'il Abner comic strip who walks around with a black cloud over his head, from which bolts of lightning regularly crackle down on him: "You've got a bad luck streak, James!"

"Not at all!" I answered, trying to sound convincing. "Didn't I latch onto you? You wouldn't call that bad luck, would you? Matter of fact, after Fate gave me you, even if I never have another lucky break ever again, I'll forever consider myself the luckiest man on the face of the earth!" [Thanks, Lou Gehrig...*you said it!*]

And that's how I felt then, and now, and always will.

It might seem strange, but Inger wasn't disturbed at all about the change in our fortunes.

She had begun working part-time at the Georgetown U. Library, and said she could always work full-time. As for me, we talked about my returning to Washington reporting. Or even resurrecting a long-buried idea of opening a Scandinavian News Bureau based in Oslo. (There wasn't a single American reporter in all of Norway.) Right now, however, Inger's main concern was that I get as far away from the whole recent "contamination" as fast as possible. Her answer to my worries about a new job was that I should be shouting to the heavens Martin Luther King's immortal words:

Free at last! Free at last! Thank God, I'm free at last!

So we picked up Jimmy and Erik and headed for Rehoboth Beach—to nature's all-curing medicines—the pounding surf and the scudding clouds, the wind and the sun and the moon and the stars, the high-flying geese and the screaming seagulls. To a refreshing world a million miles from man's minuscule maneuverings and machinations. Jimmy had finished at Georgetown Law and passed his Maryland and District of Columbia bar exams and had just spent that Summer working on The Hill for Ned Beach, now staff director of the Senate Republican Policy Committee. Jim was on his way to a law clerk position with Judge Morton of the Court of Appeals of Maryland...while Erik, two years out of Sidwell, was heading back to St. Olaf College in Minnesota.

After years of renting musty garage apartments on Hickman Street, Inger and I had found some small, rustic, well-scrubbed apartments on little Lake Comegys south of Rehoboth—the House of Stuart, it was called, after the industrious, attentive owners, Al and Helen Stuart. Here, the eye could reach out over both Lake Comegys and Silver Lake and the sanddunes to the restlessly pounding, endless Atlantic Ocean. It was a lovely bit of Denmark planked down on the outermost edge of America, and we referred to the area as *Eventyr*, a harmonious norsk word for fairytale, adventure.

As we drove past Annapolis and over that engineering masterpiece, the 5-mile-long bridge sweeping over Chesapeake Bay, I could almost hear John Masefield speaking...in rhythm with tires thudding over concrete joints...those appealing, beckoning words from his moving poem, *Sea Fever:*

I must go down to the sea again, to the lonely sea and the sky,
And all I ask is a good stout ship—and a star to steer her by.

The "Gang of Four" assembles at another Washington university—this time to celebrate Jimmy's graduation from Georgetown's acclaimed Law School. This also gave Inger a chance to show off her traditional bunad *gown from the Oslo area, plus the* lue *cap she became entitled to wear after completing her* artium *studies and entering the University of Oslo.*

Chapter VIII

"How would you like to take on the toughest PR job in Washington?"

It was Paul Theis calling from the White House, and I was listening carefully. A former newsman and congressional aide to Gerry Ford, Paul had recently moved to the other end of Pennsylvania Avenue as a speechwriter and advisor to the man he now called Communicator- in-Chief. His boss had taken over the Presidency just two months before and was trying to put Watergate to rest and prop up the nation's badly shaken morale. At the same time the economy, shocked by the Arabs' 30 percent cut in oil production the previous year, was sliding into recession. The new President was trying to restore openness, candor and integrity to government. It was an awesome challenge, and he needed all the help he could get.

What did Paul have in mind? William E. Simon, a sharp Wall Street investment banker, had moved from the Federal Energy Office, where he had established a record as a tough administrator during the oil crisis, back to Treasury as the new Secretary. He was replacing the venerable George Shultz, who made it a tough act to follow. Since Simon was also chairman of the President's Economic Policy Board, this was THE critical Federal economic policy job...and he wanted a PR pro ("no political hack, *please*") to serve as both his personal press aide and Treasury's Director of Public Affairs. The catch: Simon was an apostle of free enterprise in a city enamored with big government, and the Washington press was having a field day attacking him as a "rightwing fanatic." Ford's economic policies were thus going nowhere.

Could I do something—*anything!*—about this? Paul wanted to know.

Could *anyone?* I asked, in turn. Filled with doubt, I promised to talk with Inger. Our decision: I should at least meet Secretary Simon and get a feel for both him and the job.

And what a feel it was! I met first with Treasury's Deputy Secretary, Stephen S. Gardner, a soft-speaking ex-banker from Philadelphia with impeccable manners. I must have passed this test, for the very next day I was asked to come back to the big, colonnaded Greek-Roman-style building just east of the White House...for an interview with Simon himself. The Secretary was impressive. He was wiry, sparked energy like a dynamo, was about the same age and size as me and, with his thick, horn-rimmed glasses, looked for the world "like the brightest boy in class" (as Theis described him). He also had a good smile. Besides his grasp of issues, what really hit me was the *intensity* and concentration he displayed. Piercing blue eyes magnified by strong glasses, he scrutinized me like a drill sergeant sizing up a suspicious new recruit. He expressed keen interest in my background, smiled wanly over the sad state of his press relations ("those dummies think the economy's a branch of ecology"), then got down to serious business.

Treasury Secretary William E. Simon makes a point during a planning session on an upcoming interview. So why my big smile? I had just suggested his using that well-worn line, "Washington is the only place on earth where sound travels faster than light." "Oh, no, not the only place," Bill replied. "What about Hollywood and Madison Avenue? AND Wall Street!"

The central problem the nation faces, he said, is too much government. It is growing out of control, choking off initiative and innovation, triggering inflation and unemployment and pointing to worse domination—*much* worse!—in years to come. Most news people, particularly those here in Washington, don't realize what is happening, and "haven't the faintest idea" of underlying causes or cures. Nor do many seem to care. Their partisan minds appear already made up. Yet, their uninformed reporting sets the tone for everything the new Administration tries to do about the situation.

"Our public policies aren't worth a damn without public support," he declared with feeling, adding, "And a better informed press is absolutely essential to that."

He leaned forward: "Think you can do anything about that, Mr. Sites...er...Jim?"

"Well, I'll sure try!"

"No, no!" he shot back. "Just *trying* won't do. This job demands all-out effort. Day and night! That's the only way we'll get anywhere. Are you up to that?" (What a response! It led me to believe the rumors were true—that he was one demanding and difficult person to work with. But it was also said that he was totally supportive of those who supported him.)

"Sure, but there's one problem, Mr. Secretary: I'm a political independent. Do you really want an independent in this job?"

"You gotta be kidding!" he barked, prompting me to think the interview was finished (me, too!). He continued as before, though: "If you can get the job done, I don't care if you're a Manchurian monkey. This managerie is filled with Democrats. We can damn well use one independent 'round here! And, incidentally, can that 'Mister' stuff. Just call me Bill...."

All this was duly reported to my partner. Inger's reaction: "So now you're going to hop from the APRC frying pan into the Treasury fire. Hope you survive!"

We had just come back from three glorious weeks at the ocean (the boys had gone on their way after the first weekend)—and, suddenly, here was this new job possibility. It meant that after 23 years of working *around* the Federal government, I would now have a chance to see this colossus from the *inside*. Inger didn't like the idea of my taking on this new perspective at all. Our experiences since WWII had only strengthened her feeling that politics was corrupting and contaminating...and that politicians, at best, were but poor actors on the public stage, doing anything to get applause—and, at worst, dangerous megalomaniacs never to be trusted in their single-minded pursuit of power and influence. Still, she recognized that *someone* with some values should go into public service, an attitude she assumed had motivated Simon...and agreed to let me try as long as my self-imposed "sentence" was kept short.

It *had* to be short. Going into government would mean cutting my previous income by a full third. Yet nothing would be cutting the costs of our Kenwood home. There was one happy note, however: With Jimmy now finished at Georgetown Law School and Erik heading to the University of Oslo for his "junior year abroad," those monstrous college tuition bills that were driving middle-class families to the wall would be eliminated in one case and postponed in the other. We thus sharpened our pencils and found that if I took on this daunting job, we could hold on at Kenwood for two years. By then, we would be flat broke, and rows of bill collectors would be pounding on the door, demanding payment...or else.

So I called Simon's office and said I was coming to work. And work there was, right off the bat...on reams of forms and applications, a full field investigation by the FBI, etc. Worst of all, I had to submit to an IRS audit of my tax returns for the past three years. Seems the new Administration wanted to make sure that no one working on the Treasury Secretary's staff would embarrass him with a tax scandal. Inger interpreted all this fuss to mean that the government was trying to scare away all qualified people being considered for appointive positions. Not us, though. I passed through the needle's eye!

The day I walked into my spacious, high-ceilinged office in the grand old Treasury Building, I felt I had entered the fiery furnace itself. A disheveled, harried-looking man—the acting Public Affairs Director—rose from behind a massive, ornate desk (it was once Franklin Roosevelt's, moved over from the White House), handed me a radio-phone alert device and said, "Boy, will you ever need this!"...*and walked out.* Without one word about the problems the office was working with. Nothing about here's how we're organized and who's who on your staff. With no suggestion whatever on dealing with the wider bureaucracy and getting it to move—not to mention *surviving* it. Upset at Secretary Simon for not moving him into the job, and upset at me for getting the job, he simply left...and left me holding the bag, plus the device that would allow Simon to reach me instantly anywhere, day or night.

To make matters worse (if possible!), a courier appeared just then with a note from Theis asking me for a 2-page insert on the energy situation the US faced...for a speech by the President. Me? An energy expert? *For the PRESIDENT!?!* Dumb-founded, I rang for the secretary I was inheriting—Gail, a Civil Service career employee who turned out to be a tireless, cheerful aide—and asked in no little bewilderment where in the vast Treasury labyrinth I might turn to for help. Oh, she said, that's easy: Gerry Parsky, our Assistant Secretary for International Energy, etc. And that's how I came to meet this bright, young, rising star on our staff...*and* found out about a magic document called the "Briefing Book." This contained in concise, pointed form the best thinking of Treasury's top authorities on every question that news reporters and others might ask the Secretary. So, I weeded out the pertinent energy answers and smashed them into speech form and rushed the draft over to the White House, thinking with a sigh of relief....

Here, Mr. Ford, is precisely what you need: Now you, too, can speak like an expert on the subject!

I next made the rounds of my own offices and introduced myself to each of the 27 people on the Secretary's Public Affairs staff. A strange mixture, indeed! Here were men and women of wide-ranging skills, most of them brought in by several past Administrations for widely differing purposes—many purely as a political pay-off. Included were two retired US Army colonels, double-dipping their way along to easy retirement; they seemed to know something about military affairs but precious little about communications. The staff appeared to have no goals and no sense of purpose...except handling the most routine chores in the most routine manner. A key question I asked each was, *how do you see your work fitting in with the department's over-all mission?*

One of the more honest replied: *What the hell IS the mission?*

Well, I got the picture. As I told Inger that evening, it took no genius to recognize that my staff had to be shored up internally before much of anything could be accomplished externally. She put it better: "Just try building a cathedral on a swamp!"

The second day on the job, we were up at 5:a.m. so that my partner could drive me far out into southeast Washington to Andrews Air Force Base, where I joined Simon and two Secret Service agents for a flight in a racy 8-passenger jet to New York City. The Secretary's aide—John Gartland—showed up a couple minutes late...and was greeted by an unbelievably caustic dressing-down by Simon. *Lord, what've I gotten into?* I wondered. But suddenly the mood changed. Bill relaxed in the plane's rearmost seat and went over with me, sitting across the aisle, the crunching schedule for the day, plus a pile of briefing materials on economic issues. As though I knew the slightest of what he was talking about!

At LaGuardia we were met by two local Secret Service agents and whisked into Manhattan for a dizzying dash "all around the town." First came a half-hour morning TV interview with phone-in questions. Next came an interview with a syndicated business columnist, a news conference with a score of reporters, a luncheon talk to business leaders, an editorial board meeting at *Forbes Magazine* in the afternoon. Then came a major dinner speech at the New York Hilton. Finally, an amazingly still-fresh Secretary and two thoroughly bedraggled aides (Gartland and me) returned to La Guardia and back to Andrews...and home by midnight. With my being convinced that there was no way to keep up with this non-stop performer. Now I really wondered, *what have I gotten into!*

Inger greeted me with a hug and a kiss, a glass of hot milk and some unwelcome advice: "Don't ever take a drink when you're this tired."

She was dying to know about Simon's performance on the stump—which, of course, I had been following with an appraising eye all day. My conclusion: He *looked* great and was well received everywhere BUT had to be rated *poor* in reading a written speech, *good* in speaking from notes ("talking points") and *excellent* in handling interviews and Q&A sessions. Most important, he conveyed sincerity and conviction in what he said, and struck people as highly credible (unlike many political leaders). So I felt we really had a winner in terms of moving ahead with a nationwide campaign to rally public opinion. One minor point: Simon's thick eyeglasses kept slipping down on his nose during the TV interview, creating a glaring light spot under his eyes. What to do? Inger suggested he simply keep the glasses pushed back on his nose. It worked! And this we noticed he did ever afterward.

Another thing that impressed me was Bill's spontaneous response to questions with a full, persuasive answer. And where did he get that? Right out of the "Briefing Book." He had a fantastic photographic memory, and seemed able to recite verbatim anything he read. It was like pushing a button on a computer and getting a precise read-out from the printer. He also showed a solid sense of ethics and great judgment, instantly eliminating the chaff from kernels of information and knowing instinctively what a public official could do...and could not do.

Was he an original, creative thinker, though? Inger wanted to know. I couldn't answer that...at least not yet. But how many such people do you meet, even in an entire lifetime?

In bed at 1:a.m., I was up at 6:a.m. in order to get to the office by 7:30 a.m. By then, the Secretary had already arrived (by chauffeur-driven car), had skimmed en route through the *Washington Post,* the *New York Times* and the *Wall Street Journal,* and was ready to bark about things I had to do re the press: "Call this guy and tell him I thought he did a fine job on this story. Call this S.O.B. and straighten him out—he obviously doesn't know what he's talkin' 'bout." Etc, etc—with the resulting contacts providing opportunity to both mend fences in one case and develop further coverage in the other.

At 8:15 a.m. we were off to the Roosevelt Room at the White House for the daily meeting of the Economic Policy Board—with members like Arthur Burns, Alan Greenspan and Bill Seidman joining in with selected others from across government, depending on the subject for that day. President Ford also came in occasionally, mainly to pat everyone on the back and urge us on to greater exertions. (With Simon in the chair, that was absolutely unnecessary.) Then it was back to Treasury for Bill's senior staff meeting at 9:a.m.

In short, the business day had barely begun elsewhere, and the Secretary had already put in a half-day's work! I wondered if he ever slept.

By 10:a.m., when I finally got back to *my* office, an additional week's work had already been unloaded onto my creaking back—and I was ready to hold my own staff meeting and unload as much of it as possible onto my subordinates. Noting the quality of these back-ups, however, most of it stayed right on my desk. With the phone ringing off the hook from "the man upstairs." (He *was* upstairs—one floor above my own first-floor office beside the ornate south portico of Treasury. The view for both of us ranged out over the beautiful Ellipse, as it did from the famed Oval Office at 1600 Pennsylvania Avenue immediately to the west.)

One strange call that came in was from my old familiar boss, The Chairman of APRC. When Gail indicated who was calling, my first reaction was to say I was in a meeting, as he had done with me. But

President Ford's Economic Policy Board meets in the stately Roosevelt Room at the White House, with Secretary Simon (back to camera) conducting the discussions in his role as EPB Chairman. Among the participants: Alan Greenspan, then head of the President's Council of Economic Advisors (second on right), and Arthur Burns, chairman of the Federal Reserve Board, smoking his ever-present pipe at the table's far end. I'm the "spear carrier" far back on the left.

curiosity won out. I answered...and got this unbelievable spiel about how glad he was that I had "moved over" to this new post, how important it was to the nation, and how lucky Simon was to have "a PR pro like you" at his side.

What crust! Here was a man I had worked with closely for six years, who at the end didn't have the guts to tell me to my face that he was firing me...BUT who, now that I was working side by side with one of the most influential men in America, was trying to mend fences.

Now I used the meeting excuse and hung up...and almost threw up. Inger summed up our feelings with the understatement of the year: "Guess you won't be recommending him to anyone needing PR help...right?" *Right!*

Two weeks after joining Treasury, Simon and I sat down for a crucial meeting. With Inger's help, I had worked up the outlines of the national PR plan he had challenged me to come up with and execute. It went like this:

Right now the Ship of State is like the *Titanic* speeding into a sea filled with icebergs. Danger lies ahead, and the Secretary has to take the lead in warning the nation about our worsening problems—(those icebergs) of government overspending and massive deficits, burdensome taxes, stifling regulation and a red-tape-ridden bureaucracy. *This* is the crucial central message. Will the press report it? Will anyone listen? The answer has to be YES!

As a government leader warning about government excesses, in raising warning flags and sounding alarms, I felt he would get heavy press attention, for there's nothing in news circles like "man bites dog" stories. And in Simon we had that in spades!

But impact must be generated by means other than through news channels alone, AND for a lengthy period...if public opinion is really to be turned around. Since no money was available within government for such broader campaigning, I felt we would also have to mount a determined effort through influential national organizations, using *their* communications resources, as well. ['Way back in 1835 Alexis de Tocqueville, in his famed *Democracy in America*, observed that Americans set up groups for every purpose under the sun—almost like another branch of government.] This provided a big, additional, effective target for PR...but was something beyond normal government information approaches. Wasn't it worth a try?

Simon nodded vigorously, then got to the key question: "What do you need to get rolling and do all this?"

Mainly staff changes, I answered...for Treasury already had the reproduction/distribution machinery in place; it was either sitting there idle or wasn't being targeted properly. Needed, therefore, were (1) a deputy who knew how to get things done within the bureaucracy, (2) a writer who could actually write (surprisingly few communications/PR people can), (3) a solid radio-TV director, (4) an organization-contact person and (5) an office manager to handle the increased contacts and flow of paperwork...and make *me* more efficient

Where could I get such capable people? was Bill's next question—the tough one! I knew such people existed, for I had worked with a few right in Washington...and promised to go to work on this mission immediately.

Inger contributed to the over-all plan with one key aspect—maintaining that better speech *targeting* was essential. In short, we needed not only to crystallize our message but also to direct it into the right channels. So I suggested that Simon name me his "speech coordinator." I had found that requests for his speechmaking were handled in his office on a catch-as-catch-can basis, scattering his shots and wasting valuable time. He announced this new role for me at Treasury's next senior staff meeting, telling everyone that whenever I came to them for help, they should consider that as coming from the Secretary himself. What clearer support could you get!

A word about speeches: As a listener, Inger maintained she couldn't stand any speech that ran over 20 minutes. So we kept them less than that...*unless* something truly BIG was involved. I also felt that if an audience were to remember anything at all in a speech, it had to be focused on one compelling point—though this could be worked over in many different ways. Then came a helpful approach to press coverage: We pulled the key points out of the speech and led off the written version with a page of these in quotes (*thank you!* said reporters). Another effective approach was to draft the news story we wanted the press to report *before* writing the speech—then build the speech text around this. Everything was thus aimed at talking not only to the immediate audience but *beyond* through the press to the outside public—our real target.

I managed to write one speech for the Secretary. It took two days—or, to be more exact—two nights. Enough to convince Inger that we had to find another speechwriter *right now!* And John Gartland did. In the bowels of the bureaucracy he located a refugee from the Nixon White House named Dave Gergen—and he got the job, in Simon's office. Dave turned out to be a fluent writer, with a knack for saying the right thing in the right context, with appropriate quotes, quips, etc. What a relief! (Thanks, Dave!)

As for my own staff, I talked the IRS information director into transferring a top radio-TV man I knew over to my office, Al Hattal. Gerry Parsky agreed to transfer one of my press people to his own staff, thus creating an opening for me to fill with a capable outside writer, Doug Trussell. Gerry Warren, the President's Communications Director, came to the rescue with a transfer from HEW, Jack Mongovin, who became my Deputy Public Affairs Director...and proved indispensable in getting things done within Treasury, as well as across the whole Federal bureaucracy. A good friend then recommended a jewel of a secretary/office manager—June O'Neill. And what personal help she was!

So the circle was now complete except for the key organization-contact person. This took some further tall doing...for that kind of PR expert, we found, either didn't exist or simply wasn't available.

My efforts to fill this position led to my one and only head-on collision with the Secretary. I finally located a woman who seemed ideal for this assignment, but she was in Bill's old domain, the Federal Energy Office, now headed by Frank Zarb. On a plane to an international conference in Nassau, I told Bill about this possibility. It was like lighting a firecracker. He *exploded!* You're ruining my reputation in Washington! he yelled. I recoiled, then shouted back that my contact was only exploratory, that I was reading him in now in order to get his permission before proceeding. Carol, his attractive, alert wife (and mother of their eight children) intervened, and I returned to my seat livid with anger—determined to return to Washington with the plane next morning and quit.

Once on the ground, Bill, in another complete mood change, asked in the friendliest tone if I would join Carol and him at dinner. "No, thanks," I replied, "I'm completely fed up."

At the stately lodge we stayed in that night, I found I couldn't sleep...so went down to the dining area, where there was a refrigerator full of snacks. And there I ran into a senior editor from *Fortune Magazine*. A kindred spirit, he and I talked for a couple hours about politics and the economy and Bill Simon's critical role in "saving the nation." And wasn't giving him every possible support *my* role? I then phoned Inger (in the middle of the night!) and told her I was *really* fed up...and was quitting. Her answer? She said I was behaving like a spoiled child. She then rubbed salt in my wounds by recalling Harry Truman's sage advice:

If you can't stand the heat, stay out of the kitchen.

So I swallowed my wounded pride and stayed on. (Thanks, Inkie!)

When Simon came barking over my office phone, his calls were usually intercepted by June O'Neill, who, using a truly singular skill in dealing with people, answered with such sweetness and light that he was completely taken back. She disarmed the roughest Washington reporters the same way.

"Who the hell is June O'Neill?" the boss demanded to know one day.

"Oh, she wouldn't be at all suitable for your office," I answered.

Bill peered at (and through) me, chuckled and said, "Okay I won't."

Inger got involved in another revealing contretemps. Bill was to fly to Russia with Gerry Parsky and some others for a conference and asked me to prepare a needed document and get it to him before departure. By the time this was finished, however, he had already left the Treasury building...so I gave it to Gerry for hand-delivery on the plane. That same day Inger was conducting a tour of Norwegian visitors around Washington, and was scheduled to stay with the group overnight at the Midtown Motel. I got invited, too...and, as usual, duly informed the Treasury phone operators where they could locate me in case something came up. It did. At 2:a.m. Bill phoned from the airplane far out over the Atlantic.

"Where's that paper I ask you to put together?" he growled.

Groggy with sleep, I told him Parsky had it...right beside him. *Bang!* He hung up.

"Are you a floosie?" I turned and asked Inger.

"Wha...wha...what?"

"That's what I think Simon believes. The operators probably told him I was at this funny downtown motel, and he's probably concluded I'm here with some sort of floosie."

"Fine...as long as I'm your floosie," she joked. She never forgot that phone call, though.

This incident added fuel to Inger's smoldering fire over my job. A couple months into this hot spot, she was already so irritated she could scream over what she called "Simon's killing crusade"—a round-about reference to me as the one being killed. It was virtually eliminating my family life and the crucial time I should be spending with our two sons. Even our golden-furred dog, Bowser, was upset. I had charged him with watching over Inger during my absenses, but he now spent the long, lonely days running from window to window on the first floor of our Kenwood home, perking up his ears at the slightest sound...then leaping in delirious abandon when I finally appeared. He camped out with big, watchful eyes wherever Ink and I sat, ready to *scramble* to keep from getting stepped on whenever we moved. All of which reminded us of another Trumanism:

If you want a friend in Washington, get yourself a dog.

Well, at least we had Bowser.

Inger did not pretend to understand economics, but she did know that no family—and she assumed no government—could long live beyond its means. Nor can a nation continually import and consume more than it produces and exports. She tended to shrug off dialectics anyway, seeing society's gathering problems more in moral terms—as the inevitable end of a people awash in self-indulgence, pleasure seeking and unrestrained greed.

Government's impact in "people areas" like the busing of school children was of more concern to her. Almost alone among her friends, Inger felt this distressful development was another miscarriage of "social engineering"...which amounted to making children pay for the discrimination sins of their parents. She considered court orders on busing a trampling on the sanctity of neighborhood life and the principle of free choice—one that would lead to new waves of cynicism about government as blind and unresponsive to individual feelings.

Similar feelings were expressed on the hot issue of equal employment opportunity. Inger felt that liberals were cynically abandoning the great goals of providing opportunity for all and were now using government to force equality of conditions and results. She sadly predicted that any society that imposes and rewards any standard other than *quality* and *excellence*, whether in schools or on the job, is doomed to fall behind others...and fail.

I must confess to getting irritated at such arguments occasionally, cutting as they did across the grain of *avant garde* thinking. What irritated me most, though, was that Inger was forcing me to *think* also and to work my way through a proposal's side-effects and repercussions...and not blithely accept the latest all-knowing pronouncements from assorted Ivory Towers inhabited by academics, liberal journalists and their political friends. She wasn't about to be taken in by untried assumptions and unproved theories, especially when these came from people with lofty ideas but little experience in their real-life applications. She saw things others did not. More telling, she listened always to people and developments with a full, warm heart, and saw the effects of new approaches on the human soul and spirit—which all too few seemed to do. Or were capable of doing....

Understanding Simon was challenge enough for me. A person of morality and ethics, he was deeply committed to principle, to what he believed in...and was determined to do everything in his power to turn around the dangerous drift toward government domination he saw the nation sliding into. Within government, however, he was like an irresistible force trying to move an immovable object—the Federal bureaucracy. And, as we on his staff quipped, he *would* do so...even if it crushed all of us staffers in the process. We were the guys squeezed in the middle. But he was so totally unsparing of himself that we supported him to the limit. And, amazingly, the bureaucracy *did* move!

Personnel problems are a headache everywhere...but, in the government goldfish bowl, they're a nightmare. I had always worked with staff on an open, frank basis...trying to make my aides fully informed and mutually supporting members of an over-all team. Against Inger's advice, I tried this at Treasury, too—laying the Secretary's policies and our PR plans on the table so that everyone could understand them and join fully in what we were all supposed to accomplish. So what happened? Virtually everything said went right out the door and wound up in the newspapers—ingenuously twisted to embarrass me, the Secretary, the Administration, the President. Plans, which are the critical X factor in any sound PR program, became *plots*. Rigid walls rose wherever you turned within the bureaucracy. Yawning traps were set in every corridor by political opponents.

"The ship of state is the only ship that leaks at the top," was Simon's summation.

Nor did the leaks at Treasury sit well at the White House. President Ford was above paying attention to gossip and rumor. But not a couple of his key aides. Noting that Simon was doing a bit too well with public opinion and was becoming a potential threat for higher office, they planted detracting rumors with selected reporters: The Secretary, these held, had fallen out of favor with the President. Or, conversely, he could no longer support Ford's policies and was resigning. Or that he was leaving government for a lucrative private-sector position. And day after day, I had to call these same reporters—often wise Washington types who should have known they were being shamelessly *used*—and set the record straight. Ford finally called in the White House miscreants and put a stop to the travesty.

I myself wasn't so lucky. A sympathetic career staffer (not all are Party partisans!) told me who was doing the leaking at Treasury: A former news reporter who had already proven so incompetent that we had to stop giving her assignments. So now she spent her days on the phone talking with news people outside government and fellow agitators inside. Mongovin and I tried to dismiss her, but since she had Civil Service protection, we were told to build up a file over months proving her incompetence. This we did. Once we were ready to act, however, the Personnel Department blew the whistle, warning that we would only be wasting precious time in drawn-out hearings...and advised against proceeding.

[The result: She continued idling her time away on the public payroll, drawing steadily higher pay over many years until retirement. Leading you to wonder: How many other parasites like that exist across government?]

Staff meetings thereafter were restricted to the half-dozen people I brought into Treasury, and we proceeded to implement a national information effort that got more attention than Simon ever dreamed of. Some of the actions we took:

• As the national recession deepened and economic developments moved up to "top of the news" priority, the Secretary became a regular on *Meet the Press, Face the Nation, Issues and Answers, Agronsky & Company,* etc. (Simon was considered "good copy"—bringing out one of the great values of TV/radio interviews: You bypass news "gatekeepers"—especially the many adverse Washington print reporters — and communicate *directly* with the public.)

• Briefing seminars for the Washington press on major issues were inaugurated at Treasury, with credible, in-depth materials prepared beforehand by our experts—and with people like Sid Jones and Ed Fiedler, successive assistant secretaries for economic policy, conducting lively Q&A sessions. A good example was the Administration's investment tax proposals, where Treasury not only put together the White House background materials but also took the lead in explaining them.

• Professional news groups like the American Newspaper Publishers Association were singled out for cooperative efforts to increase reporters' understanding and coverage of economic developments. For instance, Simon and a Treasury team conducted a first-ever regional conference for news people at the Medill School of Journalism at Northwestern University, an event cosponsored by ANPA and the Inland Press Assn. The proceedings were sent by ANPA to all daily papers and US journalism schools, leading to follow-up conferences.

Meanwhile, Bill Mullen, head of the National Newspaper Association, was busily lining up speaking engagements for me—at the New England, Maryland-Delaware, Pennsylvania and Oregon press associations.

Of extra interest was a talk-plus-Q&A session arranged for Simon with an AP Managing Editors meeting. Bill made a tremendous impression—so much so that a top editor took me aside and pointedly asked:

"Say, has this guy ever thought of running for President?"

I laughed and replied: "No, he's too busy *running*, period!" (But Simon's growing exposure *was* planting seeds of suspicion, and one could almost see potential competitors warily sharpening their knives...just in case.)

• A small—or so it seemed at first—change was also made in our press relations: We "purged" Treasury's musty news mailing lists and set up a system to survey editorial and columnist comment on economic policies—responding instantly with a Simon letter to those cases where we noted unusual interest on a journalist's part. This rifle-shot letter-writing effort led to follow-up interviews with the Secretary, editorials, Op Ed articles and a long article (with handsome cover photo) in *Iron Age Magazine*.

• Another giant oak grew from a small acorn when Inger one evening drove downtown with "a sandwich and sympathy" (I was working my normal 12-hour day). Sitting on the office sofa while I typed away, she began to leaf through Simon's famous Briefing Book, and became utterly fascinated with the answers to many of the questions—questions that bothered *her* about the economy, no less than others. "Why couldn't you share all this with news people?" she asked. I looked, gulped...and thus was born a Q&A on the most pressing economic issues of the day, sharply condensed and rewritten for the average guy. This was distributed with a personalized Simon letter to publishers of 500 leading newspapers, as well as to "the usual suspects" in the Capital. It got reported throughout the country...AND filed for future editorial reference. Some papers splashed the entire Q&A over a full page.

• Shoring up our internal base, a communications briefing session was held for senior Treasury officials...on a Saturday morning! (Simon made it clear he expected full attendance, including himself.) Carroll Bateman, PRSA president, and Dr. Ray Hiebert of Maryland U. talked about the nuts and bolts of PR, opinion polling, etc, while Mongovin and I talked about how to deal with the press (as though anyone knows!). Inger and Mimbo attended, too—mainly, I suspected, to critique my own performance, which, we all knew painfully well, could stand no little improvement.

More shoring up also took place across government. Gerry Warren asked that I brief the public affairs directors of all Executive Departments on Treasury's communications activities, at one of his monthly White House meetings with them. This was followed up by our sending regularly our more important news materials—so that, on Administration economic policies, at least, everyone "would be singing from the same songbook." The same was done at my own monthly meetings with information directors from Treasury subdivisions like IRS, Customs, the Mint, Bureau of Engraving, the Secret Service and ATF (Alcohol, Tobacco and Firearms).

• Inger got into the act in still another important way...wondering out loud one day if Treasury was too remote from people's experiences: "It needs a human face," she said.

And a face it got. Mongovin and I figured out that if we cut out most of our mass mailings of news releases to non-news recipients, we could save enough money to publish a monthly summary of speeches, Congressional testimony, studies, etc, in a plain but attractive magazine we came to call *Treasury Papers*...with one mailing per month instead of the present multitude. We also viewed this not only as giving readers a better grasp of the totality of issues government was handling but also as a great morale booster among Treasury people...since it reflected so well their hard work. Simon liked the idea, and we finally got Office of the Budget approval. And, lo! out came the first issue with a striking photo (provided free!) by a friendly photographer...of the sun sifting through the beautiful south portico of our building.

After several issues had made their mark both within and outside government, Simon, in a burst of enthusiasm, wrote me a note saying that *Treasury Papers* was proving "one of the most professional and understandable educational efforts of our time." Sad to say, though, the magazine didn't prove all that grand to the opposition Party. The ink was hardly dry on the first issue before a call came in from a Congressional committee chairman demanding to know why public money was being "so extravagantly wasted." Others called it "a puff piece for the Secretary." So it was well we had done our homework on savings before launching this new ship, which, despite such political shots across the bow, sailed on throughout my short, turbulent career in government.

• Perhaps the highest-impact, most enduring thing we did started out modestly—in a phone call from an editor I had long worked with, Ken Gilmore of *The Reader's Digest*. Ken said that the legendary DeWitt Wallace would like to meet the Secretary, whose courage and crusading he had come to admire. So the magazine arranged a luncheon meeting atop the Chrysler Building in New York City, with Simon sitting to the left of Wallace (near his good ear). It turned out to be a memorable occasion, with Simon ranging with feeling over his harrowing three years in Washington. Wallace asked a lot of questions, listened intently to the answers, and finally uttered these magic words:

"Mr. Secretary, have you ever thought of writing a book about your experiences?"

Well, that was like throwing a big bone to Bowser! With the *Digest* footing the bill, a ghost writer was lined up (and later replaced by someone Simon worked with more smoothly). And, in due course, *A Time for Truth* appeared in bookstores. Though I was then no longer with Treasury, the Secretary sent me a copy of the ms. before publication. I read it thoroughly, phoned him and said:

"It's a good book, all right, Bill, but I believe that if some of the shrillness could be toned down, it'll be judged a *great* book."

"But damn it! that's just the way I feel!" he answered. And that was that.

How wrong could I be—at least in terms of the public's reception! The last Inger and I heard, sales of the hard-cover version were approaching a half-million copies, and a wealthy West Coast admirer was financing distribution of a couple million copies in paperback. With all royalties going to Bill's *alma mater*, Lafayette University. [Later, Simon bylined still another book called *A Time for Action*.]

• As for that crucial organization liaison slot, we finally brought a likely looking woman aboard...but she never really got a feel for what we were trying to accomplish. I then sent an SOS to Leone Baxter in San Francisco, the past master in this area. [Remember her role in the railroads' anti-featherbedding campaign?] Clem Whitaker had died and

Leone was now consulting on her own. We couldn't pay her a red cent, but that didn't faze her. She grasped in mid-air the need for us to get away from talking just to business/financial/investment people and to broaden the reach of Simon's message to the general public—not only through news outlets but also through women's, farm, labor, law, urban, medical groups. The upshot: A national woman's organization was singled out for priority attention in terms of both setting up a major Simon speaking platform and providing aid in creating economic-policy program materials for local use in the thousands of the group's chapters throughout the country.

• Leone also lent invaluable aid in another approach of enduring impact. The two of us began to explore setting up a new national citizens organization focusing directly on economic problems—a breakthrough I knew would interest Simon. Leone got the distinguished head of a newspaper chain interested in the idea, too. The four of us then got together, with Bill outdoing himself in wowing our guests...and promising whatever help we could provide on a personal basis. And thus was born a key Washington group that is still working to restore common sense to government economic policies. Its main theme embraced the many points Simon was already making everywhere he appeared. Some of his favorites:

• America's democracy has within itself the seeds of its own destruction. Political leaders cannot resist the temptation to spend someone else's (our) money. Spend-elect, spend-elect approaches have become THE Washington game. And like the average family's household budget, disaster lies ahead as Federal budgets become increasingly unbalanced and deficits skyrocket. [We talked at that time about the horror of $100 billion deficits; think of the clear and present danger today as they approach *many times* that level.]

• The public's servants are fast becoming the public's masters. Constantly rising salaries (Federal "comparability" studies are a recurring travesty), husband-wife-relative cliques simultaneously feeding at the public trough, lavish expense allowances and political slush funds, chauffeured limousines and the many other perquisites of Federal office...are putting our "servants" completely out of touch with average citizens, our lives, our needs. Here, indeed, is a New Royalty in the making.

[Inger found it sickening to see how people fawned over and played up to public officials—including the Secretary. Even I, his pale shadow, suddenly became a Very Important Person—a supposed channel to The Great One. Inger, with her unique insight, could not understand how Americans, of all people, could be so obsequious to those in power. Didn't they realize that they were being fleeced like sheep? Couldn't these lineal descendants of that mighty uprising 200 years ago against George III sense that every tainted breeze from Washington brought rising threats of an insidious new tyranny?

[Another insidious new tyranny was also detected by Inger. A great blessing of democratic governments is their protection of minority groups from the tyranny of the majority, she pointed out, then asked: But who will now protect the majority from the tyranny of the minority? Especially in Norway, a small minority of the public—in academia, the press and government—has come to dominate the public discourse, effectively cramming their views down the throats of the rest of the population. Anyone perceptive and courageous enough to speak out against this new tyranny is ridiculed as being out of date and out of touch...and, except in rare cases, silenced. Thus is independent thinking squashed by pressure to conform to a small clique's views. Could Plato have been wrong in extolling rule-by-the-elite in *The Republic*?]

• Only an aroused public, Simon said, can force political leaders to rein in on those ominous Four Horsemen of the Economic Apocalypse—over-spending, over-taxation, over-regulation and an overblown bureaucracy. Which spread under their galloping hooves the evils of inflation, unemployment, bankruptcies and shattered living standards.

• Simon also liked to lead off his talks with a note of relative levity—picking up that well-worn line, *Washington is the only place on earth where sound travels faster than light.* Adding that he hoped he might be able on this occasion to speed up the transmission of light....

• One of Bill Simon's comments that Inger admired the most is worth quoting here, for it applies today with at least equal force: *As a nation, we have been indulging in a massive consumption binge. We have been carelessly using up our inheritance from the past* [through inadequate savings and dwindling investment in new plant and equipment] *and borrowing blatantly from the future* [through runaway personal credit expansion as well as deficit spending]. *We are living far beyond our means—in effect, burning the candle at both ends—and the candle is getting shorter.*

[Are you listening, Mr. Bush? Congress? Is *anyone* listening?]

About Federal deficits, a hopeful theory lies in the concept of a "cyclical budget." This holds that the government should run a surplus in boom times and allow a deficit in recessions. Federal surpluses would thus act to dampen inflationary tendencies as the economy expands... and excess spending would stimulate the economy as it recedes. *Good idea*! But, except for rare occasions, it's been proven virtually impossible to implement. The reason: Congress always has a zillion ideas for new spending programs (these buy votes!) and simply can't withstand the temptation to devote *any* surplus that comes along, regardless of economic conditions, to these "worthy" purposes. Many also argue that Federal tax levels are pitched at chronically inadequate levels to produce balanced budgets anyway...except, possibly, during a runaway boom.

Speechmaking was vital to our campaign not just in terms of the immediate audience, of course. It was key to our grassroots outreach. As on my baptism trip to New York, we wove around each talk in cities outside Washington a news conference, an appearance on a leading TV/radio talk show, a meeting with the top editors of a major newspaper or magazine, etc. We tried to hold scheduling to cities we could fly to from Andrews AFB, then back, in one day—that is, to places as far away as Dallas, Denver and Minneapolis, but seldom beyond.

Once, getting up early for a trip with Simon to Dallas, I got a phone call from him saying he was moving up departure from Andrews AFB an hour earlier than scheduled...and I'd better get *moving*. I did, too—cutting up my face with the razor, throwing on my clothes and breaking speed limits to get to the airport in time. To no avail! There against the fence walling off the runway stood John Gartland, pointing at the distant horizon. And there I beheld Simon's plane rapidly becoming a dot. He wasn't waiting for anyone....

Another speaking engagement came off considerably better. The Tax Foundation (in New York) invited the Secretary to address its annual dinner meeting. As usual, Gergen and Gartland and our economic policy assistant secretary and I met with Bill in his office a week in advance to chew over what he might say. The several suggestions that came up struck me as routine—more of the same. When the session broke up, therefore, I remained seated.

"Something wrong, Jim?" Bill asked, impatient to get rolling on his deskful of crises.

"Well, yeah," I answered, readying myself for instant execution. "You're talking to a top *tax* group. They'll be dying to hear your views on one of the most serious problems the nation faces—*taxes*. So, Bill, if you feel you've really got something to say in this field, *now's* the chance to say it."

A clicking sound was the answer I got. Next morning, however, Simon called our speech group back into session, along with our assistant secretary for tax policy, and announced he was going to focus his talk on crucial changes that should be made in the national tax structure. Desperately needed, he would be saying, was *simplification* of a fiendishly complex tax code…plus deep-going changes that would make taxes more *equitable* among taxpayers and more *effective* in raising revenue for government. [Doesn't all this sound familiar today, too?] This hit the news wires like a bombshell, with Simon lauded across the country for his insight and courage in speaking out on everyone's Public Enemy No. 1.

One more speech should be mentioned, for it became truly personal. Leone Baxter used some contact magic and got Simon invited to give the commencement address to the graduating class of San Francisco State University. Here was a great opportunity to go beyond the usual palaver and provide a depth look at public problems from the perspective of life experiences…and, hopefully, extend some inspiration to young people "about to go out into the world." To avoid messing up the graduation ceremony, the University president added one condition: If the Secretary had to cancel his appearance for any reason, I would take over in his place. So what happened? A crisis did, indeed, come up…and you-know-who had to take over.

The event turned out to be a grand experience—for me and Inger, if not the students.

We worked out my comments on the long flight to the West Coast; with Simon's withdrawal coming so unexpectedly, I would have to speak from scribbled notes. And suddenly there I stood in bright sunshine before a couple hundred graduates. No Ivy Leaguers, these students knew about every wrong committed in the private sector but little about excesses in the public sector. They were also badly upset over the latest news from Saigon...where the last Americans had to flee the country in disgrace in helicopters from atop our embassy building as the Communists rolled over South Vietnam. I steeled myself for a rough reception.

I decided to talk to the class as I would to our own sons, who were in the same age group (Erik was now 21 and Jimmy, 26). So I began "telling it like it is": Of fighting my way up as an urban urchin on the streets of Pittsburgh, of shifting over during the Depression's hard times

Inger gets into the act! Here she prepares to join me and a planeload of Ford Administration economic experts in a take-off from Andrews Air Force Base outside Washington to an international conference in Jamaica.

to becoming a farm boy, of dodging torpedoes and divebombers during War II, of struggling through Wayne by sweating out onerous blue-collar jobs, of working through a half-dozen communications jobs into, finally, the hallowed halls of the Federal Government. My key message: Things may look bad to you now...BUT, as my own generation experienced so deeply, it was once even worse. Children of want and hardship, of fear and war, we *did* come through, however, and proceeded to launch America onto an unprecedented period of growth and innovation...AND, with your fresh thinking and indispensable help, we can now work together to build a still better future.

[In his recent book Tom Brokaw called us *The Great Generation.* We hardly felt "great" during those hard times, however; we were too busy trying to survive and "muddle through."]

Covering current problems with Washington, I said, "*We need government, yes. But what we desperately need is good government—the kind that comes up with sound policies and which carries these out effectively. What we don't need is a ponderous, rigid, unresponsive bureaucracy that chronically lives beyond its means, that tries to milk the economy for more than it can produce, that spurs inflation and unemployment and that, through its powers of taxation and regulation, increasingly dictates the course of our lives.*

Then came the crucial point of our remarks—the key thought we hoped the students would carry away with them and remember from this banner occasion: Inger's grand, futuristic concept of the Four-Dimensional Human. The graduates had spent some 16 years of their lives acquiring *knowledge.* But, I said, if they failed to move beyond this one area, important as it is, they would wind up as one-dimensional people. [And we've seen a few too many of that stripe!]

So I expressed the hope that if they hadn't done so already, they would move on to explore the rewarding wonder-world of art and culture and become *culturally aware.* Then, that they would absorb the inspiring world of religion and morals, ethics and philosophy...and acquire *spiritual depth.* And after immersing themselves in these three areas of self-fulfillment, move on into the critical 4th dimension—and develop an abiding *concern for others.* For only by practicing such concern can the world's peoples finally overcome history's ugly legacy of exploitation, hatred, terrorism and war...and begin to live together in harmony.

And only by *your* broadening *your* life goals to include all these four dimensions can you become a fully developed, truly civilized human being.

Concluding, I echoed another of Inger's contributions: *"I feel we Americans can solve almost any problem as long as we retain those priceless incentives our forefathers developed...to work, to produce, to achieve, to excel. And we will surely fail once these are lost. I hope that your generation will demand we return to those things that inspired our nation to greatness in the first place...and that in fighting to build a better nation and a better world, you will adhere to your ideals and to those inspiring words of that singular statesman of our century, Winston Churchill, and never give up—never, never, NEVER!"*

Was that applause I heard? The students were on their feet! Inger said I heard right...but was too winded (and wound up) to know.

As a new Presidential Election year opened up and Ford began to lay the groundwork for his campaign, Simon phoned an urgent message in to my office from a drive back from the White House: I was to meet him in his office upon arrival.

We've got to lay off, he said, referring to our whole communications effort.

The reason: "We're getting too much public attention and getting in the way of the President."

Startled, I asked if that meant cutting out TV appearances, speaking engagements, news activities and the rest of our aggressive PR programming...and he replied, *everything!*

Well, I didn't know whether to laugh or cry. I returned to my office and stared out at the Ellipse a long time...and then called Inger.

I knew Bill was absolutely loyal to the President, just as he expected everyone on Treasury's senior staff to be loyal to him. And now he wanted to head off any attempt on the part of errant supporters to push *him* forward...and to devote every effort on his part to helping Ford. But where did that leave me and the able people I had assembled within Treasury and the fantastic communications machine we had created and run like crazy over the past 15 months?

Had we reached the goals we set out toward? Simon thought so. In fact, looking back at our start-up, I don't think he had any idea then what such a program could, and would, achieve. My team had truly "hit the ground running." What had happened with the Washington press was revealing: The Secretary had fought the two-thirds that range from liberal to radical to a draw. From once feeling free to tear into this crusader for free enterprise, this group now handled him with visible caution. Simon's counter-thrusts let them know that when they attacked him, they were in for a fight. They also knew we were now in direct touch with their editors, publishers and broadcasters—their bosses—across the country. They were being held to account.

Simon was tremendous with truly objective reporters, asking only that people get their facts straight...and patting them on the back when they did so He had a unique praise-phrase for supporters: *He's a real human being!* [Inger and I hear that echoing now whenever we think of Bill.] He also had a special approach to others: He never failed to return a reporter's phone call...but in some especially worthy cases, he didn't call back until, say, 4:a.m.!

Was nun, kleiner mann? Inger wanted to know, noting my staring into space.

Well, I could have simply stuck to my seat in my grand office, doing routine things in a routine way like my predecessors...and getting public pay for "whiling away the happy hours." But, as Inger pointed out, that was hardly in either her character or mine. And as for the fantastic team I had put together, they had proven themselves too good to worry about being placed into new positions elsewhere; I would see to that.

Enter Bill McGaughey. Remember him? Some 24 years had now passed since *Business Week* sent me out to American Motors to interview George Romney—which Bill paved the way for. McGaughey had moved on to AMA (autos) and was now heading up communications for the National Association of Manufacturers. He called and said he and his NAM colleagues were following Simon's "spectacular" public opinion campaign...and would like to get together and discuss my role. Yet, McGaughey clearly had something more on his mind—something more important personally. He would soon be retiring: Would I be interested in succeeding him?

Well, that sounded at first like throwing another big bone to Bowser. But I had to say that while we could talk about cooperative efforts on our programs (NAM, the Chamber of Commerce, Business Roundtable, etc, were welcome supporters), job discussion was out as long as I was a Federal employee. That didn't discourage Bill, though. He arranged for me to meet, first, with Doug Kenna, NAM president, and, later, the Executive Committee of NAM's 200-member Board of Directors— again, so that they could hear about Treasury's outreach programs. Obviously, this also gave them a chance to "size me up."

Having laid down our communications guns, I now went to Simon and told him I was resigning. *Just what* I *would like to do, too...but can't!* was his reply. Meaning he would stick with the job at least until the election was over. I also said that wherever I wound up, I would try to continue on the outside the intense public information work we had pursued at Treasury. He liked that, and said I could count on his help wherever appropriate.

Simon held a farewell ceremony in his office, with senior staffers attending...and Inger and I heard a lot of jokes (not all funny!) about how glad everyone was to see me leaving: Simon's non-stop campaigning had worn them all to a frazzle, too! I received a "Distinguished Service" certificate signed by President Ford, plus Bill's goodbye comment—to the effect that my 15 months inside government only *seemed* like 15 years! To me, too.

The Secretary went on to say he had been reviewing what I had "forced" him to do since my arrival...and found that in just the first year, he had made 85 speeches, appeared on network television 23 times, conducted 28 press conferences, been personally interviewed 186 times and met with the Editorial Boards of 18 major newspapers.

"And all you guys thought *I* was a slavedriver!" he concluded.

As even Inger now agreed, my days at Treasury *had* been a fantastic experience. Her summing up: While I had earned a Master's Degree in International Relations through my Eisenhower Fellowship, I had earned—*really* earned—a Ph.D. in Political Economics at Treasury. And had even survived the ordeal!

The people I had worked with at Treasury would be missed. They were among the smartest, most capable I have known; not surprisingly, every one eventually ended up in high places outside government. As for me, I felt like Jonah emerging from the belly of the whale.

NAM's Doug Kenna, a former star quarterback at West Point and one bonafide "real human being," phoned Simon later for a personal recommendation. This led Bill to call me and declare: "Jim, you've got the job!"

So now I was to be Senior Vice President of the National Association of Manufacturers, in charge of communications. Inger was plenty glad over the change: Now, she might even get to see her husband again! And the boys might even get to know who that stranger was who dragged himself home occasionally. *And* we could continue living in Kenwood....

Bill McGaughey warned that the new job's territory was a minefield...and that, like him, I would have to thread my way through it *very* carefully. Significantly, one of the Board members had posed a key question at their "sizing up" meeting: *What kind of public information campaign can one carry out on a limited budget?*

My answer was that you can do a lot by rejuggling and redirecting programs and staff and existing resources, as I was sure a real PR pro like McGaughey had already done. BUT, in final analysis, I added, you have to recognize that "the bigger the buck, the bigger the bang." At Treasury we had gotten a lot of mileage out of using the communications resources of outside groups, mainly because we were dealing with a foremost public problem and because of Simon's prestige as a public leader. But, I added, such an approach could hardly be expected to work so well in a private organization like NAM.

That threw the ball back into the Board of Directors' court. I got the impression that was not the answer they wanted to hear....

Chapter IX

What can be done to turn around an organization's bad public image?

This one *was* bad, too—at least among Washington reporters. The National Association of Manufacturers was Big Business with a capital B, and you can guess how that went over with the more voracious liberals around town. Many placed NAM alongside the prehistoric Neanderthals when it came to acting on labor matters and public policy issues. [Considering the source, this was taken as a backhanded compliment by many in conservative circles: After all, when it came to public regard for the various "professions," polls consistently ranked journalists all way down in the basement...alongside congressmen, PR and advertising people and used-car salesmen.]

Bill McGaughey and Inger and I wrestled with the image question from Day One of my new job at NAM headquarters, located on 18th Street a block west of the Old Executive Office Building. With approval of the Board, Doug Kenna arranged for McGaughey to stay on as a consultant for a year. He moved out of the spacious corner office of the Senior Vice President for Communications and into an adjoining cubbyhole, where he neither complained (not once!) nor interfered in any way with the new management (me!). In terms of steering through that minefield, however, he ever offered invaluable advice—which turned out to be valuable, indeed.

NAM's executive structure seemed to me an invitation to trouble. Under the president were three senior vice presidents—meant, supposedly, to be cooperative but who, in reality, were more often competitive, especially when it came to dividing up the association's budget. Besides my post, there was one for legal affairs, headed by Dick Godown (who became a close friend)—the other for public affairs, headed by Forrest Rettgers. A third of the members of the 200-member Board, in turn, oversaw PR, while a third, each, looked after legal and public affairs activities. But *equal* the three divisions were not. Like most other Washington associations [remember AAR?], NAM was primarily a capital-intelligence and lobbying organization, and public affairs (government relations/lobbying) got the lion's share of the budget. AND fiercely defended that share.

So now I knew why that leading question had been asked at my first meeting with members of the Board. The lobby interests were saying: *No matter how grand your new ideas are, buster, you're gettin' no greater share of NAM's budget!*

Besides President Doug Kenna, the Board itself was a bright spot in this picture. NAM had 12,000 member companies, ranging from small individual-owned firms to the biggest corporations. The Board reflected all shades of opinion among these companies. A hands-on group of rotating membership, it met every three months to hear what we hirelings were doing... and to offer suggestions on how we might do better. Heading the Communications Committee was John Fisher, a tall, cooperative, engineer-trained Tennesseean, who was president of Ball Corporation (noted for their Ball/Mason canning jars, etc). The No. 2 man was Rich DeVos, the sharp, personable president and joint owner of Amway. Chairman of the over-all Board was Dick Kautz, owner of a grain processing firm in Iowa and a distant cousin of Bill McGaughey. Happily, in all three cases, we hit it off from our first meeting, with their making it clear that I and NAM's public information efforts could count on their support.

Great! They must have felt I would need it....

Another bright spot was that the Board's quarterly meetings were held at some of the finest hotels in America. Our first was at the Boca Raton Hotel & Racket Club in Florida; this was followed by others at the Greenbriar (White Sulfur Springs, W. Va.), the Broadmoor (Colorado Springs, CO), the Coronado (San Diego, CA) and the Waldorf-Astoria (NYC). Spouses were welcome to attend, as well, giving Inger a rare chance to see the country's leading businessmen close-up, in action. She found them a straight-forward, serious, hard-working lot. Janet Ball Fisher, John's wealthy, France-educated wife, was astounded to find that her husband's primary contact at NAM had a wife who both knew Europe and spoke French. She befriended Inger, introduced her around and made her feel "one of the gang." So now my favorite "furriner" got to see how "the other half" of Americans live (the -5 per cent, that is).

I talked at length with each of the half-dozen staffers I inherited, including Bob Huber, the able editor of our monthly magazine, *NAM Reports*. Bob, whom I had worked closely with when at APRC, was gradually going blind, however...so he retired, making it possible to bring Doug Trussell over from Treasury. We proceeded to revamp the magazine's masthead and layout and, after legally clearing a new moniker, renamed it *Enterprise*—announcing, in effect, that its contents would henceforth have a broader reach. Three months after my arrival, a 16-page special edition then came out bearing the front-cover headline, "GET *MAD*, AMERICA!" A distillation of the many policy materials Inger and I had worked up at Treasury concerning governmental problems—a veritable speaker's manual, this urged people to get moving and "DO Something" about them!

The "something" showed how Board members really helped. Rich DeVos, a marketing genius, maintained that a nationally distributed message would have little impact *unless* it was carried down into the grassroots by local person-to-person delivery mechanisms. Amway and its network of intensely motivated local distributors showed how well this can work. The owner of a machine shop in St. Louis then suggested NAM urge all member managements to call on each employee to "Spend a Half-Hour Today for the USA." Thus was born our "S.O.C." program—in which everyone was urged to *Support!* those public officials, organizations and newsmakers who are supporting economic freedom, *Oppose!* those who are not, and *Communicate!* your views by writing your Representative and Senators...TODAY!

We did some fine-tuning of NAM's press relations, as well. Whenever a breaking news development occurred, we issued an immediate response statement by Kenna or our chief economist...and sent out cards letting reporters know which NAM expert to contact for specific subject help. We also held a couple briefing sessions on current Washington issues. Few attended, though, showing that NAM continued to be hounded by its poor press image. A much more effective approach was needed. While Inger and I had a good idea of what that should be, its implementation would take $$$$. And that was nowhere in sight. That is, *until* I talked with another inherited staffer, our vice president for policy studies, Lee Hamilton.

Why not organize a foundation within NAM? Lee suggested. This could raise money outside the normal dues structure, bypass internal squabbling over revenue allocation, and finance qualifying public-oriented programs. *Wow!* It sounded like a solution sent right down from heaven. [Or was it up from hell?]

The Big Idea that Inger and I had in mind stemmed from my work at Treasury with ANPA and other news organizations. It involved training journalists to better understand and report on economic/political news developments. This, we felt, would not only meet a genuine current press need but, in so doing, would also deal an indirect yet decisive blow at NAM's sorry press image. So Lee and I began the grueling process of getting IRS approval to set up an NAM foundation. What would we name it? *The Foundation for Economic Freedom.* The name was Inger's contribution. Everyone liked it. In a half-year we had won approval from IRS, and the new Foundation was ready to go to work. Only one not-so-small detail remained: How do we raise the $$$$?

Well, we had an idea about that, too—and its (his) name was William E. Simon. Who in all of America had more prestige among businessmen and conservative philanthropists? Was there anyone whose appeal would be more likely to loosen up wallets and provide money for worthy news education efforts? *No one!*

So I went to Bill, told him what we hoped to do through NAM's new foundation...and, without a moment's hesitation, he signed on! *And* signed a personal letter urging their backing that went out to all NAM members and their company foundations. More than $200,000 came rolling in over the next couple months...and still more was promised.

We could now proceed to organize and carry out an unprecedented, far-reaching journalism economic education program. Here's what we planned to do:

• Economic-issue workshops would be held in J-Schools across the country, with business executives joining news leaders on-scene in analyzing problems and their reporting.

• A new journalism textbook and teaching guide would be published, authored by a dozen prominent news reporters. The title we chose: *Reporting on Business and the Economy.*

• One-day workshops on economic issues in the news would be held in major cities across the USA for working editors and commentators.

• A series of Washington seminars with top government economic officials would be held for news people from outside the Capital— with personal interviews arranged, as well.

• A university-based Center for Business and Economic Reporting would be set up, carrying out seminars and studies in the field and assisting in effective teaching.

Organizing for all this was one tough chore. Everyone and his brother had to be brought aboard (naturally, everyone knew better than anyone else how everything should be done!). Within NAM, a special group of the Board's communications committee was designated to serve as FEF's Board of Directors. This was headed by Herbert Markley, CEO of Timken Bearings, and included Dick Kautz, John Fisher and Robert Dee, CEO of Smith Kline. I myself was named FEF's president. [And who served secretly as co-president? Inger!]

More important in terms of carrying out FEF's mission was the Advisory Council we set up, which included some of the most outstanding people in journalism: Charles Bartlett, syndicated columnist; William E. Giles, editor of *The Detroit News*; Ken Gilmore of *Reader's Digest*; Dr. Ray Hiebert of the U. of Maryland; James Hulbert, senior vice president of the National Association of Broadcasters; Herb Klein, now vice president of Metromedia; William Mullen of the National Newspaper Assn.; Kevin Philips, columnist; Don Rogers, economics editor of Hearst newspapers; William Schabacker of ANPA; and Emmett Tyrrell Jr., editor of *The American Spectator.*

Criticism was occasionally heard from news sources about the use of corporate/NAM money in journalism programs (though some of the funds came from news foundations). This was expected. My own reply: "Journalists are smart enough to know if and when they're being manipulated." And as a journalist at heart, I could guarantee they were not. But the best reply came from James Elsener, editorial writer for the *Chicago Tribune:* "If the press questions the propriety of accepting corporate-funded educational programs, why doesn't it fund the programs itself?" As ANPA pointed out, the press did not. FEF did.

So where do you get people to do all the arranging and contact work required to implement such far-reaching programs? Wave a wand! Eli Lilly loaned my department a PR staffer named Dave Richards, an Englishman and talented writer. I then prevailed on Jim Kehoe, director of the US Information Agency, to lend under an Executive Placement program an assistant director, Walter Bastian. Walter was son of a DC judge and had been raised under no-nonsense discipline. Both he and Dave "had their heads screwed on straight" (Walter's favorite term) and did a bang-up job in getting our programs underway. We started with a Washington-issues workshop at the Dupont Hotel, plus two journalism school seminars—a local one at American U. and the other at Carnegie-Mellon U. in Pittsburgh. The students loved them! Particularly the chance to come to grips with real issues and discuss these with real people operating out on the firing-line.

The new book project was a classic study in cooperation between news people and journalism educators, FEF and the publisher we selected: Prentice-Hall. The book got launched during many talks with Dr. Hiebert and Louis Kohlmeier Jr., Pulitzer Prize-winning reporter at *The Wall Street Journal.* Lou signed on as one of the book's three editors, along with Laird Anderson, head of Journalism and Public Affairs at American U., and Jon G. Udell, of the Graduate School of Business at the University of Wisconsin. Anderson also authored the first chapter, "The Broad Horizons of Economic Journalism," while Dr. Udell authored Chapter Two, "The American Economy."

We then laid out more specific contents, chapter by chapter, and brought in the best news people we could find to byline each section. Included were....

• Alfred L. Malabre Jr., news editor of *The Wall Street Journal,* "Prices and Inflation."

• Abe H. Raskin, labor reporter, columnist and editorial board member of *The New York Times,* "Wages and Employment."

• John W. Hazard, executive editor of Kiplinger's *Changing Times*, "Products, Services and Consumerism."

• Dr. Udell and Roberta Hornig, of the national staff of *The Washington Star*, "Resources, Energy and the Environment."

• Ellis Haller, assistant managing editor of *U. S. News & World Report,* "Profits, Investment and Growth."

• Donald I. Rogers, business and financial editor of *The New York Herald-Tribune,* "The Inside of Business."

• Abe Raskin, "The Inside of Labor."

• Lou Kohlmeier, "Government Economic Policies."

• Harry B. Ellis, economic correspondent in Washington with *The Christian Science Monitor*, "International Economic Affairs."

A major concluding section dealt with media requirements, as follows:

• William E. Giles, editor and vice president of *The Detroit News,* "Covering Economics for Newspapers Large and Small."

• James W. Michaels, editor of *Forbes Magazine*, "Covering Economics for Magazines and Periodicals."

• Dan Cordtz, economics editor for ABC News, "Covering Economics for Radio and Television."

When our book with its star-studded cast of contributors finally appeared in print, Inger went through it page by page to find any mention of the guy who had helped lay out the contents, lined up the authors, joined in the editing and, most important, arranged the financing and publishing...and there, in the Preface, among many others, was a bare mention of my name. Inger was plenty upset:

"You mean you've done all this *for what*!?!" she wanted to know.

"But Inkie," I said, "people can get a world of work done if they don't waste all their time scrambling to see who's going to get credit for it. I don't need the credit; that should go to the contributors. More to the point, the best PR is the least seen. Let it come out in the finished product, in the performance, in the results. Like here!"

So what about that bad press relations image NAM had?

With news people swarming all over our premises, this simply faded into the woodwork! Reporters who had formerly ignored NAM were now regularly covering our doings. Our big conference room was now being used more for journalism meetings than for NAM business. (To the consternation of some NAMers!) Real reporters understood better than anyone that they, above all, were not perfect. That their field had some tall problems both *within* it and with the public. And they appreciated help in dealing with these. They were also flattered that someone *cared* about them and their reporting. For what reporter doesn't remember doing a bang-up story and then getting no response whatever? Like dropping a stone down a deep, dark well and never hearing a splashback....

A couple of my talks describing these sweeping changes promoted by NAM appeared in *Vital Speeches*. Inger and I journeyed to Dallas to make one ("Big Government: Can We Really Afford It?") while the other ("The Press, the Economy and the Nation's Future") was delivered in Akron. Both sought to dispel the multitude of economic illusions and delusions which news people often transmit to the nation. Setting these aright, we felt, was critical because these help form public opinion—and the public opinion of today easily becomes the public statute of tomorrow. For example:

• There is such a thing as a free lunch. Wrong! If the more cunning among us connive to get a rare free lunch, this raises the price for everyone else. *Someone* has to pay.

• Government can somehow pass out money that it doesn't first take away from us as taxpayers. If it tries to do so by borrowing, future generations pay the bill. Not to mention, as Inger put it, the public's paying every day in a steady, ominous *erosion of national character*.

• Business can be taxed to pay for government's largesse. Wrong again! Businesses don't pay taxes; they *collect* them. They pay out nothing they don't first take away from customers in their prices. And if competition is so stiff that a business can't raise prices, its tax payments must then come out of jobs and wages...or earnings, and this, in turn, reduces investment and modernization *and* competitiveness and jobs.

• People don't really have to work hard to produce the greater wealth everyone wants: We need only carve up the economic pie differently...and everyone gets a bigger slice. More pie in the sky! In fact, this delusion has to be the pie-est of all pies in the sky.

Right in the middle of all the effort to get FEF up and running came a mysterious invitation from John Fisher for me (*and* Inger, he emphasized) to visit Ball headquarters in Muncie, Indiana. He said he wanted to talk about NAM and its foundation. We did so, then went on to visit his and Janet's summerplace on the eastern shore of upper Lake Michigan—where they had an enormous cherry orchard bursting with delicious ripe cherries. We spent a couple days there swimming in the lake, feasting and simply enjoying the company. Then came the unexpected. When we got back to Indiana to board the plane to Washington, John took me aside and said:

"Now, Jim, you've seen how we work and live. Well, you and Inger can work and live here, too. Janet and I want you to move to Muncie...and for you to become our vice president of corporate relations."

Well! Another crossroads! Do you take this new turn? I had a hunch that Inger and her friendship with Janet had a lot to do with John's offer. It sounded fine BUT.

How could I leave this crazy place called Washington after so many years? What about all those FEF programs just getting underway? Didn't I owe all those people who had enlisted in this effort my continued involvement? And how about Bill Simon and all the money he had raised at my instigation?

John's answer: He would see that I was made chairman of NAM's PR advisory committee; then I could supervise the FEF effort from Muncie. That just raised a lot more doubts. As Inger said, everyone knows how managing by remote control works...and *doesn't.*

Inger also knew which course to take...by instinct. She was having a bad time with Washington, especially after our experiences at Treasury. And it wasn't just the daily mess being served up by the media on welfare cheating, food stamp fraud, government loan defaults, contract cost over-runs and tax evasion—on the billions being rifled from the public treasury because, as she said, "People don't seem to apply the same morality to dealing with government as they do to dealing with each other."

Yet, it was the *people* in Washington that she found most disturbing...*and* their political gatherings. Most of those attending were so busy trying to meet the "right" people and work out some personal advantage that it was impossible to hold a normal conversation. A person's eyes darted around the room even while he talked—then he would bolt away, attracted by an ostensibly brighter star on the distant horizon. The attractive, ambitious, aggressive young women-in-politics flirted flagrantly with any man they thought had influence. And constant whispering went on in every corner about new government appointments and prospective promotions. Here, indeed, was every type of scoundrel in our sky-high hierarchy of scoundrels. They shifted loyalties as rapidly as new suns rose in their me-centered skies...and old suns set.

The Flagrant Flirts got especially short shrift from Inger. At one reception in the Rayburn Office Building on Capitol Hill, I fell into a discussion with a striking brunette with slicked-back hair, slanted eyes and a full red mouth. Ink spotted us from far away and literally ran over to join us—all smiles, as usual, but with an expression I recognized as "high alert." "Remember Kalamazoo?" she asked me innocently. "And our Promise?" *Oh, yes!* I responded, then mumbled about how nice a place Kalamazoo was, quickly excused myself to attend to a "pressing matter"...and that was the end off my discussion with Flagrant Flirt.

This incident underscored Ink's firm belief was that *there's no such thing as free sex.*

By which she meant *problem-free* sex. Nor was she referring to such promiscuity-centered problems as VD and AIDS—which can be costly/deadly enough. She maintained that men should be told in their earliest 'teens that any and all sex adventures can lead to massive complications. Interpersonal entanglements of incredible complexity! Simply because these deal with the very foundations of what makes a person a person. Freud was right: Tamper with this area, man, and you've got trouble! Sex is a loaded gun, which can oh-so-readily backfire or blow up in your face. So fantasize all you want about sex adventures, if you must. But once you proceed on into reality, you run the risk of setting off a giant explosion. If you're married, you'll probably ruin not only your marriage and home but maybe even your life. So, instead of chasing the latest temptation and flirting with such danger, asked Inger, why not focus on building a good relationship with your existing mate? [Okay...*why not?*]

There's no such thing as secret sex. This was another of Inger's favorite warnings. Like murder, sex escapades will *out*. By word or deed, behavior or slips of the tongue, the participants themselves generally see to that—however hard they try not to.

Inger was under no illusions about the Mating Game...or her own sex, either. She viewed men as driven creatures—driven to make money (the more, the merrier) and achieve power and prestige. And driven by nature, like beasts in the forests, to beat out other males and capture the most attractive females. And women? Inger viewed them as driven, too—driven to *capture men* with money and power and prestige, whether attractive or not. While my wife turned up her pretty nose at people's acquisitive drives, she had too much Danish blood in her to be wholly dismissive toward money. [It's no accident that Copenhagen means *shopping* harbor.] For good or bad, money has become the West's ultimate measure of status...and of an elusive sense of security in a very insecure world.

Finally, when it comes to which sex is the most clever and calculating, Inger felt it's no contest. Women simply run rings around men.

"Can it be that men are really dolts in such a contest?" I asked.

"You said it!" came the reply.

"But now, Ink, you've gone too far," I protested. "When you married me, I had neither money nor power or prestige. So why'd you do it?"

"Love, *min elskede* [my beloved]. True love!"

That stopped me in my tracks. But, bravely still, I harked back to the inspiring poem I had memorized as a schoolboy from *McGuffey's Fifth Reader*, "So, tell me, Missus Abou Ben Adhem, do you still want to be listed as 'one who loves his fellowmen.' Or *women*?"

Inger shut her eyes and sighed. "It's getting harder," she said.

"What is Man, dear God, that Thou art mindful of him?" I prodded, echoing the Bible.

"God mindful of Man? Why should He be! When more and more people are less and less mindful of *HIM*?"

"And think of the inhuman, hideous horrors men commit in God's name! Or *Allah*'s. Or in a god by any other name."

"Well, that's not God's fault. The enemy is *US*!"

"But didn't God mean to create man 'a little lower than the Angels'?"

"Yes, but now, I'm afraid, man has lowered himself so low he's sunk out of sight."

The upshot of John Fisher's offer to come to Muncie? Inger (reluctantly) and I (less reluctantly) decided to stay at NAM and in Washington. [Had John's offer come a year later, our reaction would have been quite different. Which shows how *timing* can change everything.]

One refreshing change from Capital shenanigans came about when the Eisenhower Fellowships held a special conference for award recipients in Taiwan. China Airlines offered half-rate prices, as did the finest hotel in Taipei. So Inger and I took off for two weeks (with the NAM president's blessing), stopping over on the way in Tokyo and Kyoto. It was our first visit to the Far East, and a real eye-opener into different cultures. Inger, traditionalist that she was, fell in love with the kabuki theater's ritualistic dramas and the native-style place we stayed at in Kyoto—with shoes off in the hallways, sleeping on mats on the floor, dinners with amazingly varied food and served by kimono-clad women on low, low tables. Then came Taiwan and talks with EEF Fellows from around the world, affording rare, personal insights into global developments. My tall, blond, sparkling Inger made a big hit; she was "at home" and relaxed in an international gathering. The Orientals were not quite sure what kind of American *this* was. But the lingering trace of a lilting accent gave her away. Yes, here was another immigrant in a nation of immigrants. [Thanks again, EEF!]

As for FEF's journalism programs, Inger was especially glad that we were branching out into the education field. To this librarian, nothing was more important than education, learning, books. She treasured books as much more than just printed words on paper, however. Books bring their authors into the home as living beings...from far across the stars and the tempests of time...to share their knowledge, their feelings, their observations, their life experiences. Every bookshelf is invested with their spirits. And if you close your eyes hard enough, you can see them—writing, talking, yelling, whispering and, above all, *communicating*...hoping to reach out across the human aloneness gulf and find an echo, a responding chord in *your* spirit. Love books, Inger said, and you'll never be alone; you'll have the wisest of the ages as your personal friends. [Can today's Internet top that?]

That Fall Jimmy Carter defeated the person we had become really fond of, Gerry Ford, for the Presidency, and a flock of Georgians moved into the White House. At our own house, meanwhile, things were going awry, too. While son Jimmy had begun working as an examiner in the US Immigration & Naturalization Service (and later the Tax Litigation Division of the Justice Department), Erik hadn't quite found his footing at school, or any compelling goals in his studies. So he suddenly quit and joined the US Army. As a buck private! Inger went into shock. This was the result of my falling victim to "the Washington monster" and neglecting my sons, she said. Which was probably true.

Amazingly, however, the Army rescued us all. Erik thrived on its order and sense of purpose. I visited him at Fort Leonard Wood in Missouri, where half the mixed (and mixed up) recruits were drummed out after three months...and found he had been elected his group's platoon leader. He was then assigned to Fort Hauchuga, New Mexico...and, later, to the Defense Language Institute in beautiful Monterey, California. After a year of total learning immersion here, he emerged speaking Russian like a native.

[Sent eventually to Europe, Erik went on to get a BA in Psychology from the University of Maryland and an MA in International Relations from the U. of Southern California (both at their extension schools in Frankfurt, Germany). All thanks to the US military.]

NAM was undergoing serious upheavals of its own. A big, bold scheme came up to merge the association with the National Chamber of Commerce, thereby creating a single powerful business advocacy organization. I was handed the job of drawing up plans for merging the two communications departments, and proceeded to work closely with Doug Kenna and the Chamber's president, Dick Lesher, on the details. (For instance, the Chamber had that fine magazine I had once written many articles for, *Nation's Business*—which meant that our own *Enterprise* would have to go.)

Which group would control the resulting entity? Somewhere on the road to merger, this critical question failed to get a workable answer, and the proposed plan for union collapsed. Surprisingly, Doug Kenna, one of the nicest guys in town, was made the innocent scapegoat. He "resigned" and a new president (a.k.a. NewP) came into NAM from Big Steel. A tough labor negotiator, he never quite managed to understand why so much effort was going into "those outside journalism programs."

NewP also didn't like the NAM arrangement of having three senior vice presidents reporting directly to the president: This obviously meant a lot more administrative work for him. So a management consulting firm was hired to study the NAM structure. To get my input, their two reps talked with me all of five minutes. Then...surprise, surprise!...they came up with the designated recommendation: Forrest Rettgers, our in-house "old Washington hand," would become executive vice president—with Dick Godown and me downgraded to plain old garden-variety vice presidents. I told Rettgers that this change was a real boner: It would be interpreted by the many journalists we were working with as a downgrading of NAM's press relations. He agreed...and took the case to NewP—who did *not* agree.

Inger decided we had better start packing our bags...again.

Signs of trouble were emerging, as well, in the journalism-program paradise FEF was creating. In fact, snakes abounded in this Eden! Or, more apt, this Eden was becoming the very minefield McGaughey had warned about. Inger had also warned that anyone trying to do something so bold and beneficial was bound to run into trouble from *someone*. Look, she said, at what happened to Jesus! Well, I looked...and started clearing my desk, too.

The flow of money into FEF coffers was what, unbelievably, set the snakes a'snappin'.

First indicators of trouble came in from NAM's field troops, who were charged with enlisting new dues-paying members...and making sure dues were paid by existing members. Businessmen giving $$$$ to FEF were reported turning reluctant to make their full dues payments to NAM. After all, wasn't NAM's foundation a part of NAM?

I then ran head-on into more trouble from a Washington think-tank that was supposed to cooperate with FEF in supplying issue experts for our Washington news workshops. The head man didn't want to *cooperate*; he told me with a straight face that he would have to *control*. Sorry, sir! That was out of the question. NAM simply wouldn't buy such an arrangement. Nor would I. Worse, he said he was finding that FEF was gobbling up $$$$ that corporations would normally have earmarked for Washington-oriented programs by *his* group. And that was out of the question...from his viewpoint.

Worst of all, another foundation that was conducting journalism-business seminars like some of ours began to demand that FEF confine itself to non-competitive areas. That made no sense either because, as FEF's journalism advisory board pointed out, there was plenty of room for both foundations in this problem-ridden field. Yet, the other foundation was supported by a couple major NAM member-companies, who threatened to pull out of NAM *unless* FEF ceased and desisted. (They knew how to push the hot button. An association is a fragile alliance, and almost any strong member can veto common action.) Panic broke out within NAM: My God, we're going to *lose* some big dues-paying members! There were meetings and meetings...of the over-all Board as well as the FEF Board. And who became the target? Me!

As Rettgers commented, the dissidents know all too well that the way to destroy FEF and its journalism programs was to destroy the guy who had created and was running them.

Could anyone withstand this three-prong attack? Inger said she didn't think all the advice given by Machiavelli in *The Prince* would help at this stage. Neither did I.

A strange incident revealed why FEF was "stirring up the animals." The annual NAM Board meeting was held in San Diego that year (my third with NAM), and the governor of California, Ronald Reagan, was scheduled to be our main speaker. With Inger's help, I set up a news conference for the governor, and we both were truly impressed with his handling of the Q&A session. Here, we now knew first-hand, was a real pro. Then, we listened to his speech...and, of all things! it sounded precisely like something we might have written for Bill Simon. He skillfully addressed the same problems...and pushed the same solutions. Two peas in one pod? *Yessir!* But maybe too much so....

NewP gave the game away when he let slip, "Jim, if only Bill Simon hadn't written that letter raising money for your Foundation, there'd be no problem."

I was astounded! Simon had done this only at my instigation, and only to be helpful in carrying forward the work with news people which we had begun at Treasury. Looking into the situation, I found that the West Coast clique saw in this grand gesture something sinister. They concluded that Simon was using NAM, through me as his insider, *as one of the means to push his candidacy for President of the United States*! The West Coasters were alarmed. They already had their candidate, and his name was Ronald Reagan. Simon was out (he never tried to get "in")…and his man at NAM had to go.

The Center for Business and Economic Reporting, set up at nearby American University, became another magnate for high-level squabbling. There were charges and counter-charges, personal attacks, even a threatened lawsuit. (So much for the myth of "peaceful" academe!) It got so bad that NewP finally threw up his hands: NAM's foundation and its programs and president simply weren't worth the uproar. He sent me a memo demanding my resignation…*by noon*. More colossal crust! I felt sorry for the labor unions he used to negotiate with.

John Fisher, now NAM's vice chairman (and soon-to-be chairman), told me to sit back and relax. This, he said, was an old familiar tactic which the opposition had dusted off and was using in "a typical management power struggle."

Actually, John was wrong…at least is his reference to *management*. What I had unwittingly blundered into was a *political* power struggle. And I could see a steamroller of exactly that stripe heading right toward me.

Either way, the cannonading was unsettling the guy who was taking all the enemy fire. Inger, too. Fit to be tied, she was ready to don her Viking armor and broadsword and charge into battle. So I went back to John and said that I, too, was throwing up my hands: NAM and NewP simply weren't worth more headaches. The great guy that he was, John at first protested, then noting my resolve, proceeded to work out a deal under which I would resign and become a "consultant" for several months.

Thus, after three years-plus I said goodbye to NAM and a lot of friends and took off for Rehoboth Beach…where, by untimely coincidence, Inger and I had just gone deep into debt to buy Al Stuart's property with its priceless oceanside setting. Now 56 years old and unemployed, I felt it was high time *to go down to the sea again, to the lonely sea and the sky....*

There was a lot of spilled blood to be washed off in the briny deep. In fact, as Inger put it painfully well in appraising both APRC and NAM, if all the knives that had been stuck into my back were sticking *out*, I would look like a porcupine.

Or, as it's often said, no good deed goes unpunished.

I wrote a farewell note to the news people, educators and authors who had contributed unsparingly to FEF and our trailblazing work. Which, with my departure, died a-borning. All current programs were discontinued. All planning for new ones stopped. The foundation was shut down and its remaining funds turned over to The Center for Business and Economic Reporting. The Center became the only surviving remnant of the multitude of things FEF had set out to create. *Plus* our unique, highly useful textbook on economic reporting.

A final bit of irony: Early on, without telling me, the USIA's Walter Bastian got so enthusiastic about our journalism programs that he went to Denny Griswold, the incomparably able editor of *Public Relations News,* and suggested I be named "PR Man of the Year"—Denny's prestigious PR-upgrading award which was presented at an annual banquet in New York City. Denny liked the idea, and proceeded to interview NAM Chairman Herb Markley to lay the groundwork. At precisely the critical moment, however, all hell broke loose!

And more irony: NewP didn't last long in the association cauldron, either. He wrote a letter on NAM stationery supporting the Carter Administration position on a highly controversial issue. This went over great at the White House but NOT with a big bloc of NAM members. So he, too, shortly afterward "resigned" and went his way.

A couple morals can be drawn from this boomeranging Washington experience:

In terms of *mission*, it's obvious that the grander the concept, the more it needs to be based on a solid foundation. With the benefit of 20/20 hindsight, it can now be seen that the FEF journalism programs were simply out of place in a business organization. This was like trying to graft a rose onto a cactus. A better "fit" would have been to base them at a news organization (like ANPA or NNA) or a leading journalism school. Or back them up with a single, completely independent financing source.

In *personal* terms, you canNOT make more out of a job than it's designed for. You can't be a police-beat reporter and try to act with the authority and resources of a publisher. Anyone who's too imaginative and expansive is seen by others as a *threat*, Inger pointed out. Latent rivalries surface. Turf wars break out. Bodies are hauled out—*yours* first. So stay in your place. Keep your head down and your mouth shut. Enjoy your job. That way, it just might last a lot longer!

• • •

It was the best of times, it was the worst of times...it was the spring of hope, it was the winter of despair. That master wordsmith, Charles Dickens, said it all in thus introducing *A Tale of Two Cities*. And so it was in America, too. Still reeling from the twin blows of Vietnam and Watergate, the nation was undergoing another rough round of good and bad times, of turmoil and turbulence...and Inger was having an even rougher time adjusting to the new situation we found ourselves in. We both joined in Uncle Sam's 200th birthday celebration, helping out at the American Revolution Bicentennial Commission headquarters on Lafayette Square (and working with Chairman John Warner, later US Senator from Virginia). John Paul became Pope— the first non-Italian in 455 years. Norway's Grete Waitz won the New York marathon for the 9th time. The Shah was overthrown in Iran and the Ayatollah Khomeini set up an Islamic state, triggering portents of worse to come. Then came more ominous portents: General Saddam Hussein seized power in Iraq. Soviet forces invaded Afghanistan, unleashing a civil war all too similar to Vietnam. Margaret Thatcher became prime minister in Britain, setting off a bold conservative revolution. And an Eisenhower Fellow, Suleyman Demirel, was elected prime minister in Turkey.

With my future career up in the air, Inger went to work at the Foreign Service Institute of the US State Department in Roslyn, Virginia, teaching Norwegian language and culture to US diplomats and military officers bound for Oslo. Which meant we could go on eating!

(Her paltry pay meant we were in for some pretty lean victuals, however.) This teaching position launched a 13-year-long love affair: Ink had found her calling!.

FSI classes were never more than a half-dozen people. No lectures, please. Everyone simply gathered around a table, reviewing assigned exercises and conversing in the new language about everyday situations they would encounter in Norway, with the students getting steadily better during the six-month course. It also gave teachers a unique chance to get to know the personalities and learning strengths and weaknesses of their students. And whom did Inger rate as best? The military! Submariners like Captains Bill Hayes, Frank Caldwell and D. D. Blaha. Plus one (*only* one) USIA man, Tom Spooner. Then came an extra-special student who had been director of the Peace Corps for eight years and was just appointed US Ambassador to Norway, Loret Ruppe. Inger said she had never met anyone so alert and so able…and who so graciously gave *everyone else* credit for her achievements.

I myself spent a lot of time at Rehoboth working on the property we had bought in February. This included three vacant lots plus a 4-apartment building, an ancient farmhouse and two cottages—all in dilapidated condition and needing repair, painting and a general fixing-up. The wind howled in from the sea...and, oh, it was cold! By mid-May (three months after leaving NAM), enough was done with the place to begin renting for the Summer season…and, hopefully, bringing in some income to make the mortgage payments.

Was I worried about the future? Not any more than Inger, who, when it came to money matters, really didn't seem to care. Incredible! *We'll manage* was her attitude. So I felt much like that dubious character in the *MAD* comic books who says, *What...ME worry?* Since I was sure no one would ever hire anyone who's 56, I began laying plans to set myself up as a Washington PR consultant, even though the Potomac woods seemed full of them.

Meanwhile, I "pendled" back and forth to Washington. On one of these swings, I was lunching at the International Club on K Street with a columnist pal when I heard a hearty greeting. And there stood Bob Roland, a youthful, solidly built, articulate association executive who, when head of the National Paint and Varnish Association, used to ask me (I was then with APRC) to speak at his annual member meetings about Washington consumer issues. He was also a "good dresser"—so much so that many called him Goochie.

"You're just the man I've been looking for!" Roland said, clapping me on the back.

This put me on guard: He sounded like a bill collector or a policeman nabbing a criminal.

Roland went on to say that he had recently become president of the Chemical Manufacturers Association, that CMA was about to launch a major national PR campaign to counter the terrible image the industry was getting from Love Canal and other environmental problems...and that he wanted me to direct the effort. ME! Just like that. And when should I start? Right away! Did this mean that my days of beachcombing were at an end? You said it!

Roland knew all about my work at Treasury, APRC and AAR and as a Washington reporter. But what about my problems at NAM? Was anyone back there capable of understanding those problems...and still be willing to recommend me to another employer?

Yes, there was. And his name was Richard DeVos. The Amway president had become chairman of the NAM Board's Communications Committee when John Fisher moved upstairs, and he and I had worked closely together throughout my final storm-filled days there. So Roland phoned DeVos to get the personal recommendation he needed to take to the CMA Board. And what did this tremendous person say? Rich responded that I "had simply gotten too far out in front of a couple NAM members"—and that, considering how associations work, this was more to my credit than a detraction. [Thanks, Rich!]

So I signed on with CMA, determined to do a good job while, at the same time, keeping my head low and my mouth shut.

Inger's reaction? "NOT *another* association job!" And again: "Hope you survive!"

She lamented that by now I seemed to have earned the reputation of a Washington fireman—the guy people call on when they're faced with a blazing national PR fire that has to be put out. She also wanted to know how I could shift so readily from one crisis job to another. Well, Inkie, it doesn't happen so readily at all! But experience had taught that if you give yourself some time and do a lot of digging and talking to authorities, your brain adjusts to new situations and challenges...and you begin to see where to go and what to do. I followed this approach with staff, as well. You outline the kind of news story, feature article, speech, etc, you want a staffer to tackle...but then suggest he give it some thought and come back later to discuss it further. *His* brain then gets a chance to adjust to the new challenge and come up with ideas on meeting it. Many people panic when given a tough assignment, fearing they won't be able to handle it. But time for adjustment *can* work wonders (assuming the capability is there). All of which accords with a well-remembered verse my grandfather used to quote for my benefit:

When a job is first begun, never leave it till it's done.
Be it great or be it small, do it well or not at all!

Another small factor became important at CMA: 'Way back in my first year of college when I thought I was going in for medicine, I loaded up with science courses, including eight grueling semester hours of chemistry. So now I knew at least what an Atomic Table looks like and how really dangerous certain chemical compounds can be. This echoed the fortuitous help I received at Treasury through my college minor in Economics, and especially my course on "Financing Government." [The lesson: You never know what's going to be useful in life.]

The campaign Roland described: Chemical companies behind CMA, like Dupont, Monsanto and Dow, wanted to convince the public that the industry recognizes the dangers inherent in chemicals *and* that it is taking steps to protect people against these hazards. This in the face of attacks by environmental/governmental groups who were screaming about these dangers...and getting massive press attention. Problems to be addressed included product safety, employee safety, transportation safety and, above all, *disposal* safety—what to do with the myriad chemical dumps that were dotting the countryside and "leaching" dangerous chemicals into our underground aquifers and other water resources. Chemical contamination had become second only to atomic fall-out as a huge, scary national peril. This was the BIG issue and there was no resolution in sight, though many in the industry hoped government would eventually act on the problem and take the industry off the hook. It was obvious that chemical wastes had accumulated to such an extent over the years that requiring the companies to clean up the dumps would simply bankrupt them. And lead to no clean-up whatever.

CMA's projected PR campaign was laid out well in advance of my arrival on the scene by the association's PR advisory committee. It embraced many familiar steps: Booklets were to be produced on each of the principal safety areas, and distributed in sequence over the coming months. A first-class film was to be produced for TV and local meetings. Company scientific spokesmen would be trained and placed on radio/TV "talk shows" across the country. Then came something special (and very expensive): A major advertising campaign in national magazines would target thought leaders. The total over-all cost to CMA and its member companies: $4 million a year, three-fourths of which was for advertising. It was this money that I was now charged with spending in such a way as to get maximum public opinion impact...while placating everyone and his brother who would be looking over my shoulder.

My only question, which neither Roland nor anyone else seemed able to answer was, how long would the industry put up this kind of money for such an intangible thing as communicating, building good will and convincing people that "chemicals are good for you"?

Like NAM, the PR department at CMA was made up of a half-dozen people under a vice president, Vic Peterson, who turned out to be a genuine PR pro and totally cooperative. Roland thought the new PR effort could somehow be implemented separately from CMA's ongoing information programs. Vic and I took one look at this suggestion and agreed that it was unworkable: I needed the same staffers on the new national campaign that Vic was supervising on the old one. Just try driving a car with two drivers! So Vic transferred to another department, and I went to work.

Some of the campaign highlights:

• A speech training genius at the national Chamber of Commerce somehow got industry scientific leaders to become first-class spokesmen on radio-TV talk shows. I was the first to take the course (with Inger howling with laughter off-stage) and can attest to his skill. The key: *Relax!* Act as though you're talking in the viewer/listener's livingroom and make your points in everyday terms. We hired an outstanding DC PR man, John Adams, to place these spokesmen on radio/TV stations…and soon they were blanketing the nation with the industry's story.

• The best footage was pulled out of the motion picture film and made into five short TV clips, which were placed with TV stations across the country. One that showed a *black* chemist at work in an industry laboratory had spectacular success: It was shown time and again by the Washington NBC affiliate between evening primetime programs, giving Capital-area (government) viewer impact that could never have been bought for love or money.

• The ads that were developed by company advertising directors and a top ad agency were also person-oriented. Each showed a chemical worker talking as an *individual* to the public about his job...and what *he* was doing to assure public safety. Surveys showed the ads were noted by people leafing through target magazines and made good impressions. I myself put together a double-spread "info ad" that briefly summed up the industry's case. It ran in *Time Magazine*, etc. (Inger might have been the only one who read it!)

Environmental groups weren't at all impressed by our campaign (or maybe they *were* but wouldn't show it). If anything, they intensified their own counter-efforts. Inger's conclusion was that the professional staff running these groups was the real problem, not the public or even average environmentalists: The more that industry did to protect the environment, the louder these staffers screamed—simply because that's the way they got attention, members and money...and protected their jobs. It was a blatant case of more banging on the hollow steel drum that modern people have to live in…and survive.

News people covering the environment also seemed frozen in fixed positions. Inger and I put together a speech, "Chemophobia, Politics and Distorted Images" (reprinted in *Vital Speeches*) summing up the sorry state of reporting in this area...and its political repercussions. Chemophobia struck us as not just an attack on the chemical industry and its contributions to living standards but was also, in broader terms, a reflection of a pernicious anti-science, anti-technology, anti-growth mood that could have unfortunate consequences for the future, both within the USA and abroad.

Two years into this effort came signs of trouble *within* the CMA membership. The campaign, as feared, was falling victim to its own success. Through it, the industry was beginning to convince people it was doing a better job; its image was improving, and government was moving toward solving the massive waste disposal problem by setting up a "Superfund" to clean up the worst dumps. As a result, members began asking, why keep spending all those $$$$ on PR? Besides, the economy, including the chemical industry, wasn't doing all that well under Jimmy Carter—one reason that Ronald Reagan beat him hands-down at the polls after just one term in office.

To shore up the industry's flagging resolve, the advertising reps and agency came up with a study showing that *billions* of impressions were being made by our ad campaign on the public consciousness. This was to be presented to the CMA annual meeting in Phoenix. I gagged at the validity of the study: It seemed to come right out of *Confessions of an Advertising Man.* This led Inger to propose—facetiously—that we collaborate on a companion book that would be even more revealing, to be called, *Confessions of a Washington PR Man.* [Like now?]

In any event, I suggested the study might have at least a little credibility if Roland himself made the presentation to the Board instead of CMA's vice president for communications (me), who had an all-too-obvious self-interest. He did so...and did it well—while I gagged some more in the audience. Inger, too. We both felt I had been hired to run a national information campaign, not to fight some dubious, losing battle for PR funding. Besides, as I had proved long ago when selling insurance, I wasn't worth an *oere* (1/7 of a cent) at that sort of thing.

Back in Washington after the Phoenix meeting, Roland and I talked over the industry PR campaign's foreseeable end and came up with an agreeable result regarding my role: I would again become a consultant—this time for CMA, for eight months. This, hopefully, would give me time to develop that long-dreamed-of independent consulting business. Thus, three years into another big national information effort, I was once more "free at last!" And, at 59, clearly unemployable, according to my housemate. Or was I?

My first step was to join forces with John Adams—as Senior Consultant to the firm he had built up over the years, and its clients. Another likable, able Englishman, John proved a pleasure to work with. We set out to convince our myriad personal contacts around the country that they simply *had* to hire us to help solve their Washington PR problems. And problems the US itself had plenty of, as well. Iran had trampled on foreign embassy rights and seized numerous American Embassy hostages, releasing these (by coincidence?) at the same time as Reagan's inauguration as President. Reagan was shortly afterward shot outside a hotel in Washington, the Pope was shot in Rome and Anwar Sadat, the only Arab statesman around, was killed by Islamic extremists in Cairo. Reagan announced a huge increase in the US defense budget aimed at bankrupting the USSR. [It eventually did. The USA, too—almost!] Russian planes shot down a South Korean airliner near Japan, killing 269. In Lebanon, terrorists blew up a military barracks, killing 241 Americans and 58 Frenchmen. And Britain and Argentina went to war over the Falkland Islands.

Taking off from these developments, John and I tried for a year every approach known to man to develop new clients—yet, nothing seemed to work. We seemed to be spinning our wheels, proving anew the old adage that PR isn't sold, it's *bought*. Meaning that when people get into trouble with public opinion, *they* seek PR help—the same way you run to a doctor when sick. Nor did anyone seem particularly interested in *preventive* PR. We did pick up a couple minor jobs along the way—enough to pay for a cup of coffee or two for the staff. And we gave far too much free advice to far too many people, who thanked us (for our stupidity!) and proceeded to put the advice to good use without paying a red cent for it.

Remember the APRC Chairman's warning against giving free advice? Inger did...and asked plaintively, "How many years do you have to live, Candide, before learning *at least a little* about human nature?"

Well, I was at least learning more about my wonderful wife's former homeland. Since we had extra time, we spent more of it surveying Norway's fjords and fjells (which isn't a bad way to spend your time). We also located an apartment with a fantastic view over Oslofjord...

and *bought* it without blinking. Or maybe, as in Kenwood, we bought the view and the owner threw in the property! The 11-story building sat on a hill, and our apartment was on the 10th floor—so, on a clear day, you could see across the fjord, with its ships and sailboats, almost to Sweden. Or take an overnight ship south down the fjord and across the Skagerrak to Denmark.

And where did we get the $$$$ for this wonder? By selling the Old Farmhouse in Rehoboth. But what about all the debt incurred in buying that house and the rest of the property in Rehoboth? Well, we got lucky (though Inger insists that the harder you work, the luckier you get). We converted the apartments to condominiums, sold four and kept one…and paid off the mortgage. So now we could enjoy beach-combing without sinking under waves of debt.

These grand places were not just for us, either. Inger thought they should be enjoyed no less by Jimmy and Erik…and their families. Both sons had recently gotten married, making Inger and me into those dreadful beasts known as *in-laws*. But if *we* were to be in-law beasts, what, Inger wanted to know, would that make our daughters-in-law?

My extra time also went into renewed free-lancing writing, particularly for my long-favorite outlet, *The American Legion Magazine*. A lengthy article on consumerism was followed by one on Norway's critical role as NATO's northern defense anchor, written on the scene. The ink was hardly dry on this piece when a letter suddenly appeared in our mailbox from the former *TALM* editor, ol' pal Joe Keeley. His surprising message: The American Legion was thinking of overhauling its 65-year-old magazine (it really needed it)…and would I object to Joe's recommending me for the job?

Oh-h-h! How do you respond to that one? My first reaction was to wonder if Joe had lost his mind. We lived in Washington and the Magazine was published in Indianapolis. And I couldn't even imagine how the twain would meet.

Inger helped: Why not? she said. We were both dead-tired of public relating—sick of all the slings and arrows thrown my way on the Washington PR beat, sick of lobbyists, politicking and politicians and all their hangers-on. And here, right before us, was something new. Maybe even a chance to leave the whole discordant PR field and return to my first love, journalism (which must surely be no less discordant).

But hold on! Inger cautioned, abruptly reversing course. [What else could you expect?] You wouldn't move to Muncie—remember? And you're not about to get me to move to "that other Indian place"!

Nevertheless, a meeting was arranged for me in Washington with Robert Spanogle, the executive director of the Legion. Bob wanted to hear my ideas on reshaping *TALM*, which were literally *legion*—dealing mainly with editorial focus and graphic appearance. He had some ideas, too...on the kind of work arrangement that could bring me on board. Since internal relationships made it impossible for the Legion to match my CMA salary, Bob proposed an ingenious solution: I would get what they could afford but work less than full time, thus letting me continue independent consulting with others. The Legion would rent an efficiency apartment for me at Riley Towers, a block from headquarters, and I could fly out to Indianapolis on Mondays and return to DC on Thursday or Friday. With all expenses paid. The solution was, indeed, *ingenious!*

More meetings followed with key players, plus on-scene talks in Indiana. And before Inger and I knew it, I had been enrolled as the new Editor-in-Chief and Publisher of *The American Legion Magazine*. Circulation: 2,500,000. Readership: 7,000,000.

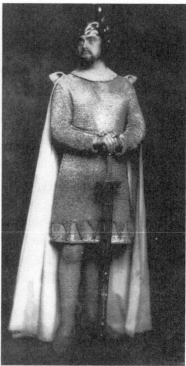

(Upper Left) Inger's father, Erling Krogh, at his 80th birthday celebration as one of Norway's great opera and folk singers. (Right) Performing in the lead role in Lohengrin, *staged in Oslo. (Below) Inger's Mamma (our "great Dane") and Pappa visit the nation's capital...and love it!*

Chapter X

Inger always wanted to be editor of a national publication. And now she was going to be not just editor but *editor-in-chief.* Vicariously, of course. Which didn't daunt her at all: She knew she could horn in on copy planning sessions and influence my editorial decisions at will... and, through me, the magazine itself. And she did!

The first official thing I did after taking over *The American Legion Magazine* was designed to gladden the hearts of all freelance writers: We *doubled* the maximum payment for their articles: From $750. to $1,500. This also gladdened Inger's heart. She was tired of seeing me put in a month's work as a freelancer for a few days' pay. So now *everyone* was happy (except, of course, the magazine's owner, the Legion, which had to foot the higher bill).

This change also boosted *TALM* into 12th place as "most desirable market" for freelance writers. Meaning we could now appeal to better writers and raise the quality of contributed articles. Which we promptly set out to do.

Once I got settled in at Riley Towers, with Inger's help, we set out to find out more about the Legion and to meet the people at headquarters. The Legion building itself turned out to be a classic design located prominently in the city's landscaped central five-block area known as the World War Memorial Plaza. Happily, the corner office I inherited had an unbeatable view over this parklike setting. Of most interest to Inger, though, was Clowes Memorial Hall, center for the performing arts and home of the Indianapolis Symphony. As expected, the wildly popular annual Indy 500 Auto Race came in far down her list as an "also ran."

We found out a lot we never knew about the Legion, too. For instance, that it sponsors the annual Boys State and Boys Nation and, in cooperation with the (women's) Legion Auxiliary, Girls State and Girls Nation. That it sponsors nearly 2500 Boy Scout troops (plus hundreds of Girl Scout troops), making the Legion a foremost backer of these good-citizenship activities. That popular, highly rated American Legion Baseball has produced more than half of today's major league stars. And that in 1944 the Legion authored and pushed the GI Bill of Rights through Congress—an action that came to change the face of postwar America (though it did nothing whatever to help merchant seaman veterans, as Inger again sadly pointed out).

Incredibly, my having been in the US Merchant Marine during WWII continued to plague me even in my newest job. Despite my three-plus years of hazardous sea duty, some Old Guard legionnaires began a whispering campaign as to whether the new editor and publisher of their magazine was a "proper" veteran, or even qualified to be a Legionnaire (I had already joined National Press Club Post 20 in Washington). This brought Bob Spanogle riding to the rescue. He pointed out that, after all, I *was* a member of the US Navy Reserve during those tough WWII years...and that I served my country just as heroically (his word) on merchant ships as I would have had I been on Navy ships. (Not that we Merchant Mariners ever once felt like heroes; we were just doing a job and hoping, by the grace of God, to make it through to the end of the war.) Spanogle's explanation stilled the hounds' howling but never really settled the issue...as I was to hear repeatedly afterward.

After partially shaking off those nipping at my heels, I turned to the areas on which Inger and I had decided to concentrate in building a better magazine: Editorial focus, graphic appearance, staffing and advertising. A big order! Involving a complete overhaul....

A special, authoritative identity for the magazine seemed to us a first urgent need. As the originator 26 years before of the continuing "Washington: Pro and Con" feature and contributor of many articles since, Inger and I knew personally of the magazine's widely varied contents. It is by no means a "house organ" but, rather, a broad-reaching, general-interest magazine. Yet, a refocusing was clearly necessary to better reflect what the Legion itself stands for. So we introduced this subtitle under the masthead on the contents page, "The Magazine for a Strong America." This seemed a worthy supplement to the Legion's expressive traditional motto, which continued to be carried on the cover, "For God and Country."

Having worked closely with *US News & World Report* on several interviews that its editors did (with Bill Simon, for one), we proceeded to draw up plans for a series of "Headliner Interviews" as a means of getting top national people involved in the magazine...*and* thereby both raising its stature and attracting greater reader and advertiser attention. This was supplemented by adding a new layer of in-depth "Reports to the Public" on issues of major current significance, such as national security, terrorism, economic problems, better health, the future of the labor movement, organized crime, communism, the USSR and the many ramifications of the Cold War.

News about the Legion itself—member and local Post activities (there are over 15,000 community-level Posts) plus national meetings and headquarters developments—were consolidated in the middle of the magazine, immediately following the general-interest features, and given distinctive layouts. These items had formerly been scattered throughout the "book," giving a chopped-up, thrown-together appearance. Yet, what was more important to Legion members than seeing their own names in print?

It's hard to believe, but we also found that the editorial staff was operating with no plan beyond piecing and pasting together the upcoming issue with whatever was coming in over the transom from Legion officials and freelance writers. NO plan! This amounted to trying to find your way through a dense forest without either a compass or a blazemarked trail. So a new planning process was instituted...laying out general coverage goals for 12 months into the future, with more specific implementation carried out over each approaching 3 months. Weekly staff meetings were then inaugurated to check on progress toward these designated targets, including assigning major articles to the most capable, most relevant freelancers...and to give staffers a chance to come up with *their* ideas on future directions and copy inclusions.

(Inger knew a lot about woods without trails, from hard experience. She and I had set out once from a lodge near Stowe, Vermont, on an all-day crosscountry ski trip. As the shrouded sun neared the horizon at day's end, we found ourselves far from base...so decided to take a shortcut home through the forest, along a trail that seemed to lead in the right direction. But the trail dwindled away and disappeared and, with darkness and the thermometer both falling rapidly, we wound up in the middle of nowhere, struggling and stumbling through fallen trees, thorny bushes and deep snowdrifts...*on skis.* Desperation drove us on...until, finally, exhausted and freezing cold, we escaped from calamity as the last glimmer of daylight disappeared. I don't think many women other than Inger could have managed such a ordeal. And in her late 50s! Her only reaction: "No, no, NO more wandering through trackless wildernesses for me!")

Graphic redesign turned out to be fun, echoing many of the things I had learned at the *Chrysler Motors Magazine* 35 years before. A top layout artist (whom I had worked with in Washington) was engaged to come up with a bold New Look, from cover design and contents page all the way through to the popular concluding "Parting Shots" page of humor. Included were new type faces and column widths, greater use of color and more dramatic photos and artwork. Shunning the fancy and superficial, we set out to achieve a feel of *strength and solidity*— elements the Legion itself stood for. Thus, the cover logo and section heads were newly set in Bolt bold, happily capturing exactly this effect.

The first issue of the magazine incorporating this New Look and our myriad editorial changes rolled off the presses four months after my arrival in Indianapolis. The cover was an eye-stopping piece of Star Wars artwork, heralding a Q&A interview inside with Casper Weinberger, US Secretary of Defense. The New Look hit Legion readers with the impact of an Outer Space missile. We were off and running!

Personal interviews with myriad top public figures followed during the months ahead, commanding rising reader attention (and teaching Inger and me a lot about the art of interviewing). The April issue featured Secretary of State George P. Shultz. Then came Secretary of Commerce Malcolm Baldridge, CIA Director William J. Casey, UN Ambassador Jeane J. Kirkpatrick, Joint Chiefs of Staff Chairman Gen. John W. Vessey, Secretary of Labor Raymond J. Donovan (appearing in September—a Labor Day special), FBI Director William Webster, disarmament negotiations Ambassador Edward L. Rowney, IRS Commissioner Roscoe Egger (April), Secretary of Agriculture John R. Block, Secretary of Education William J. Bennett (whom I would interview two more times over coming years), James W. Rouse (urban redevelopment expert), NATO Secretary-General Lord Carrington, Arnaud de Borchgrave, *Washington Times* editor-in-chief and expert on Soviet disinformation...etc., etc.

Just listing these authorities provides an idea of the broad range of subject matter covered...and the public/reader interest in what such notables had to say. All were interviewed by tape recorder — with the tape breaking in one case halfway through and the microphone conking out in another. With both interviews requiring writing the entire interview down from memory later. Making and re-making appointments with busy people was no less a hazard. But the main challenge was to research the subject (and person) involved to the point where you came to know almost as much as the interviewee did. Pertinent questions were drawn up beforehand to guide the information flow, but you had to be ready at all times to pursue an unexpected comment...and make the result come out as close as possible to actual conversation. In each case, I rehearsed the whole sequence with Inger to get her reactions and input before charging off into "the lion's den."

Inger got her licks in directly on one magazine edition—a special headlined "Travel, America!" Taking off from the inside experience she had chalked up as a Capital tour guide, she wrote a glowing byliner on Washington as a foremost travel destination. A fine spread, it was... with great photos. But where was the freelance payment? she wanted to know. Sorry, Inkie, I had to say. It simply would not have looked "seemly" for the editor to be paying out Legion funds to his wife. She reluctantly agreed...*and* decided (sorry, Jim!) to sell her writings elsewhere next time.

The magazine we were most proud of? That of December 1984— our "Pursuit of Peace" issue. Ronald Reagan had just been re-elected President of the USA, and Inger suggested the magazine do something special as a follow-up. So by extraordinary effort we managed to get statements of 300-to-500 words from each of the four living Presidents: Reagan, Jimmy Carter, Gerald Ford and Richard Nixon. These headlined that month's Christmastime issue on an inspiring cover de-sign of a dark-blue sky filled with stars. Richard Nixon's comments were especially memorable...for he urged America and other advanced nations to come to grips *now* with problems of the misery-ridden Third World, which is being left far behind the West's progress—left wal-lowing in the debris of starvation, disease and ignorance, which gener-ates rising resentment and a craving for vengeance. The result of the West's failure to act? The likelihood of a "Third World war."

A Third World war! The terrors of terrorism! Islamic fanaticism run amok! Muslim-Hebrew, Muslim-Hindu, Muslim-Christian, Catho-lic-Protestant conflicts! Cross-border conquests! Class, racial, geno-cidal hatreds!

Upon reading the former President's remarks, Inger turned to me with a stricken look and said, "What he's saying is that *unless we all learn to live together on this tormented planet, we will surely die to-gether.* Desperate people take desperate action. Western nations could well be inundated by waves of asylum-seekers, migrants and immigrants...and our precious democratic institutions and prosperous societies destroyed. But there's got to be a way out! Isn't it far better to help these desperate people help themselves *where they live*? In their own countries? Just throwing money at the problem seems only to make it worse: The money drifts into a few pockets and makes these few richer while everyone else stays poor.

Inger went on: Couldn't the UN *or someone* convene a world con-gress of statesmen—*real* statesmen—to come up with practical, work-able *people-oriented* solutions? For example, most of Africa is almost a basket case; but why couldn't Africans themselves create an all-Af-rica Peace Corps that would put the most developed Aficans to work helping the least developed?

"*Why* not?" I answered, throwing up my hands. "Unfortunately, Inkie, you've put your finger on the X factor, the missing ingredient. It's those statesmen. Where do you find truly wise, objective people—and not wind up with just the same old power-hungry debating crowd—or with people already tarred with corruption and just looking for an-other handout?"

Where?

Besides meeting a long row of outstanding people (*in addition to* the many at Legion headquarters!), my greatest pleasure as editor-in-chief was returning in small ways some of the big favors people had extended to me over the years. Thus, I was able to get my former *Business Week* boss, Stan Brams, the ultimate authority on the auto industry, to do a couple of bang-up, top-dollar byliners on Detroit—one on America's long love affair with the motor car, another on where the US auto industry's going (?). John Adams of *US News and World Report* turned in a timely April-issue article on taxes. Ol' Pal Dick Godown from NAM days, now president of a biotechnology association, got into the magazine with some incisive comments on this exciting, pioneering field. Bill Simon got a chance to damn deficit spending again in a no-holds-barred interview. Dr. James Fletcher, who tried to hire me at NASA, talked about coming space developments. And some long-standing PR contacts contributed articles from their own areas of expertise (yes, many PR people *do* have solid stories to tell!).

When I put on my hat as *TALM* publisher, the results were not always so rosy. The magazine was a going business with an annual budget of more than $9 million. Questions came up right off the bat about getting the right printing firm for the magazine; once the presses got rolling for each issue, it took *10 days* to churn out enough copies for our 2.5 million members. And what about the massive purchases of paper that were needed? To save enough money for higher staff salaries, we tried going to a cheaper paper. This didn't work at all; it simply made the magazine *look* cheap. Fortunately, we were able to land a top production manager, who seemed to have solutions for all such problems. (Thanks, Bill Poff!)

Other staffing changes came apace, including bringing in a new art director and filling two editorial positions. Half of *TALM*'s 30-member staff worked in our circulation department, which had long since been thoroughly computerized and modernized, freeing me of headaches in that area. The able woman manager served up a startling statistic: Each month *8,000 Legion members* had to be taken off the rolls, mainly because of death! These were mostly aging veterans of WWII (*my* generation) and the last surviving vets from WWI—a dismal fact behind the Legion's current drive to sign up new members from

America's Vietnam agony.

One inherited assistant editor caused a personnel ruckus: She announced that she would no longer proofread copy. I told her I personally proofed every major article and interview. Couldn't she do the same? *Oh no!* she said, implying that such routine work was beneath her dignity...even though it was included in her position description. More entreaties followed, along with a legally required written notice. All without result; she said she would rather be fired. Which, at last, had to happen. Leaving me feeling completely baffled. How could anyone do something so dumb! Yet, she wasn't dumb at all...and the sister she relied on for advice was a judge. So it seemed a case of pride carried to the ultimate irrational, self-destructing extreme.

Not so! said Inger: Here was another "victim of the times." Woman's Lib had taught her all about assertiveness...and she finally asserted herself right out of a good job.

Building a new editorial staff reminded me again of how difficult it is to find truly able, suitable people—those who both *know* what to do and *will* do it. Inger warned that her own job experience indicates that while the communications field has an abundance of fine performers, it is also beset with many "climbers" and "con artists." The first are generally the bright young—people who come from nowhere and don't know a lot BUT are willing to work hard to get ahead. Given solid guidance, many of these work out. And the second group? Forget it! These are people who look great on paper and talk a great game BUT don't perform. So you've got to become an expert at poring over resumes` and weeding out such undesirables. Despite such precautions, however, I still occasionally got "stuck and stung."

Deadlines are another test. People with journalism training know all about completing assignments on time. To them a deadline is sacred. But that's not always the case with PR types and others with a general communications background. So how do you get such non-performers to perform? Inger's advice: *Don't even try!* It's not worth expending your limited life-energy trying to get such people to work. Better to sign off and do the job yourself.

[Re bright people in communications, TV news anchorage is decidedly different, as the well-paid performers in this field will tell you.

That is, you must not only *be* sharp but *look* sharp, too—with a melodious voice and pearly white choppers through which you utter with measured authority the words usually written by ground-level journalists off-camera—who are no less bright but may not have quite your captivating personality. As the Great Bard put it, *the PLAY is the thing!* But is it journalism?]

TALM's inherited editor turned out to be a "quick read" and willing worker—*the* aide who made it possible for the editor-in-chief to be away from the scene so much. He also knew the Legion and its internal politics and which skeletons were rattling around which closets. Knowledge essential for survival! He also had a super-secretary who deserves special praise. Joan Berzins was unbelievably productive and forever pleasant to work with. I had been in close touch with her since my first freelance work was turned in to Joe Keeley and *TALM*...and never experienced or heard one negative thing regarding either her or her performance. She was one of those hard-working, unsung assistants in journalism who make editors look good, even when they're not. (Thanks, Joan!)

What about staff morale? One way Inger suggested the magazine build this up: Have a monthly dinner "idea exchange" meeting with the editors—with drinks, good food and a relaxed mood of camaraderie. And this we did (with Spanogle's OK re $$$$) at the distinguished Indianapolis Athletic Club. In announcing this revolutionary treat, I suggested that if the staffers couldn't bring ideas for new articles, etc, they should at least bring questions. Inger flew out to Indianapolis and joined in the first evening session, where a thoughtful youngster (who later became editor of a major magazine) asked: "Where are we going, Jim Sites?"

Taken by surprise, I barely managed a "huh?" Did he mean *TALM?* America? Pop culture? People generally? Life itself? The human soul? Or was his question a take-off on *Quo Vadis, Domini?* His answer was "all of the above."

Well, I didn't know anyone [do you?] who was capable of providing even minimalist answers to such questions. Unless it was Pope John Paul II. Or Inger. And who ever heard of an editor interviewing his *wife?* So we kicked this question around for months...and never resolved anything. The closest we came was a suggestion that we interview that great evangelist, Billy Graham—whom Handly Wright and I once met on a fishing pier far up the St. John's River in Florida. But the Legion represents a cross-section of all American faiths; would the Board go along with our choosing a spokesman for any one? Well, couldn't we get comments from, say, four different spiritual leaders, as we did with the four Presidents? Yes, but which four? So Inger and I are still waiting and hoping some other national magazine will one day pick up this challenge...and do us all a great service.

[Years later I did an interview for *TALM* with Gary Bauer, then head of the Family Research Council and a one-time candidate for the Presidential nomination...on America's pop culture and where *it's* going. It turned out to be a devastating indictment of Hollywood and television and the rest of the Media/Entertainment Complex for its pervading emphasis on sex and violence. Bauer singled out particularly the avid promotion in films, publications, CDs and the Internet of permissiveness, pornography, promiscuity and perversion. He then posed the jolting questions: Is *this* the kind of society we want to build? And have our children grow up in? Inger added her own question: *Is it?*]

Getting Legion clearance for controversial articles and editorial departures could have been a real problem (one Joe Keeley had warned about)...but, surprisingly, this went well. The magazine answered to and worked with a score of legionnaires headed by a good-humored, soft-speaking southerner named Milford Forrester (from, suh, South Carolina!). These Magazine Commission worthies didn't know much about journalism but, man, did they ever know about the Legion! And what readers liked and did not like...and what could go and what would not go. So I met with them regularly, talked about major changes *before* making them, and listened carefully to their reactions and suggestions. For, above all, they were our indispensable bridge to the National Commander—at that time the warm, cordial Keith Kruel—and the over-all Legion ruling body of past Commanders.

The Magazine Commission's value was underscored when a new National Judge Advocate was hired to replace the astute Bertram (Bertie) Davis, a great guy who, along with Bob Spanogle (and Joe Keeley), was responsible for my joining the magazine. Out of excess zeal, the replacement proceeded to set himself up as sort of a Supra Editor, not just checking copy for legal/libel and policy implications but also muscling in on editorial prerogatives. Well, Inger and I had experienced such problems before. (The AAR President Tom Goodfellow liked to say that he "didn't need lawyers to keep him *out* of trouble...but to *get him out* when and if he ever got *in*.") I tried direct persuasion, with no results. I then brought Spanogle into the act, also with no results. Finally, when two articles got sidetracked, I felt we had had enough. I went to Forrester, who went to a tough former National Commander, who went to the new Judge Advocate...and that was the end of the problem.

Advertising proved one hard nut to crack. Ad revenues covered a third of the magazine's costs. Yet, much of the pedestrian appearance the magazine had fallen into was, unfortunately, due to its hard-sell mail-order ads, so we set out to try to encourage general advertising. Defense contractors were an obvious target. So were "institutional" advertisers—those seeking to attract public support for their public policy positions (Legion members are famously active in public affairs). And what about beer ads...for this greatest generation of veteran beer drinkers?

Alas, nothing really worked. *Except* that old PR pal Marshall Lewis, now with the US Committee for Energy Awareness, saved one day by contributing a full-page (high revenue) ad to our inaugural New Look issue entitled, "Nuclear Energy: Is America Being Left Behind?" Otherwise, company ad directors and ad agencies alike seemed to be mired down in the attitude that *TALM* was just another of a whole group of "fraternal" publications...and if they broke the line by appearing in one, they would have to include others. Bah humbug!

Inger came up with one idea that helped move the ad mountain a centimeter or two. She looked at the dozen interviews we had done over the first year and said, hey, *These national leaders talk to America through The American Legion Magazine: YOU can, too!* (Meaning all you advertisers.) And that's the key line that finally appeared in an attractive six-page, two-fold brochure, showing interviewee photos galore, which we put together specifically for our advertising agents' use with the ad community.

Something good *did* come out of my explorations in this ad waste-land. One of the advertising people I talked with was Chuck Deasy, a retired US Navy Captain and aircraft carrier commander, who revealed that a Washington-based magazine he worked with was looking for a new editor. Its name: *Wings of Gold* (named after the gold wings Navy aviators get when graduating from flight school). Its publisher: The Association of Naval Aviation (ANA).

My ears perked up on this bit of news. So did Inger's. It had been a long 1 1/2 years since we took over the *Legion* magazine, and air commuting to Indianapolis was wearing us both down. I was weary of flying in bad weather, of delays and round-about routings, and of equally bad on-board food and service. The same for my barren room at Riley Towers. And as for my own indigestible cooking, who could stand that for long? Inger, in turn, was tired of seeing me taxi off to National Airport every week...and of wondering when (and if) I would come back. She was still enjoying teaching Norwegian at the Foreign Service Institute, but wasn't enjoying at all rattling around our big house in Kenwood alone.

Then, too, there were family changes to consider. Jimbo was winding up seven years at the US Department of Justice and was heading out to Billings, Montana, to become a partner and tax specialist in that state's biggest law firm, Crowley, Haughey, Hanson, Toole & Dietrich. This would leave Inger even more alone in Washington...since Erik was now with the US Foreign Service in Germany. There, he was intensely interested in the immense changes now going on in the Soviet Union, where Mikhail Gorbachev had just taken over and proclaimed *glasnost* (openness) and *perestroika* (restructuring) as the orders of a new day for a badly troubled system. Would such unprecedented approaches work? Hardly! Erik saw even more portentous changes ahead....

Chuck Deasy arranged an exploratory meeting for me with Mac Snowden, another retired Navy captain who was Executive Director of ANA. Tall and pleasant and an endless source of jokes, Mac said that the present editor of *Wings of Gold*, M. W. Cagle (VAdm-Ret) was giving up his post in order to devote more time to his cattle farm and "Pride of Virginia" meat business. Mac cautioned, however, that, unlike the Legion, the ANA was small (10,000 members and a half-dozen staffers), low budget ("meaning we can't pay much") and publishers of a quarterly whose 100,000 readers are a far cry from the monthly *Legion Magazine*'s 7,000,000 readers.

"You couldn't possibly be interested!" he concluded with a laugh.

Why not? was Inger's rejoinder.

My former Washington PR counseling partner, John Adams, had asked earlier if we would like to get back into PR in the Capital, and Inger and I had simultaneously blurted out *NO WAY!* No more big national campaigns and infighting among conflicting interests and colossal headaches, thank you! Besides, Inger and I liked magazine work and weren't about to leave journalism again. And as for the pay, we were now in our early 60s...and what was becoming far more valuable than money? *Time!*

So Mac got me to meet with ANA's authoritative president, retired Admiral James L. Holloway III, former Chief of Naval Operations. As forthcoming as Mac, he nonetheless wondered how in the world a non-aviator was ever going to write intelligibly about and champion Naval aviation. I wondered, too! Yet, I was no stranger to the sea, as my resume indicated. To which he seemed to have still more reservations:

How could a former merchant seaman ever relate to high-flying US Navy "top guns"? Well, hadn't I managed a few tougher challenges over the past 35 years? And couldn't *Wings of Gold* profit from an outsider's fresh touch?

We finally got down to the lowly subject of $$$$. This posed no problem for me since we were discussing what looked like a half-time job at half my CMA pay...leaving me free to freelance elsewhere, do editorial consulting, etc. Over-all, it appeared we were on track, and we parted promising to think the matter over further.

Back in Indianapolis, I broke the news of my leaving to Spanogle, who had proved to be a real pal in times of need, and we set termination date three months ahead to allow for a smooth transition. This went well except for a lot of behind-scenes pulling and hauling over who would become the new editor-in-chief/publisher. I argued that the current editor and the new staff created over the past 20 months were ready to go it alone, and the decision-makers "upstairs" finally agreed. Actually, except for advertising, the goals that Inger and I set out to reach had, indeed, been attained: The magazine looked great, and editorial coverage was now more attuned to the times. It was time to bow out.

Heart-warming personal memories would accompany me and Inger, too...with many enshrined in a farewell present—a big plaque with four covers of the magazine sculpted thereon: The amateurish-looking edition produced just prior to our arrival; the first of the "New Look" series; the four Presidents' "Pursuit of Peace" number; and that of May 1985—the last one bearing our personal imprint. I wasn't leaving entirely, in any event. The new editor-in-chief expressed hope that I would continue doing Washington interviews for *TALM. Absolutely!* was my answer. And I did....

• • •

Try going to sea on a giant aircraft carrier and seeing it in full-throttle operation. It's one of life's truly fantastic experiences. It's deafening, eye-boggling! Controlled chaos! Hi-tech at its highest, human ingenuity tuned to its finest! Inger was overwhelmed by the sheer magic of it all. Small wonder Naval aviators feel they're the greatest....

Inger and I sailed out of Jacksonville, Florida, on the *USS John F. Kennedy* under sunny skies, with the carrier heading at speed into a chill wind, which raked the deck and sent us into the lee of the superstructure, clutching coats tighter. Fighter planes roared down the flightdeck in ear-splitting precision, charging off like snorting bulls released from a paddock, soaring into the sky at ship's end and setting the ship, the sea, the very air to vibrating...while planes aloft screamed in to land, their tailhooks grabbing cable and screeching to a halt. Thumbs up! the pilots signaled. And our thumbs up to you!

Has man ever contrived such an intricate joining of man and machine...or ever run it with such skill and pinpoint precision? Not to our knowledge. Inger thought everyone involved, from the bilge to the bridge, should get a medal.

So this, we learned, is what Naval Aviation is all about. Not "all", though, because this was only a *demonstration* for us landlubbers. Think beyond! Think of trying to land a high-speed jet on a carrier that, from cloud-height, looks no bigger than a postage stamp—then of doing this at night or in storm and pitching seas. What's more, carrier crews are fightingmen and women—thousands of them—and have to be prepared to enter battle anytime anywhere in the world. Carriers are the vital instrument America uses to project power across all the seven seas, and protect national and Free World interests. What a gang! And what a challenge!

This is the crucial, amazing field Inger and I now found ourselves in the middle of. And entrusted into our hands was Naval Aviation's magazine, *Wings of Gold*, the main means of communicating the members' story among themselves and to the outer world. We vowed to give the mission our best.

It all started with a letter from Admiral Holloway welcoming me aboard ANA that Fall. Inger and I wound up at the Legion in June, spent six weeks in Norway fixing up our apartment overlooking Oslofjord and taking long, long hikes all over Nordmarka. The trip was a hearty reminder that while my wonderful wife *lives* in America, she *thrives* in Norway. Like a child returning home. We then spent September and part of October at Rehoboth surfing through white-caps and fighting jellyfish. (The Fall's the ideal time at the beach—the crowds are gone and you have all those marvels at the edge of the sea to yourself.) Noting that my income was now sharply reduced (it went from the Legion's two-thirds of that at CMA to ANA's one-half), we sold our money-devouring house in Kenwood and bought Jimmy's much smaller house in Bethesda (as he and family took off for Montana). We next tackled *Wings of Gold.*

Is it really true that one picture is worth ten thousand words?

That was Inger talking. My own feeling: This is an understatement! An unusual, high-impact picture changes your whole *perception* of what's being communicated, not only in terms of its own message but of any accompanying word-text. Remember Clem Whitaker and his emphasis on coming up with a *visual* symbol of a political or public-opinion campaign goal? And don't dreams unroll in your brain like a projected movie? Does anyone ever dream of *words* and sentences? Our conclusion was that people seem to learn best by *pictorializing* messages whenever possible.

So Inger and I put "extreme makeover" of its graphics at the top of our list in making *Wings of Gold* into an enviable, class magazine.

The editorial content, we found, wasn't really a problem. Admiral Cagle was doing an unusually good job—*really* unusual for a non-journalist—in rounding up news on worthwhile events and reporting these well. He deserved praise and ANA's thanks. The magazine's problem centered on *style*—on the way the copy was pointed up and presented. So how do you change this with a bang? You meet with Fred Maroon....

I knew Fred to be one of the top photographers in Washington, or even in the nation. He and retired Navy Captain Edward L. Beach (besides writing *Run Silent, Run Deep,* Ned was skipper of the atomic submarine, *Triton,* when it became the first vessel to circumnavigate the globe under water) had just co-authored a big, handsome book called *Keepers of the Sea,* published by the Naval Institute Press. Ned and wife Ingrid gave Inger and me a copy for Christmas...and, at first glance, we were bowled over by Fred's photos, many of which portrayed aircraft carriers and their winged progeny in dramatic, eye-arresting action.

Man-oh-man! we thought, if we could only get to use such pictures in *Wings of Gold*. What a lift they would give!

So Ned arranged for me to meet Fred in his Georgetown (DC) home. I told him that ANA had no budget for such grand things as his photos, but that they would be seen by and bring great cheer to some of the finest people in America's military forces. The happy result: Fred loaned me a million-dollar selection of his best photos at peanut prices! The first appeared on the cover of our "maiden" edition. Taken directly into the sun, it showed a carrier in the background knifing through a sun-splattered sea with a flight of airplanes coming straight at you in the foreground. It was spectacular! A fitting introduction to a new era for the magazine....

This Spring 1986 edition of *Wings of Gold* also came out with completely new and different graphics, much like the first issue we created of *The American Legion Magazine.* In this instance, however, since our budget was strictly "slim pickin's", we used a bright young artist at our printer's shop. And continued to use him—he was a *find*! The editorial content (which provided a chance to include every key player at ANA, and then some) further boosted the magazine over the top. A few standouts:

• Admiral Thomas H. Moorer, the salty, outspoken, gruff former CNO and Chairman of the Joint Chiefs of Staff and now chairman of ANA, appeared in a recorded interview, with pointed remarks on the Soviet threat and US military priorities.

• Admiral Holloway did a Q&A on "Combating Terrorism." [A score years ago!] The ANA president, who recently served as executive director of a White House Task Force on Terrorism, summed up the report's conclusions by stating, "the best solution [to terrorism] lies *in good intelligence* and such effective reaction forces that *potential terrorist actions can be preempted before they occur.*" [Italics added by Inger who, as we write this, still cannot believe the horrendous failure of US Intelligence leading up to the destruction and death of 9/11.]

• Vice President George Bush made it, too. A one-page feature related how the once-and-future President of the USA was the youngest commissioned aviator in Naval Aviation history during WWII, fought through 58 combat missions, was shot down in the Pacific and, by sheer luck, was picked up by a US submarine...and survived to go on to the White House.

• Secretary of Defense Casper Weinberger wrote a byliner on the upcoming battles in Congress over the defense budget.

• Cap's piece was reinforced by a recorded interview which Clarence "Mark" Hill (RAdm-Ret), the ANA's vice president for government affairs, and I did on Capitol Hill with Senator Phil Gramm, of Texas. Subject: How the new Gramm-Rudman-Hollings budget-control, deficit-reduction process would work. [It worked well, indeed, for many years...but not now!]

• A special treat was then added: The inside story of how the action-packed movie, *Top Gun*, starring Tom Cruise and released that very year, came to be produced. Like the film itself, the behind-scenes story was almost as exciting, featuring pilots from the Navy's Fighter Weapons School at Miramar, California, and breathtaking dogfights above the carriers, *USS Ranger* and *USS Enterprise*. (Tom Cruise later appeared as a special guest at the ANA annual meeting in Washington during the premier showing of the film in the Capital.)

Did our new approach work? Did it impress anyone? Well, it did in at least one key instance—with the guy who signs the payroll. Shortly afterward, Admiral Holloway came by my office and, casting aside his earlier reservations about the lowly seaman, said, "Jim, you're almost ready to start flying!"

As the magazine's coverage indicates, our editorial range extended far and wide... purposely...for external status-building was just as important for *Wings of Gold* as developing a solid readership. Advertising from defense contractors provided most of the magazine's budget...and, through strenuous effort by Chuck Deasy and ANA's admirals, we were able to hold that up at a cost-covering level. (As journalists learn sooner of later, *someone* has to pay the bill for printing all their fancy words!)

One of the pernicious problems ANA tried to help the Navy deal with involved flyer retention. It cost Uncle Sam more than a million dollars to train an accomplished aviator. Who puts in a few years of service—and then what happens? He is spirited away by commercial airlines! Who can obviously offer him a better deal...*plus* being home with his loved ones a lot more. So frequent coverage was devoted to this area—with Inger concluding that we were all wasting our time with "jawboning": The bleeding off of naval aviation's best went on and on.

Another problem surfaced with the magazine's editor himself. Or was it the typesetter or printer? A picture caption somehow got into print indicating that a certain ship's speed was so many "knots per hour." *Horrors!* Even the greenest seagoing greenhorn knows you can talk about knots or even nautical miles per hour, but never, never knots per hour...since the very word "knot" sums up both distance and time, or speed. A flurry of outraged reader letters followed. To which The Editor's Corner added this footnote: "The culprit has been sent back to sea to learn the ropes all over again...*and* the knots."

One other special edition of the magazine should be mentioned, for it got to the heart of ANA's *raison d'etre* itself. This was the issue of the Summer of 1987. Our Board took a look at the budget battles raging across Washington and decided we had to make a clear, convincing case on behalf of voting some of those taxpayer sums for carrier aviation. And giant sums they were. An aircraft carrier is a seagoing airport, complete with the highest-tech equipment, costly airplanes, sophisticated ammo and over 3,000 skilled crewmen and flight personnel, plus all the supplies they need to keep going. Building, equipping, operating and maintaining such a ship-of-war *costs*, period. Yet, such a printed presentation also costs—and ANA had to cut expense corners wherever possible. So we met and talked and talked...and finally decided to include in the middle of that Summer's issue a 36-page special insert—one that would not only go out as part of the regular magazine but which could also be printed separately and sent to all Members of Congress, Executive officials, news and thought leaders, etc. Included would be nine special articles featuring authorities...all the way from Navy Secretary James Webb Jr. and Congressman Norman Sissify to Navy Journalist 1C Steve Lawton. It also meant I had my work cut out for me—lots of it!

Thus it was that ANA soon came out with a hard-hitting Special Report headlined *The Aircraft Carrier: America's Indispensable Response to the Threats of a Violent Peace.*

Graced by three of Fred Maroon's most striking color photos, it had *impact!* [And hopefully helped keep our carrier fleet moving ahead...and ready for the endless crises of the Mideast.]

Dealing with the ANA's cadre of retired naval aviation officers has to be counted the greatest reward of all from the nearly three years I spent editing their magazine. Here are people who are intensely trained (Annapolis and Pensacola), who have lived their lives with danger, and who are accustomed to command (and *being* commanded). All this develops real people—no-nonsense types with, conversely, unexpected *flair*...plus a warm, ingrained spirit of camaraderie.

Inger and I take our hats off to them all—especially Mark Hill, who had the office next door to mine, Mac Snowden and Captain Fred Orrin, Mac's successor. Not to mention Admirals Moorer and Holloway and the latter's successor at ANA, Admiral Wesley McDonnell.

What did these illustrious U. S. Navy officers like to talk about most? *Midway!* The battle that, like Stalingrad in Russia and El Alamein in North Africa, marked the turningpoint of WWII in the Pacific. It was Navy Air's finest hour! One that Inger, as a European, had heard little about...and wanted to know more. So here's the story she got:

A bare half-year after the horror of Pearl Harbor, the grueling three-day Battle of Midway stopped cold one of the most awesome naval forces ever assembled...*and* rolled back Japan's last all-out attempt to clear US forces from the Pacific. It was a classic of great seamanship...and airmanship. But a string of coincidences also played a decisive role, leading many American fliers, like the veterans at ANA, to think that God must surely have been their co-pilot:

First was having our aircraft carriers out on maneuvers during the terrible destruction of Pearl Harbor. They survived to fight another day...at Midway, and beyond.

Second was catching the four huge carriers in the Japanese fleet trying to recover planes sent earlier to bomb the US base on Midway Island—their decks cluttered with planes, ammo, fuel-lines, crewmen and massive confusion.

Third came right after our torpedo planes had been shot down while attacking without fighter-plane cover...when 36 US carrier-launched divebombers, their gas running down to "the point of no return," suddenly spied the Japanese armada through a break in the clouds and unleashed their fury...squarely on target. A heavy Japanese cruiser and all four giant carriers were destroyed, along with their planes and many of Japan's most experienced aviators, many of whom had bombed Pearl Harbor. The US lost the carrier *Yorktown.*

Many came to add another factor to this victory at Midway: We had broken the ultra-secret Japanese communications code—so knew exactly what the enemy was up to. But this was hardly a coincidence; it was the result of hard work and ingenuity by our cryptologists. As Inger said, their penetration was like having a US spy right in the camp of the enemy—which indeed proved to be worth 10,000 men in the field. Score a big one for US Intelligence!

While toiling away on *Wings of Gold*, I had not forgotten my promise to continue recording Q&A interviews for *The American Legion Magazine*, and, with Inger's help when she could get away from her teaching at the Foreign Service Institute, we turned these in at the rate of one every two or three months. Then, when Congress in its wisdom finally passed a law declaring that WWII merchant seamen were (really, actually and truly!) to be considered WWII veterans…and thus entitled to at least an American flag at the time of burial…I contributed an article in tribute to my few surviving buddies called "Heroes of the High Seas."

This followed another feature Inger and I did earlier in connection with a National Press Club trip to South America, "Brazil: The Next Frontier." The trip, conducted by our peerless NPC tour leader, Betty Wason, was not only informative and fun but also provided a chance to meet Inger's aunt (originally from Denmark) and her family in Curitiba. Also, one of the fellow travelers we hobnobbed with turned out to be the golden-voiced announcer and commentator, John Cameron Swayze. Yet, boiling down an Andes-size mountain of material into an 1800-word article proved one tough challenge. What we learned in the process: This vast, diverse, resource-rich "land of tomorrow" may finally be getting its act together…promising to begin making tomorrow happen *today*.

We later got in touch with friends at *The Reader's Digest* and arranged to do a joint byliner which would appear first in *TALM* and later, in shorter reprint form, in *The Digest*. The subject was a "natural" for both magazines: Alfred Nobel and the Nobel Peace Prize. This was written on the scene in Oslo, where the prize that year was awarded, amid widespread controversy, to Mikhail Gorbachev. But he *did* turn East Europe loose…without bloodshed. (*Tusen takk, Gorbie!*) Some 30 years before I had tried mightily to get a story into *The Digest*… unsuccessfuly. And now it finally came about. As Inger said, "You gotta have patience!"

As our 65th birthdays drew near, Inger and I took a hard look at the years ahead, where, because of my free-wheeling hopping around and across a dozen different jobs (all of which you've followed on these pages), we would have the barest minimum of retirement income. And we concluded we had to do something extreme (*crazy* is a better word) to make ends meet. So we talked, and talked some more, and finally decided to throw all our savings into a bold, risky construction project at Rehoboth on the Atlantic.

Before embarking on this hazardous venture, however, we began to look around Washington for an editor to take over my position at

Wings of Gold. Obviously, you can't just walk out and leave your pals and the ANA ship (or carrier) sitting there high and dry. We already knew where there was one ideal candidate: Captain Rosario "Zip" Rausa, the experienced, thoughtful, capable editor of a Navy publication—a true Officer and a Gentleman. But what can you do to land someone who's already fully employed? Well, you ask. And, lo and behold, Zip told me he was thinking of retiring from the service! So we got Zip cleared by all at ANA and on the job...and cleared out. With a whole shipload of good memories....

Chapter XI

What about that "bold, risky construction project" at Rehoboth on the Atlantic?

Knowing we had to continue working and earning a living (which Inger considered a blessing cleverly disguised as a burden), we asked ourselves, well, why not build a house? On our vacant land at the ocean, that is. And, hopefully, assuming such a risky investment works out, use the profit for extra income. *Profit?* You gotta be kidding!

Inger, naturally, thought I had gone *berserk* (an old Viking word). Even more so since I had expanded the project to include *three* houses, not one. As the plan unfolded, she came to see that I was berserk, indeed...and blasted away:

"I hope you'll never try to build another house!"

Inger was plenty upset at all the trouble we were running into...and, of course, I got blamed for leading her into such a morass.

I really deserved blame, too. Being an architect had always seemed to me one of the great professions in life. So why not try your own hand at it? As though you know what you're doing—and getting into! Well, you do learn....

Besides, Inger had always said that you're given this one blessed life and you shouldn't hesitate to use it to do the things you want to do, regardless. She also said that if there had to be regrets later, she would rather regret taking action that turned out poorly than regret not having dared to act at all. She then clenched her position by quoting this fine line from Shakespeare:

Our doubts are traitors and make us lose the good we oft might win by fearing to attempt.

So Inger joined, ever so reluctantly, in wrestling our traitorous doubts to the ground...and we set forth. Once we settled on the design, we faced the often hilarious matter of getting zoning approval from the local Building Engineering Office. Don't even think of trying it!

This bureaucratic travesty took myriad altered plot-plans and months of "friendly" negotiations before the office gave us the nod, and I believe it was only because of Inger's winning ways that we finally succeeded.

The builder we selected was agreeable enough. It was just that, as project developer, we had to be on the site and on our toes continuously...for we found that the on-site supervisor loved short-cuts. These raised the builder's profits!

Addition of a third floor to our house led to more problems, since supporting walls underneath had to be reconfigured. And why did we want three floors instead of two? For my house-wide office, with bed, sitting area, WC, et al—a place where a worn spirit could find repose...or soar with the gulls, geese and the two giant blue herons that fish our lake...and look eastward over a sweeping, inspiring panorama of sand and surf. Inger got so riled up over the extra trouble this caused that she vowed never to visit the third floor. [And she hasn't. Which, you might say, was not altogether a sorrow.]

One design detail she did like, however, was our making the first floor into virtually a separate apartment, with kitchenette, two bed-rooms and two baths and a big screened porch. What better place for visits by our two sons! Not to mention their families, for each son-and-wife couple now had two children each—Philip and Teresa in Montana and Walter and Erika in Germany. With hardly any effort whatever, we had become grandparents! Inger's 45-year America ad-venture had expanded to cover six descendants, and now she could fret over the whole half-dozen instead of just one—me.

Now came the big question: Would the two two-story houses *sell*? An astute realtor allayed our fears. The Delaware beaches, she said, were one of the last remaining uncrowded recreation areas in the whole populous Northeast, and attractive real estate was in rising demand. She was right. One house sold fairly quickly...and our longterm friends, the Spragues, moved into the other. We, in turn, rented out our house in Bethesda and moved all we had into the three-floor unit. Rehoboth

Beach, Delaware, long the entire family's favorite vacation spot, became our new permanent address. Building/investment project completed!

(When it comes to investments, Inger found this capitalist society unforgiving... and no, no place for amateurs. This applies especially to the stock market—a veritable Las Vegas gambling casino—where, it seems, only insiders make real money. Unless you're a Warren Buffett and have a whole stable of honest analysts, you never know what's really going on within a company...so, full of hope, you buy its stock and the next day a dreadful announcement comes out and sends the stock into a tailspin. Or even when you're lucky enough to guess right and buy right and the stock rises, you never know when to sell. Like the dumbest sheep, we ourselves got into some highly touted stocks over the years—on *my* recommendation!—almost always buying high when the market was rising and selling low when it collapsed. The result was that we got thoroughly sheered. The

This is the house that Jim (had) built...on the edge of the American continent at Rehoboth Beach, Delaware—with no little verbal "aid" from Inger. The view reaches eastward over Lake Comegys and the wide beach to the turbulent Atlantic. The setting, with its geese, ducks, herons, and smaller birds of every description, is so special that Inger calls it Eventyr, *for fairytale, adventure. Apt name for a rapt place!*

same for that most volatile of speculative arenas, commodities. So please don't try to persuade us to get into the stock market...ever again! We'll stick to real estate, where, if you buy a house in the right location-location-location (the three things you should always look for), the value grows and grows even while you're enjoying the property's use.

Living a three-hour drive and a million spiritual miles from Washington did not keep us from keeping in touch with that distinguished citadel of pomp and pomposity, political turmoil and traffic jams. (The area had grown during our 40 years there from a sleepy southern town of 1.2 million to an unmanageable DC-suburban donut-like sprawl of 4 million, rivaling the population of all of Norway.) During the 1980s, Ronald Reagan cut taxes and raised defense spending (and piled up massive budget deficits) and pushed the Soviet Union into bankruptcy and dismemberment...and was succeeded by George Bush at the White House. Then, barely one term later, President Bush came to be succeeded by that personable young talk-talker from Arkansas, William Jefferson Clinton (plus-plus wife Hillary). These events brought big change-overs in appointive positions throughout government, providing equally big opportunities for us to do "inside dope" stories and interviews with new faces.

At the *Legion Magazine*, for instance, Inger and I collaborated on a couple payback Q&A sessions with close contacts from our Naval Aviation days: Admirals Tom Moorer and Jim Holloway. They made great copy. After dealing with DC political types, it was also wondrously refreshing to work again with such solid, frank, plain-speaking people.

An unusual interview we did next took place in Oslo with the top authority on the Viking era, Helge Ingstad. Over 90 years old at that time, he rattled off a treasure-trove of information on how the Vikings discovered America—knowledge based not only on the Icelandic sagas but also on the revealing excavations of an actual 1,000-year-old Norse settlement that he and his wife had carried out at L'Anse aux Meadows in Newfoundland. From this base, he pointed out, such adventuring seafarers would undoubtedly have felt compelled to explore the North America coastline and rivers much farther...but how far remains shrouded in the fog of unrecorded history. Unfortunately, the settlement was short-lived. Hostile *skraelings* (native Indians) made things so hot that the Vikings finally had to pull up stakes and pull out. And left Columbus the honor of opening the New World to permanent European settlement.

We then embarked on a blockbuster series of headliner interviews for *TALM.* Inger posed this thought: Why couldn't we throw light on all the interlocking aspects of government by doing a Q&A with an expert in each area—at the rate of, say, one per month? The resulting package would be far more informative than dry articles. *TALM*'s editor gave his enthusiastic approval, and we forged ahead with this singular series, all appearing under the cover-page heading, "Inside the Government Machine":

• *The White House*: "The World's Toughest Job"—featuring Dwight Ink, veteran of high positions from Federal agencies all the way to the White House and now president of the Institute of Public Administration in New York City.

• *Congress:* "Is Congress Still the People's Forum?"—Norman J. Ornstein, former Congressional staffer and now Resident Scholar at the American Enterprise Institute.

• *Regulatory Agencies:* "How Much Regulation Do We Really Need?"—James Q.Wilson, professor at UCLA and president of the American Political Science Association.

• *Lobbying:* "Washington Lobbying: Blessing or Curse?"—Jeffrey Birnbaum, *Wall Street Journal* Washington reporter and author of the new book, *The Lobbyists.*

• *The News Media:* "The Power of the Press"—Stephen Hess, Senior Fellow in Government Studies, Brookings Institution.

•*State & Local Governments:* "The Crisis CAN Be Solved"—Richard P. Nathan, professor of Political Science and Public Policy at New York State University, Albany.

• *Think Tanks*: "Idea Brokers and the Rise of the New Policy Elite"—James Allen Smith, adjunct professor, New School for Applied Social Research, and author of book on subject.

The impact of this last area—that of think tanks—is one that the public generally appears least aware of...unfortunately. For these collections of scholars and old Washington hands, as at liberal

Brookings and conservative AEI, work day and night to come up with new ideas for new laws, plus refinements of existing laws. And their research finds its way directly into the corridors of power all over Washington. Inger and I have had frequent contact with people working at and running think tanks and can attest to their influence. It's not to be underrated.

What's missing in our over-all mix of Washington impact areas? An expert's views on the Supreme Court, for one thing. Plus, possibly, an expert's views on the over-all Federal bureaucracy—aside from the Office of the President. These areas are no less fundamental than the seven listed here, for while the President and Congress may team up to *produce* legislation, the courts determine how it is *interpreted,* and the bureaucrats determine how it is *implemented.* In either case, or both, the final product can be quite different from that intended by the President and legislators.

The series made a big splash—the last of its kind for Inger and me, as it turned out. Our 70th birthdays were at hand, and we decided to get out of the interviewing business. As Inger pointed out, my graying hair and years of Washington experience somehow didn't fit in with quizzing the "young whippersnappers" coming into government. Too often we felt that some of these — particularly those acceding to their lofty positions as a pay-off for helping in a political campaign — should know more and be more balanced and capable than we found them. So why give their half-baked views broader visibility?

What do next? Inger suggested we begin a newspaper column. Alas, she had forgotten!

Back in our Washington reporting days, I had teamed up with a wise, good-natured reporter named Harley Murray to launch a weekly column called "The Pocketbook Impact of Politics." The idea was to go beyond political commentary and the personality skullduggery coming out of the Capital and provide people with some solid reporting on how Capital action (or inaction) affects the economy, your job, income, taxes, quality of life, etc. Good idea...BUT. For a half-year we churned out columns and tried to sell these to newspaper editors across the country. And we did, indeed, sign up a couple dozen. Since these turned out to be smaller-circulation papers, their payments were discouragingly low. Meanwhile, our printing, mailing and promotion costs were discouragingly high. The result: We finally threw in the sponge...and refunded the signed-up editors' payments, with thanks. Leaving the field to the big news syndicates who know the business a bit better...and who didn't mind our competition at all, or miss us at all.

Inger and I had other plans, regardless. There were two books I had long been hoping to find time to write—two chronicles of discovery: My own discovery as a boy of "the real America" with its priceless traditional values...and the discovery of modern America by an attractive, sympathetic newcomer to these shores—Inger (who else!), my own private, personal, perceptive Valkyrie. Meanwhile, Inger hoped to spend more time in her beloved Norway, with all those relatives and friends she had grown up with. The chance came soon, too...but by no means as we had planned: Our beloved Mamma died. At 95.

Astrid Philip Krogh—a great Dane, a fantastic person! Which she proved to be at life's end...once more. When she could no longer take care of herself in her own apartment, even with visiting nurses' help, Inger and brother Erling arranged for a move into the Oddfellows Home, one of Oslo's coziest. Here, unlike the score of other patients, Mamma never once uttered one word of complaint, over anything. However much discomfort or pain she felt, her only answer to anyone's asking how she was doing was *straalende!* [wonderful!] Jokes about mothers-in-law abound—for good reason, I suppose. But I myself had the opposite experience. Mamma was a no-nonsense disciplinarian (which helped make Inger herself so *straalende)* but, toward me, she was invariably friendly and considerate and *fun* to be with.

Mamma was interred in the Krogh family grave under stately birch trees adjoining the Honored Dead section of Vaar Frelses Gravelund (Our Savior's Cemetery) in Oslo. Alongside Pappa and Grete, our ever-smiling, ever-helpful sister (who had died of cancer five years before). The site is next to a towering stone marking the grave of Peter Asbjoernson, the famed compiler, along with Joergen Moe, of Norse folklore and fairytales like "The Three Billygoats Gruff." I got the feeling she would have liked nothing more....

Today, Mamma lives on in our daily reference to her remarks, for she seemed as wise as Confucius with such sayings as...

...*It takes a strong back to carry good days.* Meaning that affluence can be one of mankind's toughest challenges. Or, as she herself
interpreted it, "people who have everything often wind up enjoying
nothing."

...*The big problem with getting old isn't trying to remember; it's
trying to FORGET!* Meaning that, somehow, you've got to put aside
all your mistakes and failures in life, the losses of loved ones, the slights
and injuries inflicted by others, etc, etc.

Mamma had outlived her devoted husband, Erling Krogh, by a
remarkable 26 years...and her death started Inger to thinking that
we should do something to honor him, too...before his memory as
one of Norway's greatest singers faded away, along with his generation. So how do you honor an acclaimed singer who organized
one of the nation's first opera companies? Well, why not through
opera itself? And what better way than to support young singers
just getting started on their careers? We went to *Den Norske Opera*
and talked with its executives at length. The result: A special fund,
the Erling Krogh Legat [trust], was established to award 15,000
norske kroner (some $2,500.) every other year to a promising young
Norwegian singer.

[Today, at two-year intervals, Inger and I (and sometimes our sons)
join DNO President Bjoern Simensen and Director Bernt Bauge in
their Oslo offices to celebrate the latest Legat recipient. Eight have
already been so honored. It's a grand occasion for a grand idea! All
thanks to Inger's foresight. It's also singularly timely, fitting in with
the striking new national opera building Norway is developing on the
Oslo waterfront.]

Inger's hands-across-the-sea activities struck me as further testament to the unusual role she has long played as an unofficial, unher-
alded goodwill ambassador for Norway in the United States, and vice
versa. This extends far beyond her Scandinavian contacts. Indeed, it
extends across the outermost reaches of our continent and through all
levels of society, from the innercity mess of Detroit to the White House
and the highest ranks of business and journalism, through three universities and several libraries, Washington tour guiding and Foreign

Service Institute teaching…as well as through the half-dozen key communications positions I myself have held.

The two of us have also served in a small role in the other direction, promoting goodwill for America in Norway and elsewhere overseas. And now our two sons, both of whom speak Norwegian fluently, are completing the bridge-building across the Atlantic. Erik spends much of his time in Norway, and attorney Jim is Norway's Honorary Consul for the state of Montana. Talk about people-to-people diplomacy!

And what role has Inger played for me personally? Just read this book! I can only add here that Inger has truly become Valkyrie herself, my fearless fighting comrade who has stood ever ready to pick me up when I fell in battle (which was not seldom), dress my wounds and spirit me off for R&R to our Valhalla home. What a wife! What a Viking! Watta gal!

Son Jim's work as Honorary Consul is also noteworthy since it puts him into direct contact with Norway's Foreign Service and such key Scandinavia-US groups as the Sons of Norway, Nordmanns-Forbundet (the Norse Federation) and the Norwegian-American Chamber of Commerce. He thus learns anew daily what Inger found out here early on: That Norwegians and other immigrants from Scandinavia readily became solid citizens of America, their new home on the western side of the Atlantic…and have gone on to contribute mightily to the nation's growth and development and ongoing progress.

Upon completing our work with *Den Norske Opera*, Inger proposed we travel on to northern Norway, the storied Land of the Midnight Sun, which, surprisingly, she had never visited. Sure, I said, but who's going to foot the bill? Why not land a writing assignment? she replied: "That way, it won't cost. It'll *pay!*" Her thought was that we might write an article on that most impressive saga of Norwegian seamanship—*Hurtigruten,* the coastal express steamers that, day and night, the whole year 'round, in rain, wind, snow or shine, ply the dangerous, reef-strewn, storm-ravaged coastline from Bergen to Kirkenes on the Russian border. Wasn't this another exciting natural for *Reader's Digest?* she wanted to know.

Gunnar Arneson, editor of *Det Beste*, the Norwegian edition of the

Digest, liked the idea. But with one daunting variation: Instead of sailing this far-north route during the Summer when the sun shines all the time, we would do it in mid-January—when the sun doesn't shine at all! Since we had previously sailed the southern legs of this route, once from Bergen to Trondheim and later from Trondheim to Bodoe, Gunnar suggested we fly to Tromsoe far above the Arctic Circle and catch the ship there for its final rough run to Kirkenes—which, amazingly, lies on a longitude as far east as Istanbul.

This gave me pause. The sea way north (which gave *Nor-way* its name) is inshore from the notorious shipping route to Murmansk, where so many Allied merchant ships were torpedoed by enemy submarines and bombed by enemy planes flying from airfields in occupied Norway during WWII. It was also the scene of howling arctic storms that whipped up mountainous waves, capsizing ships and freezing survivors who made it onto rafts and into lifeboats. There were also painful memories of my first trip to sea during WWII, at age 19, when my ship ran headlong into a hurricane east of Nantucket and battled all night to stay afloat...finally limping back to New York to reload our shifting cargo and replace the four lifeboats the storm had torn loose. Scenarios right out of hell! I decided I simply couldn't risk having Inger go along.

Oh, no, you don't: We're in this together! was the reply I got.

So together we flew from Oslo to Tromsoe, landing in a blizzard in pea-soup visibility that confirmed my worst suspicions of the mayhem to come. But, then, a miracle happened. By the time our ship sailed, the storm began to blow itself out...and we had calm sailing and mild weather, riding the remnants of the Gulf Stream all the way north across the roof of Europe. At the North Cape, we stood in eerie stillness in daytime darkness, looking almost straight up at the North Star and beholding the flashing, greenish, shifting patterns of the *aurora borealis*. When we put ashore in Kirkenes, however, the weather gods turned angry again just as we returned from a frigid, windy visit to the Russian border (which brought back memories of my long-ago contact with Russian guards at the USSR border with Iran). Another blizzard hit! Snow piled up over the airport runway and all across Finnmark. Our plane was canceled, and we trudged around a brave city for an extra day, thankful we were on solid land and not at sea with the ship we had just left—which was sailing back southward to Bergen in this wild, wild melee.

This experience in the far north convinced even Inger that we had had enough of Arctic *sturm und drang*. So, returning to America, we set off for Florida with the intention of finding a suitable rental for a few weeks during the Winter. Norway was a fine place to be during the snow-swept, dark, wintry months IF you stayed at one of the country's cozy lodges in the countryside...but Oslo was different. By February, as repeated snows were trampled down on streets and sidewalks, this fair city became one monstrous sheet of ice, with people slipping and falling all over the place and breaking hip bones, ankles, wrists, etc. Nor was Rehoboth's Winter weather much better, with its wild winds raking the deserted shoreline...and our house.

Florida thus got the nod. Here, we knew from past visits, was a booming state of sun-drenched beaches and hurricanes, of golf and bridge, of over-eating and over-drinking, of limitless luxury and migrant misery, of the newly wed and the nearly dead, of facelifts, cosmetic dentistry and an endless—and endlessly frustrating—search (a la Ponce de Leon and Hernando De Soto) for the fabled Fountain of Youth. Here was the state we said we would never retire to; yet now, suddenly, we found ourselves driving straight into this brave new world. Our destination: Southwest Florida, which was in the early stages of a hectic building boom.

Here, south of Fort Myers and north of Naples, we found a place we really liked: An attractive, brand-new development, Sawgrass Point at Pelican Landing in Bonita Springs. A realtor showed us a small apartment overlooking a lake and fairway, with swimming pool across the street, an unspoiled Robinson Crusoe beach on a nearby island in the Gulf of Mexico and the world's friendliest people. And Inger got roped into *buying*, not renting!

And what's impressed my wife most about our modest new Winter home? Our neighbors! Most hail from the upper Midwest, and we've never witnessed such successful marriages. Here are couples that have spent a lifetime together (really *together*)—who are devoted to home and family and church and country and who walk together, talk together, have fun together. Here, indeed, are people representing the backbone of America. They put into daily practice Inger's own formula for a successful marriage, which she expresses in these apt lines from a little verse she's picked up:

The grammer of marriage sounds like a lie: It's first person you, second person I.

After our Florida venture, Inger promised that there will be no more changes of addresses…or additions. This meant I could now turn to my first book project.

From her arrival in the United States and first attempts to find out what makes this unique nation tick, Inger has been fascinated with my own childhood—especially my jarring transition at age10 from the steep streets of industrial Pittsburgh to a Bible Belt environment immersed in traditional American values. Like hard work, dedication to home and family, strict "raisin'," tough schooling, religious devotion, neighborliness and love of country.

Wasn't this the real America? she wanted to know. And if not honored so openly nowadays, weren't these values the real foundation of presentday America—however blurred over by avant garde, permissive, if-it-feels-good-it's-good posturing?

Yes, I agreed, she had something there. Uprooted from my urban urchin existence and "farmed out" along with brother Ernie and Sis during the Great Depression [why is such a wrenching experience called *great?*] to our grandfather's place in the nation's heartland, I spent the next seven years growing up in a Tom Sawyer-like setting on the north bank of the Ohio River…at the very juncture of the Midwest, Appalachia and the South. Here, I found myself following those priceless guiding stars of the American epic: The *Holy Bible, McGuffey's Fifth Reader,* the *Boy Scout Handbook* and our historic documents on mankind in a free society.

"If all this doesn't add up to the hallmarks of the real America of your fathers and forefathers, what does?" Inger asked.

"Okay, you're on!" I answered, and began to lay out *the* book forthwith.

An editorial flop from my days with *The American Legion Magazine* was another motivating factor. At Inger's suggestion, I had once written a dozen prominent people proposing that each reach back into his growing-up years and write an article for the magazine developing the theme, "This Is My America." Easier planned than done! Every single person contacted pleaded unable to spare the time to do so. I then concluded I would have to do it myself, for my own past had precisely the elements we were looking to bring out. Yet, I also concluded that doing the story justice required a full book. And now, hopefully, this would come about....

Still, there were doubts as to whether anyone would read such an account from so long ago. Especially young people, our real target. For is anyone more completely absorbed in the demanding, arresting *present*, with all its exciting changes? Nevertheless, we wanted youngsters like our own grandchildren to know about this fantastic world that was—a world whose values, however diluted by current cultural shifts, continue to shape their future.

Action, we decided, was the way to appeal to young readers. So Inger and I began by listing the most dramatic action incidents I had lived through during that period, from 1934 through 1941. Our plan was to build individual chapters around the most compelling, coming up with not just a recital of the passing years but, rather, with a chronicle of exciting action that young people would *want* to read—an autobiographical novel or, as it's often called, dramatic non-fiction. We would also include an element of suspense, keying the whole running narrative to two daunting missions that my schoolteacher mother posed upon my leaving Pittsburgh:

1. Search out the real America.
2. Find "the ultimate secret of life."

And what would we name this book? *America: The Search and the Secret*. Nothing else, Inger said, would be more fitting.

The devastating Great Flood (Ohio River, 1937—another two-edged use of that tricky word, *great*) kicked off the book, with our house barely escaping being swept away, along with hundreds of others, under the mammoth wall of muddy water that pounded down the valley. This was followed by grade-school recitals, spelling bees and demanding l'arnin' ("taught to the tune of a hickory stick"};

hellfire-and-brimstone revival meetings and being "saved", then baptized in the river to the booming chorus of "Swing Low, Sweet Chariot"; almost starving through the late winters when the food canned during summers ran out; picking buckets of blackberries and working for 10 cents an hour on neighboring farms with Grampaw under a scorching sun from dawn to dusk; making the grade as a First Class Scout; jawboning with a wise Justice of the Peace while working in his tomato patch...and learning about life from my Aunt Emma and a beautiful neighbor nicknamed "Amazin' Grace"; suffering through Grampaw's death down by the riverside, and, finally, trembling and mumbling my way through the valedictory speech when graduating from highschool.

Inger's towering human-development goal of becoming a Four-Dimensional Human was also developed in the book. (Actually, knowing readers have detected no little resemblance between Inger and Amazin' Grace, the first to teach me to love classical music, the visual arts and good literature.) The 4-D Human was posed as an incomparably superior alternative to the narrow, job-related objectives of an increasingly crass, technology-driven, commercialized, entertainment-obsessed age.

But, you might ask, what did the book conclude is "the ultimate secret of life"? The answer lies right there in the open, in the *Search and the Secret* title itself: The secret is *searching*. Sonny, the main character, finally came to realize that however hard he searches, he would never find any absolute answers to life's mysteries. That looked about as frustrating to him as chasing a rainbow. Yet, he also concluded that perhaps man's greatest glory lies in keeping up the searching, the striving, the upward reaching, the quest for answers. And if you do, he asks, wouldn't you always remain young in spirit, regardless of age?

Putting all this onto paper was like living my childhood all over again [just as now, on these pages, I'm re-living my years with Amazin' Inger]. And I came to feel that even if *A:TS&TS* never sold a single copy, the very experience would be worth all the effort. To me, that is—*not*, naturally, to a publisher!

As all authors and would-be authors find out PDQ, writing a book is one thing; getting it printed is another. Publishing houses are over-whelmed with manuscripts, and precious few ever get into print. We talked with a couple literary agents (who are also overwhelmed and tend to fend off newcomers) and tried different approaches to different publishers. Sorry, Charlie! was the kind of response we got.

Then, as luck would have it, Inger and I went to Eastern Kentucky on an Elderhostel program and found ourselves sitting at lunch one day across from Dr. James M. Gifford, the dedicated, enterprising CEO of the Jesse Stuart Foundation, regional publishers and booksellers headquarted in Ashland, KY. I knew about Jesse Stuart from my mother's avid readings, having met him in print as the prolific Kentucky writer of virile poetry and such bestsellers as *Taps for Private Tussie* and *Beyond Dark Hills* (with its echoes of Mom's own Kentucky). Inger got a chance to admire his work, too—liking especially a gripping autobiographical story about the ruinous impact of politicking-with-education called *The Thread that Runs So True*. We've found him to be one of America's finest grassroots writers, and the foundation bearing his name deserves praise for promoting his works and his memory.

Inger also found much to admire in Kentucky. Besides, that is, the courageous, fiercely independent people (who reminded her of the Norwegians of her childhood) and the green-pastured, white-fenced horse farms around Lexington...*plus* the bourbon! The eastern part is a harsh "hard scrabble" land but one of singular drawing power, still felt despite the widespread havoc inflicted by strip mining. Best of all for Inger, though, was discovering the deep, abiding love the people in these dark hills have for music. Plus the exotic musical instruments they fashion by hand.

Our key question for Dr. Gifford, though, was whether he and his foundation would be interested in publishing a book about a boy coming of age right across the river in southern Ohio—a book reflecting the priceless values of this heartland area. The heartening answer was *yes*. He liked our youth-oriented goal, then zeroed in on the book's crucial value in these words:

"Teenagers desperately need a guide through the modern moral wilderness. They need help in deciding not only what to *be* in today's confusing world but also what to *become* in the future. And here it is!"

Dr. Gifford also joined us in the essential job of signing up four prominent people to serve as "shills" on the book's jacket. We finally put together a quartet that, as Inger stated, "harmonized beautifully." Their illustrious names: Gary L. Bauer, president of the Family Research Council; William E. Simon, my old boss at Treasury and then head of his own Wall Street investment firm; R. Emmett Tyrrell Jr., editor-in- chief of *The American Spectator*; and Ronald G. Eaglin, president of Morehead State University.

At this point the wheels began to turn and, in 1998, after much recasting and proofreading, *America: The Search and the Secret*[1] came out, designed by the Foundation's Brett Nance and illustrated with eye-catching line drawings by artist Jim Marsh. With all our thanks to you, Jim Gifford, Brett and everyone else at JSF!

Shortly after our book appeared came the turn of the century. As a young girl, Inger believed there was something magical about a brand-new millennium, and that she would never live long enough to see such a milestone in time. Yet, here she had made it...and in one piece! Minus, that is, a foot-long section of her colon and a leaking aorta heart valve—both hangovers of the American "school of hard knocks" she's attended for over a half-century. However, unlike most of those living in Florida, we don't talk about medical problems any more than we have to. *Living* is too important. Thinking, too. Not the least because we're into our 60th year together. While I'm now officially stamped as a fossil, fogey, croak, geezer and wheezer, Inger maintains an amazingly youthful, refreshing, childlike (*not* childish!) outlook on life. How does she do it? By staying *interested!* In our two sons, four grandchildren, three homes, two countries, the uproarious passing scene, the world.

It's said that time flies. But that was before the era of jets and space exploration came into being...so, now, it seems more fitting to say that time *rockets*. You try to grasp and stop it, and it slips right through your fingers like air. [Remember those appealing lines by poet Elizabeth

---

[1]*AMERICA: The Search and the Secret*, by James N. Sites (c), is available at $22 from the book's publisher, the Jesse Stuart Foundation; 1645 Winchester Avenue; P.O. Box 669; Ashland, KY 41105. Telephone: 606/326-1667. Email: jsf@jsfbooks.com

Akers Allen? *Turn backward! Turn backward, O Time, in your flight! Make me a child again...just for tonight.*] We're finding that if you live long enough, your circle of contacts steadily narrows and you're increasingly left with few people you can instinctively relate to. (One recent tragic loss was that of Inger's brother Erling, a deeply respected attorney who befriended and helped hundreds...and who, without warning, fell dead of heart arrest on an Oslo street adjoining the Royal Palace.)

In terms of relating, whom do you meet now who personally experienced the grinding poverty of the 1930s or survived the monumental challenges of WWII, including, like Inger, the harrowing five-year enemy occupation of her homeland? Or lived through the Cold War and M.A.D., Korea, Vietnam, a *doubling* of America's population, the massive post-WWII technological, social and economic upheavals that have changed our whole way of life? Or learned firsthand from those turbulent years—not just with your head but with your *bones*?

This longer view is more urgent than ever today, and Inger and I have lately found ourselves frequently cast in the unaccustomed role of having to field myriad questions on both continents about current events. And no one gives a more honest, objective answer than the lady who runs our home—the fair one with the startlingly open, direct gaze, who ever shines a Diogenes-like light on whatever she touches. For instance, the new millennium's dawning saw the election of former President George Bush's son, George W. Bush, and America's deadly involvement in Afghanistan and Iraq...where we stuck our hands and feet in the Muslim terrorist tar baby and found ourselves unable to shake loose. Bush No. 2 then got re-elected by appealing to traditional values and patriotic fervor fired by the 9/11 horror...even while the Iraq mess went from bloody to disastrous. So what, we're asked, do people with our background and experience (which you, the reader, have been following on these pages) think about these situations and other big issues of our times? A tall order to fill! But we try....

What about Iraq? We find it almost impossible to talk about this subject without screaming...out of anger, frustration and heartbreak over those being murdered and maimed, as well as over their grief-stricken families. Our leaders evidently went into Iraq with the noble objective of getting rid of a despicable dictator but without either adequately weighing the consequences this would have in triggering internal insurrection and stirring up Islamic extremists throughout the Middle East (and beyond), or planning how to respond to these grim consequences. As suicide attacks, bombings, kidnappings and assassinations by Muslim finatics increased in savagery day by day, casualties escalated apace...and, as with Vietnam, Inger wept tears of blood. News reports on Iraq were eliminated—she simply couldn't stand their devastating impact.

The tragedy in Iraq has raised pressing, unanswerable questions as to whether civilization can coexist with international terrorism on the scale of viciousness now being experienced, where every street corner, train station and public gathering place becomes a potential death trap. Prodded by radical Muslim clerics no less than by Osama bin Laden, countless "holy" warriors slipped into Iraq and turned it into a slaughterhouse...while other terrorists extended their butchery to wherever people incurred their displeasure—to Kenya, Turkey, Russia, Bali, Madrid, London. All the while the world waited for signs that the responsible sectors of the Muslim community would come to grips with their internal extremists. And waited....

Within the US, meanwhile, arose questions—publicly ignored by officials—as to whether our priceless economy can exist with Washington's methods of financing the mammoth, mounting costs of the combined war in Iraq and the battle against world terrorism. Indeed, one wonders:

If the American people had to pay a stiff additional tax to finance the war in Iraq, would they have supported that deadly mission at all?

And if some US leader were courageous enough to propose a special supplemental Anti-Terrorism Surtax (or World Freedom Tax, as PR "spinmasters" might call it) on taxable annual incomes of, say, more than $100,000, how would that rich man's club called Congress react? And how would the wealthy backers (and indirect decisionmakers) of both political parties react?

You can already hear the moaning and groaning!

Inger saw this as a saddest commentary on human nature: It's one thing to have young men and women paying with their lives fighting ruthless terrorists but quite another to ask the well-to-do—or even people generally—to back up that fight by paying higher taxes. Maybe that's being overly cynical, though. As she adds, you never know how the American people might react to real statesmanship advocating a pay-as-you-fight approach to the war on terrorism. Not to mention to a global war against chaos-causing poverty, ignorance and disease.

The newer world *can* help build a better world.

Not to worry about footing the bill, though. Washington prefers to talk only about *cutting* taxes, not raising them. The talk-of-the-Capital has it that if any taxes were to be increased, these should hit spending and consumption, not income—like a national sales tax or Value Added Tax, which Europe has long imposed. *And* which proponents know would be highly regressive, hitting hardest the great mass of consumers, *not* the well-to-do.

You have to wonder if some kind of strange madness has seized Washington when it comes to economic policies. For example, the White House periodically sent requests to Congress for "supplemental appropriations" to finance the war in Iraq. But did *anyone* suggest raising taxes to do so? Massive new borrowing was resorted to, instead. What you heard on The Hill was, "we must pass these bills to support our troops." Which was a colossal dodge: *The* way to support our troops is to pay for the war's costs *now*, however painful that might be.

It <u>can</u> be done. There are now 430,000 US households (an amazing, accelerating figure!) with a net worth of more than $10 million. While only one percent (1%!) of the population—the super-rich—controls *one third* of the nation's personal assets. And who has more to gain than the well-to-do from contributing more to building a stronger nation and a more stable, terror-free world?

Yet, what we're seeing, instead, is abandonment by many conservatives of genuine concern over deficit financing of government programs. In this perverted view, the only way to restrain the liberals' huge spending schemes is by running huge government deficits. Madness! This is like trying to diet by gobbling up huge helpings of fast foods, chocolates and ice cream. As Inger sadly points out, such an approach would bid farewell forever to any hopes of reining in on the politicians' profligate spending and balancing the Federal budget.

It's instructive to note that Norway's VAT (*Moms*, it's called there) is 25%. But this pyramids in practice and is a major reason, along with systemic inefficiencies, why price levels in that country are some 50 per cent higher than in the USA. Automobiles, gasoline and alcohol are taxed, and priced, at far higher levels. Completing the picture are stiff income taxes whose rates escalate at much lower income levels than in the USA. So, is there any doubt as to who pays for those generous-seeming Welfare State benefits? It's the *recipients!* (A huge part of whose contributions are first bled off to support the vast bureaucracy set up to administer the system.)

A startling statistic reported in Norway recently indicates that nearly 60 per cent of the work force is now employed by government. With untold others dependent on government contracts. What kind of an Orwellian society will there be...and what kind of life will individuals lead...when that ratio rises to 70 per cent? Or 80? *And the nation's high-priced oil runs out?*

It seems that only Inger asks such questions.

Mammon rules Washington today—the President and Congress kowtowing to this money god along with everyone else. Money from big donors has become *the* absolute requirement in politics. With campaign costs skyrocketing, you can't win elections without paying out fortunes. And you collect not only from wealthy individuals but also from Political Action Committees and big organizations—business as well as labor, like the powerful teachers and public employees unions. So who can blame Inger for concluding that Mammon has now turned our democracy upside down, creating a government of the wealthy, by the wealthy and for the wealthy.

Our Founding Fathers must be turning in their graves!

Can America survive politicking with its economy? This might once have seemed a silly question, but not today. Reason for concern lies in the tightening crunch of at least five major economic problems:

• Those horrific Federal budget deficits *and* the growing slice of present outlays eaten up by interest payments on debt.

• Our huge foreign trade imbalance—spurred by chronic dependence on high-cost foreign oil imports and China's manipulation of dollar-yuan exchange levels to spur ever-increasing exports to the US.

• The colossal, unsustainable expansion of private debt, permitting people to continue living in a virtual fool's paradise while constantly postponing the evil day of reckoning.

• The mounting costs of medical care, which can only increase when and if the millions without medical insurance coverage finally get adequate medical care...and the Baby Boomers move into retirement and staggeringly expensive terminal illnesses.

• Higher-education cost hikes far beyond over-all cost-of-living increases.

Regarding this last point, Inger has never quite understood the costly medieval administrative/faculty structure embraced by universities. Or why many professors, hiring themselves out as consultants and cashing in on the "publish or perish" dictum, should get paid more and more for teaching less and less. Or why Washington should continually bail out higher-education extravagance by slavishly increasing student loan programs, saddling young people with a painful burden of debt for years into their working future.

Is there any way to make these citadels of voodoo economics cut costs and become more efficient? Inger's answer: Congress should require that no Federally guaranteed student loan could be used at any school whose total annual costs to students (tuition, dormitory, books and fees) exceed the BLS Cost-of-Living Index.

Oddly enough, the 2004 election campaigning almost totally ignored such problems (not to mention Social Security's). Or maybe that wasn't so odd after all: There are no easy answers, and the tough ones win no votes. Yet, while politicians might be able to dodge such issues when facing voters/taxpayers, they can't fool the financial markets. The more obvious results: A dwindling dollar on foreign exchanges and steadily rising interest rates at home. And how long can the US rely on foreigners to buy US bonds and finance a governmental system based on borrowing? Which must surely be the ultimate in voodoo economic policies.

While America remains a nation of unparalleled opportunity, the gap between the wealthiest and the poorest citizens grows and grows—just as the gap between the world's richest and poorest nations grows apace. Our middleclass is rapidly becoming an endangered species. In a global economy, business operations naturally gravitate to low-wage countries, and so do high-paid jobs in US manufacturing, forcing many in America to work two jobs in the lower- paid service sector to make ends meet. All the while politicians turn handsprings to avoid raising the minimum wage to keep up with living-cost increases. Which Inger finds the unkindest cut of all—the ultimate expression of unfeeling, uncaring public policies.

Meanwhile, the business world has been rocked by shocking revelations of fraud and corruption in high places. Think of Enron, WorldCom, Tyco, Adelphia Communications. This is only half the problem, however: Business' new managers and business consultants have promoted a cult of compensation for corporate CEOs and other top executives that seems to be interpreted as giving them license to plunder their firms for all they can get *for themselves*, with little or no regard for the interests of customers, employees, stockholders or the broader community they are supposed to serve.

Is this plague of plunderers what free enterprise has finally come to? Inger and I have devoted much of our lives to promoting and defending the competitive enterprise system...as a more broadly beneficial and workable alternative to government takeover and ever-tightening centralized controls. BUT, we can assure you, today's misfirings and the sorry spectacles of unrestrained greed on part of so many executives are *not* what we had in mind.

Treasury Secretary Simon liked to say that *in Washington the long term is the next election.* In today's business world, on the other hand, the long term now appears to be the next quarterly report to profit-hungry stockholders—all those clamoring for a pumped-up price for the company's securities. Thus are long-term goals being sacrificed for short-term advantage.

Nor do politicians and business executives stand alone in this regard. People's infectious desire for immediate gain has led to an explosive growth of gambling across the country...and not just in plush new casinos and on TV and the Internet but also via state-sponsored lotteries. Yes, *state*-sponsored. State governments, presumably responding to public desire for huge winnings as well as a brake on tax increases, are avidly promoting appeals to one of the worst traits in human nature—one that often leads to incalculable human misery. *Our* government!

It's said that people get the kind of government they deserve. Alas, so did the Romans....

When Inger was growing up in Norway, she and her friends thought of far-away America as "the land of a thousand dreams"—where, if you studied and worked hard, many *could* come true. More important to the world's peoples, America also came to stand as a shining, god-like beacon of hope, offering not only freedom from want but also freedom from oppression...with liberty and justice for all, including society's lowliest. However, looking at today's depressing scene of abuse, neglect, political chicanery and leadership failure...and pyramiding problems in both the public and private sectors, one can't help but wonder if we're witnessing the twilight of the America god. Are we?

If the old gods and their tough moral restraints against anti-social behavior are, indeed, dying, as Inger fears, what will replace them? As the money chase, pleasure-seeking, the Seven Deadly Sins and dog-eat-dog attitudes become the New Order, what can possibly replace the accompanying loss among people of the feeling of community—of the sense that we're-all-in-this-together? Or the loss of intensive human development aspirations? In a smaller society like Norway, one can see more clearly that as religion's influence declined (the churches are almost empty), government became the new god—everyman's guarantor of succor, however illusory, throughout life. And sex and "the good life" became the new goals, the new religion.

Yet, while such goals also seem to captivate more and more Americans, there remains a deep distrust of government on this side of the Atlantic. President Ford pointedly summed up these fears in warning that *any government that can give you everything you want can also take away everything you have.*

Inger's life has been a strenuous personal crusade against every form of tyranny over the development of the human being and the human spirit—development summed up in her ideal of the Four-Dimensional Human. And what are those subtle forms of modern tyranny? Just look around you! They're everywhere in modern society. Television is the most visible, its dubious lures turning people into snack-filled sleep-walkers and utterly flattening out the human personality. Then comes the rest of the Media/Entertainment Complex, the more onerous segments pervasively promoting pornography, promiscuity, perversion and permissiveness.

Inger refers to these influences as crimes against the human spirit—crimes that are all the more deadly because their effects are so camouflaged, so insidious. Yet, as our long involvement in communications and public opinion formation shows, people's eyes *can* be opened to these influences' degrading, dehumanizing effects. Inger long ago discovered that Americans have a fabulous capacity for correcting problems once they become aware of their impact and effects. The pendulum has swung far in one direction. It *can* swing back again....

Norway commands attention in this regard because here's a country that, capitalizing on rich reserves of North Sea oil, has...incredibly...shifted in modern times from one of the poorest lands in Europe to one of the wealthiest, rivaling Mideast oil kingdoms. To Inger, this is a mixed blessing: She worries that a wholesome, hard-working people could well be ruined by affluence. Not to mention by a spreading "anything goes" morality. Or by the rising tide of narcotics, prostitution and crime brought into the land by Third World migrants. It sometimes seems that in the name of *snillisme* [doing good for others] and carrying out the social engineers' dream [nightmare?] of building "a multi-cultural society," Norway is inadvertently abandoning the values that created a great people and committing cultural suicide. Will it?

When William Faulkner received the Nobel Prize for Literature in Stockholm, he said he believed that mankind will not only survive the problems besetting us but will *prevail.*

It's on this note that Inger joins in saying *so long!* to the readers of her America saga. Thanks for letting us share with you our trials and failures and rare triumphs, thoughts and dreams from a fascinating, eventful half-century. It's been an *experience!* Both living it and writing about it.

In concluding, we would like to quote another author we've come to admire: Alfred, Lord Tennyson—and not just because of his famous *Crossing the Bar.* At the conclusion of his powerful poem *Ulysses,*

Tennyson wrote these ringing words that Ulysses addresses to his shipmates of a lifetime of exploration:

> *...Come, my friends,*
> *'Tis not too late to seek a newer world.*
> *...My purpose holds*
> *To sail beyond the sunset, and the baths*
> *Of all the western stars...*
> *Though much is taken, much abides; and though*
> *We are not now that strength which in old days*
> *Moved earth and heaven, that which we are, we are:*
> *One equal temper of heroic hearts,*
> *Made weak by time and fate, but strong in will*
> *To strive, to seek, to find, and not to yield.*

Inger surveys another special part of the world from our 10th-floor apartment on Oslo's westside. In the distance is Oslofjord, which runs southward 60 miles to the Skagerrak and North Sea and beyond. Here, Inger has returned from her decades-long Norway-America saga of discovery to where she started, life immeasurably enriched by her experiences. Moreover, she now has two countries instead of one. And so do I. Plus a whole new world...of music. Thanks, Inger!

Index